Approaches to Translation

Other titles of interest include

ELLIS, Rod
Classroom Second Language Development

ELLIS, Rod
Second Language Acquisition in Context

KRASHEN, Stephen
Language Acquisition and Language Education

KRASHEN, Stephen
Second Language Acquisition and Second Language Learning

KRASHEN, Stephen
Principles and Practice in Second Language Acquisition

KRASHEN, Stephen and Tracy Terrell
The Natural Approach

NEWMARK, Peter
A Textbook of Translation

NUNAN, David
Language Teaching Methodology

PECK, Antony
Language Teachers at Work

ROBINSON, Pauline
ESP Today: A Practitioner's Guide

ROBINSON, Gail
Crosscultural Understanding

WALLACE, Catherine
Learning to Read in a Multicultural Society

WEIR, Cyril
Communicative Language Testing

WEIR, Cyril
Understanding and Developing Language Tests

WENDEN, Anita and Joan RUBIN
Learner Strategies in Language Learning

YALDEN, Janice
The Communicative Syllabus

Approaches to Translation

PETER NEWMARK
Centre for Translation and Language Studies,
University of Surrey

PHOENIX
ELT
incorporating
PRENTICE HALL MACMILLAN
New York London Toronto Sydney Tokyo Singapore

Published 1995 by
Phoenix ELT
Campus 400, Spring Way
Maylands Avenue, Hemel Hempstead
Hertfordshire, HP2 7EZ
A division of Prentice Hall International

First published 1982 by Pergamon Press
This edition first published 1988 by Prentice Hall International

Printed and bound in Great Britain at
the University Press, Cambridge

British Library Cataloguing in Publication Data

Newmark, Peter
Approaches to translation.
1. Translating and interpreting
I. Title
418′.02′01 P306 80-41008

ISBN 0-13-043795-6

11 10 9 8
99 98 97 96

For Pauline

Foreword

In this Volume *Approaches to Translation* Professor Peter Newmark of Polytechnic of Central London has made an important contribution to a more satisfactory understanding of the real nature of translation. Wide acquaintance with the literature on translation theory, many years of experience in teaching translation techniques, and obvious expertise as a translator have all contributed to this well-illustrated and highly useful contribution to a better comprehension of the many phases of the translator's task.

Professor Newmark's major contribution is in a detailed treatment of semantic vs. communicative translating in which semantic translation focuses primarily upon the semantic content of the source text and communicative translation focuses essentially upon the comprehension and response of receptors. This distinction becomes especially relevant for the wide diversity of text types which Professor Newmark considers.

This approach to translation flatly rejects the proposition that translation is a science, but it does insist on treating the basic propositions of translation in terms of a theory of communication, one which is not restricted to a single literary genre or text type but which has applicability to a wide range of discourse and related problems. Accordingly, this volume deals extensively with the problems of figurative language and proposes a number of valuable suggestions as to how these can and should be handled.

Professor Newmark's teaching experience leads him to deal with a number of matters which most books on translation largely overlook—e.g. the rendering of proper names and titles and the translation of metalinguistic texts, which, with the exception of lyric poetry, are perhaps the most difficult types of texts to render without considerable readjustments in content and form.

The second part of this volume treats not only a wide range of practical issues, including punctuation, translation techniques, and technical translating, but also some elements of central importance to any student of translation—e.g. the significance of linguistics for translation and the relevance of translation theories to the translator's task.

Probably some of the most insightful comments in this volume are those which suggest a basis for a critique of translation methodology—something which one could well expect of someone who has had such a long and rich experience in teaching prospective translators and evaluating their effors.

EUGENE A. NIDA

April 1981

Preface

I first wrote on translation in 1957 for the long-defunct *Journal of Education*—an article which is duly recorded in the Nida (1964) and Jumpelt (1961) bibliographies. In 1967 I started writing again, not long after Anthony Crane and I had launched the first full-time postgraduate course in technical and specialized translation at what was then the Holborn College of Law, Languages and Commerce. In fact, I am something of a compulsive writer, but I am first a teacher, and though I owe much to Nida and the Leipzig School (or rather, as I saw them when I first became interested in translation theory, the *Fremdsprachen* writers), the main source of stimulation for my papers, and more particularly my propositions, is my classes.

Linguistics, in the modern sense of the word, did not exist in Great Britain 25 years ago except perhaps at J. R. Firth's SOAS (School of Oriental and African Studies) of the University of London. In its wake, translation theory is slowly developing from a series of rather general reflections and essays on the merits of faithful and free translation—interspersed with clichified epigrams identifying translation with women, carpets, traitors, coats, mirrors, Turkish tapestry (the reverse side), copper coins, false portraits, clear or coloured glass, musical transcriptions, wives, heroism and folly—to represent an identifiable and somewhat peculiar discipline. It is an academic pursuit that is dependent upon and apparently subordinate to a practical exercise. In a sense it is at third remove. Those who can, write; those who cannot, translate; those who cannot translate, write about translation. However, Goethe and a host of respectable writers who wrote well, translated well and wrote well about translation are an obvious disproof of this adapted Shavianism.

The fascination of translation theory lies in the large scope of its pertinence, its basic appeal (the concern with words) and its disparate levels, from the meaning within a context, of, say, a full stop to the meaning within another context of, say, the word 'God'. Translation theory's present standing is not yet secure. To begin with, 'everyone' has views about translation, many have written about it, few have written books about it. It is taught at various universities in the Federal Republic, the GDR and in other Eastern Bloc countries; at the universities of Paris, Amsterdam, Montreal, Ottawa and Tel-Aviv. 'Verrons-nous un jour figurer aux programmes des universités un cours de "Sciences de la Traduction" qui placerait à leur juste rang le traducteur et l'interprète dans la communauté culturelle?' M. E. Williams, Président of the École de Traduction et d'Interprétation of Geneva University, wrote wistfully in *Parallèles*, 1978. As far as I know, such courses are unknown in most anglophone countries. In the United Kingdom there have been undergraduate courses for the last 6 years at the Polytechnic of Central London; the University of Dundee and Portsmouth Polytechnic run a course in conjunction with their German options, and

Bristol Polytechnic is about to start a course. There is still no chair in translation theory.

I have always intended to write a textbook of translation theory and practice when I give up full-time teaching. I should then be in a better position to understand the bounds and to grasp the scope of my subject. As it is, I still see many virtually neglected areas and topics. In the meantime, I am happy to follow Vaughan James's invitation to publish some of my papers.

I have selected two introductory papers; three on communicative and semantic translation, which is my main contribution to general theory; one on texts related to language functions, to which I shall later add papers relating to the expressive and informative language functions; one on the translation of encyclopaedic and cultural terms—which is perhaps the most practical aspect of translation theory—and two on synonymy and metaphor; and, finally, from three papers I am reproducing nearly 150 so-called propositions on translation (these a not too distant echo of Nietzsche's paragraphs, I hope) which range from large topics such as the status of translation as an academic exercise and its relation to language-teaching and etymology to indication of the sense-values of the various punctuation marks.

I am aware of many gaps: such topics as lexical and grammatical ambiguity, the translation of poetry, technical translation (I have published papers on medical translation in the *Incorporated Linguist*, vol. 14, nos. 2 and 3, 1976, and in the *British Medical Journal*, Dec. 1979), synonymy (discussed in 'Some problems of translation theory and methodology', *Fremdsprachen*, 1978–9), the translation of plays, the history of translation, translation's influence on culture are hardly touched on. Other subjects such as the unit of translation, translation equivalence, translation invariance, detailed schemes for assessing translation, I regard as dead ducks—either too theoretical or too arbitrary.

With many limitations, these papers attempt to discuss certain significant aspects of translation and to give some indication of its importance in transmitting culture, in revitalizing language, in interpreting texts, in diffusing knowledge, in suggesting the relationship between thought and language and in contributing towards understanding between nations. That is a mouthful, so I would add that some of the unending fascination of the pursuit of words and things and utterances rubs off onto the pursuit of translation rules and recipes.

I thank Eugene Nida for writing the Foreword, and I gratefully acknowledge help from Pauline Newmark, Elizabeth Newmark, Matthew Newmark, Anthony Crane, John Trim, Vera North, Derek Cook-Radmore, Ralph Pemberton, Ewald Osers, John Smith, Alex Auswaks, Michael Alpert, Duncan Macrae, F. Hirst, Rosemary Young, Roger Lambart, M. R. Weston, Roger Barrett, Katharina Reiss, Bernadette Millard and Dominique Steggle.

PETER NEWMARK

Polytechnic of Central London

Acknowledgements

The author and publishers gratefully acknowledge permission to reprint extracts from articles in the following journals:

'A note on translation and translators', *Incorporated Linguist*, April 1969, October 1969.
'On lexical correlativity', *Audio-Visual Language Journal*, March, Winter 1969.
'Teaching Italian translation', *Incorporated Linguist*, April 1971.
'The case for literature', *Universities Quarterly*, June 1972.
'Twenty-four restricted rules of translation', *Incorporated Linguist*, January 1973.
'An approach to translation', *Babel* xix (1) 3–19, January 1973.
'Further propositions on translation parts I and II', *Incorporated Linguist* **13** (2 and 3) 34–43 and 62–73, 1974.
'The case for précis', *The use of English* **25** (3) 226–8, Spring 1974.
'Book review (*The new Muret-Sanders' Encyclopaedic Dictionary*)', *Incorporated Linguist*, April 1975 and Winter 1976.
'Book review (D. von Horvath: *Jugend ohne Gott*)', *Times Higher Educational Supplement*, p. 23, May 1975.
'Learning a foreign language', *Education and Training*' **17** (6 and 7) 141–3, June/July 1975.
'Book-review (G. Steiner: *After Babel*)', *Incorporated Linguist* **14** (4), October 1975.
'European languages: some perspectives', *Curriculum Development*, (10) 8–33, University of Sussex, Winter 1975.
'The theory and craft of translation', *Language Teaching and Linguistics: Abstracts* **10** (1), CUP, January 1976.
'A layman's approach to medical translation, part I', *Incorporated Linguist* **15** (2) 41–43, Spring 1976.
'A layman's approach to medical translation, part II', *Incorporated Linguist* **15** (3) 63–68, Summer 1976.
'The importance of accuracy', *CILT Reports and Papers 13* (German in the UK, Problems and Prospects), pp. 60–62, 1976.
'A tentative preface to translation', *AVL Journal* **14** (3), Winter 1976.
'The translation of proper names and institutional terms', *Incorporated Linguist*, 1977.
'Translation and the metalingual function of languages', *Lebende Sprachen*, 1977.
'Communicative and semantic translation', *Babel* (4) 1977.
'Some problems of translation theory and methodology', *Fremdsprachen*, (Leipzig) 1978.
'Componential analysis and translation theory', *Papers in Traductology*, University of Ottawa, 1978.
'Thought, language and translation', *Babel* (4) 1978.
Article on 'Applied linguistics' in *Aretê Encyclopaedia*, 1979.
'Sixty further propositions on translation', *Incorporated Linguist*, March 1979.
'The translation of metaphor', *Babel* (2) 1980.

Contents

PART ONE

Aspects of Translation Theory

1. The theory and the craft of translation

The first traces of translation date from 3000 BC, during the Egyptian Old Kingdom, in the area of the First Cataract, Elephantine, where inscriptions in two languages have been found. It became a significant factor in the West in 300 BC, when the Romans took over wholesale many elements of Greek culture, including the whole religious apparatus. In the twelfth century, the West came into contact with Islam in Moorish Spain. The situation favoured the two essential conditions for large-scale translation (Störig, 1963): a qualitative difference in culture (the West was inferior but scientifically acquisitive and receptive to new ideas) and continuous contact between two languages. When the Moorish supremacy collapsed in Spain, the Toledo school of translators translated Arabic versions of Greek scientific and philosophical classics. Luther's Bible translation in 1522 laid the foundations of modern German and King James's Bible (1611) had a seminal influence on English language and literature. Significant periods of translation preceded Shakespeare and his contemporaries, French classicism and the Romantic Movements.

* * *

The twentieth century has been called the 'age of translation' (Jumpelt, 1961) or 'reproduction' (Benjamin, 1923). Whereas in the nineteenth century translation was mainly a one-way means of communication between prominent men of letters and, to a lesser degree, philosophers and scientists and their educated readers abroad, whilst trade was conducted in the language of the dominant nation, and diplomacy, previously in Latin, was in French, international agreements between state, public and private organizations are now translated for all interested parties, whether or not the signatories understand each other's languages. The setting up of a new international body, the constitution of an independent state, the formation of a multinational company, gives translation enhanced political importance. The exponential increase in technology (patents, specifications, documentation), the attempt to bring it to developing countries, the simultaneous publication of the same book in various languages, the increase in world communication, has correspondingly increased requirements. UNESCO, which up to 1970 published an *Index translationum*, recorded a 4½-fold increase since 1948, with translations into German nearly twice as many as into Russian, the second most numerous. (Correspondingly, most theoretical literature is in German.) Scientific, technical and medical journals are translated wholesale in the USA and USSR. The EEC now employs 1600 translators. In 1967, 80,000 scientific journals were being translated annually (Spitzbart, 1972). Some 'international' writers (in the age of 'international' culture and world-literature) immediately sell more widely in translation than in the original, whilst others in Italy and the smaller European countries depend for a living on the translation of their works as well as their own translations.

The translation of literature in the 'minor' languages, particularly in the developing countries, is much neglected.

* * *

In relation to the volume of translation, little was written about it. The wider aspects were ignored: translation's contribution to the development of national languages, its relation to meaning, thought and the language universals. It was mainly discussed in terms of (a) the conflict between free and literal translation, and (b) the contradiction between its inherent impossibility and its absolute necessity (Goethe, 1826). Cicero (55 BC) first championed sense against words and said a translator must be either an interpreter or a rhetorician. The classical essays are those of St. Jerome (400), Luther (1530), Dryden (1684)—all favouring colloquial and natural renderings. Tytler wrote the first significant book on translation in 1790, stating that 'a good translation is one in which the merit of the original work is so completely transfused into another language as to be as distinctly apprehended and as strongly felt by a native of the country to which that language belongs as it is by those who speak the language of the original work'. In the nineteenth century, the important essays and references by Goethe (1813, 1814), Humboldt (1816), Novalis (1798), Schleiermacher (1813), Schopenhauer (1851) and Nietzsche (1882) inclined towards more literal translation methods, while Matthew Arnold (1928) favoured a simple, direct and noble style for translating Homer. In the twentieth century, Croce (1922), Ortega y Gasset (1937) and Valéry (1946) questioned the possibility of adequate translation, particularly of poetry. Benjamin (1923) saw translation filling in the gaps in meaning in a universal language. He recommended literal translation of syntax as well as words: 'The sentence is a wall blocking out the language of the original, whilst word for word translation is the arcade.'

The above is a brief conspectus of views in the pre-linguistics period of translation. On the whole, they make no attempt to distinguish types or quality of texts (which are mainly Biblical or literary), and while they are strong on theory, they are short on method and practical examples. They show a gradual transition from a natural or free treatment towards a literal analysis, if not translation, of the original, but there is no development of a theory, and many of the writers were not aware of each other's work.

* * *

With the increasing number of translator and reviser teams for documents and glossaries, the formulation of some translation theory, if only as a frame of reference, becomes necessary. The need is reinforced by the proliferation of terms of art, in particular of technological terms—in chemistry, for instance, a hundred internationalisms a month, in electronics, a few thousand a year (Spitzbart, 1972)—and by the desire to standardize the terminology, intra- and interlingually. But the main reason for formulating a translation theory, for proposing methods of translation related to and derived from it, for teaching translation, for translation courses is the appalling badness of so many published translations (Widmer, 1959). Literary or non-literary translations without mistakes are rare. Already in 1911, the *Encyclopaedia Britannica* stated in a good article absurdly restricted to literary translation, 'Most versions of modern foreign writers are mere hackwork carelessly executed by incompetent hands.' Now that accurate translation has become generally politically important, the need to investigate the subject is urgent, if only to agree on general principles.

* * *

Translation theory derives from comparative linguistics, and within linguistics, it is mainly an aspect of semantics; all questions of semantics relate to translation theory. Sociolinguistics, which investigates the social registers of language and the problems of languages in contact in the same or neighbouring countries, has a continuous bearing on translation theory. Sociosemantics, the theoretical study of *parole*—language in context—as opposed to *langue*—the code or system of a language—indicates the relevance of 'real' examples—spoken, taped, written, printed. Since semantics is often presented as a cognitive subject without connotations, rather than as an exercise in communication, semiotics—the science of signs—is an essential factor in translation theory. The American philosopher C. S. Peirce (1934) is usually regarded as its founder. He stressed the communicative factor of any sign: 'the meaning of a sign consists of all the effects that may conceivably have practical bearings on a particular interpretant, and which will vary in accordance with the interpretant'—no sign, therefore, has a self-contained meaning. Typically, to the reader an iced lolly may mean a flavoured frozen confection on a stick (as a non-participant, the purpose of the object is not important to him), but to the manufacturer it means a profitable source of income, to a housewife a messy nuisance for which she gets a demand all the year round, to a child a satisfying cold drink on a stick which lasts a long time. If one puts oneself as reader of a translated text in the place of the manufacturer, the housewife or the child, the importance of Peirce's theory of meaning for translation theory is clear. Charles Morris's (1971) division of semiotics into syntactics, the relation of signs to each other; semantics, the allocation of signs to their real objects; and pragmatics, the relation between signs and their interpreters, has been taken as a model by the Leipzig translation theorists (Neubert, 1968, 1972; Kade, 1965, 1968) who have been particularly sensitive to the pragmatics of political statements. Thus what is approvingly translated as *Fluchthelfer* in the Federal Republic would be rendered pejoratively as *Menschenhändler* in the GDR.

A translator requires a knowledge of literary and non-literary textual criticism, since he has to assess the quality of a text before he decides how to interpret and then translate it. All kinds of false distinctions have been made between literary and technical translation. Both Savory (1957) and Reiss (1971) have written that the technical translator is concerned with content, the literary translator with form. Other writers have stated that a technical translation must be literal, a literary translation must be free—and again, others have said the opposite. A traditional English snobbery puts literary translation on a pedestal and regards other translation as hackwork, or less important, or easier. But the distinction between careful, sensitive and elegant writing—'proper words in proper places', as Swift put it—on the one hand, and predictable, hackneyed and modish phrases—in fact, bad writing—on the other, cuts across all this. A translator must respect good writing scrupulously by accounting for its language, structures and content, whether the piece is scientific or poetic, philosophical or fictional. If the writing is poor, it is normally his duty to improve it, whether it is technical or a routine, commercialized best-seller. The basic difference between the artistic and the non-literary is that the first is symbolical or allegorical and the second representational in intention; the difference in translation is that more attention is paid to connotation and emotion in imaginative literature. The translator has to be a good judge of writing; he must assess not only the literary quality but the moral seriousness of a text in the sense of Arnold and Leavis. Moreover, any reading in stylistics, which is at the intersection between linguistics and literary criticism, such as a study of Jakobson (1960, 1966) and Spitzer (1948), both of whom discuss translation as well as comparative literature, will help him.

Logic and philosophy, in particular ordinary language philosophy, have a bearing on the grammatical and lexical aspects of translation respectively. A study of logic will assist the translator to assess the truth-values underlying the passage he is translating; all sentences depend on presuppositions and where the sentences are obscure or ambiguous, the translator has to determine the presuppositions. Moreover, a translation-rule such as the following on negations (my own) derives from logic: 'A word translated by a negative and its noun or object complementary term may be a satisfactory equivalent.' (Thus a 'female' is 'not a male'.) A word translated by a negative and its verb or process converse term is not a satisfactory equivalent, although the equivalent meaning may be ironically implied. (Compare 'We advanced' and 'We didn't retreat'.) A word translated by a negative and its contrary term is not a satisfactory equivalent, unless it is used ironically. (Compare 'spendthrift' and 'not stingy'.) A word translated by a negative and its contradictory term is a weakened equivalent, but the force of the understatement may convey equivalence: e.g. 'false' is almost 'not true'; 'he agreed with that' is almost 'he didn't dissent from it'. Lastly, a word translated by a double negative and the same word or its synonym is occasionally an effective translation, but normally in a weakened form (e.g. 'grateful' may be 'not ungrateful', 'not unappreciative'). A translator has to bear all the above options in mind, in particular where the contrary, contradictory or converse term is plainly or approximately missing in the target language, which should be his own.

Philosophy is a fundamental issue in translation theory. When Wittgenstein 'abandoned the idea that the structure of reality determines the structure of language, and suggested that it is really the other way round' (Pears, 1971), he implied that translation was that much harder. His most often quoted remark, 'For a large number of cases—though not for all—in which we employ the word "meaning", it can be defined or explained thus "the meaning of a word is its use in the language"' (Wittgenstein, 1958), is more pertinent to translation, which in the final consideration is only concerned with contextual use, than to language as a system. Again, when Austin (1963) made his revolutionary distinction between descriptive and performative sentences, he illustrated a valuable contrast between non-standardized and standardized language which always interests a translator: for a formulaic sentence such as 'I name this ship *Liberté*', there is normally only one equivalent in, say, French, 'Je baptise ce navire sous le nom de *Liberté*', and the translator has no options such as would be available if the sentence had read: 'I wish the *Liberté* all success.' Further, Kant's distinction between analytical propositions which are linguistic, e.g. 'All bachelors are unmarried', and synthetic referential propositions such as 'The bachelor hid in the cupboard', provided the rest of the passage clarifies the type of cupboard he hid in, gives the translator more licence in his treatment of analytical propositions. Lastly, Grice's 'meaning means intention' helps the translator to see that 'Would you mind doing it?' and 'I refuse to believe it' and 'Would you care to come?' have nothing to do with minding or refusing or caring. Usually, a text's or a proposition's intention can be ascertained only *outside* the utterances, by examining the reason and the occasion for the utterance. 'I'll murder you if you do that again' may be a mother exercising discipline. 'Demain c'est samedi' may mean 'Tomorrow, the holidays begin' (Seleskovitch, 1979).

Translation theory is not only an interdisciplinary study, it is even a function of the disciplines I have briefly alluded to.

* * *

Translation is a craft consisting in the attempt to replace a written message and/or statement in one language by the same message and/or statement in another language. Each exercise involves some kind of loss of meaning, due to a number of factors. It provokes a continuous tension, a dialectic, an argument based on the claims of each language. The basic loss is on a continuum between overtranslation (increased detail) and undertranslation (increased generalization).

In the first place, if the text describes a situation which has elements peculiar to the natural environment, institutions and culture of its language area, there is an inevitable loss of meaning, since the transference to, or rather the substitution or replacement by (Haas, 1962)—the word 'translation', like so many others, is misleading, due to its etymology—the translator's language can only be approximate. Unless there is already a recognized translation equivalent (but will the reader be familiar with it, and will he accept it?—here we must bear Peirce's pragmatics in mind) the translator has to choose from transcribing the foreign word (say, *directeur du cabinet*), translating it ('head of the minister's office'), substituting a similar word in his own culture ('Permanent Undersecretary of State'), naturalizing the word with a loan translation ('director of the cabinet'), sometimes adding or substituting a suffix from his own language (e.g. *apparatchik,* Prague, *footballeur*), defining it, or, the last resort, paraphrasing ('head of the Minister's departmental staff'), which is sometimes added in parenthesis or as a footnote to a transliteration. However, there is no 'referential' loss if the situation is on neutral, non-national ground with participants without specifically local features (e.g. a mathematical study, a medical experiment using standard equipment), i.e. if there is cultural overlap.

The second, and inevitable source of loss is the fact that the two languages, both in their basic character (*langue*) and their social varieties (*parole*) (bearing in mind Jakobson's (1973) gloss on Saussure), in context have different lexical, grammatical and sound systems, and segment many physical objects and virtually all intellectual concepts differently. (Usually, the closer the language and the culture, the closer the translation and the original.) Few words, phrases or sentences correspond precisely on the four lexical scales which interest the translator (Newmark, 1969): (1) formality (cf. Joos, 1967) (from frozen to uninhibited); (2) feeling or affectivity (from overheated to deadpan); (3) generality or abstraction (from popular to opaquely technical); and (4) evaluation (four subscales: morality (good to bad); pleasure (nice to nasty); intensity (strong to weak); dimension (e.g. wide to narrow)). I have proposed a translation rule that corresponding words, collocations, idioms, metaphors, proverbs, sayings, syntactic units and word-order must be equally frequent (in the appropriate style and register of the text) in the source and the target language; but the translator can never follow this rule to the letter, since it even has inherent contradictions.

Thirdly, the individual uses of language of the text-writer and the translator do not coincide. Everybody has lexical if not grammatical idiosyncrasies, and attaches 'private' meanings to a few words. The translator normally writes in a style that comes naturally to him, desirably with a certain elegance and sensitivity unless the text precludes it. Moreover, as Weightman (1947) has pointed out, a good writer's use of language is often remote from, if not at cross purposes with, some of the conventional canons of good writing, and it is the writer not the canons that the translator must respect.

Lastly, the translator and the text-writer have different theories of meaning and different values. The translator's theory colours his interpretation of the text. He may set greater value than the text-writer on connotation and correspondingly less on denotation. He may look for symbolism where realism was intended; for several meanings where only one was intended; for different emphasis, based on his own philosophy or even his reading of the syntax. The different values of writer and translator may be parodied through a school-report, where words like: competent, fair, average, adequate (cf. *adäquat*), above average, satisfactory, passable, middling, may mean all things to all men (cf. Trier, 1973). Thus diagrammatically one may see a target language text as an object in a magnetic field which has seven or eight conflicting forces exerted upon it. The resulting loss of meaning is inevitable and is unrelated, say, to the obscurity or the deficiencies of the text and the incompetence of the translator, which are additional possible sources of this loss of meaning, sometimes referred to as 'entropy' (Vinay, 1968).

* * *

This, then, is the problem, and in the last 30 years, a considerable theoretical literature has been devoted to it. A few professional linguists, as well as translators, began to turn their attention to translation theory at a time when philosophy was substantially concerned with language and later when with the decline of Bloomfieldian or behaviourist (rather than structuralist) linguistics and rapid progress in applied linguistics, semantics was being (grotesquely) 'reinstated' within linguistics. Prior to this period, translation theory was almost exclusively the concern of men of letters, with the notable exception of Humboldt.

The literature is dominated by Nida, whose work is informed by his experience as a linguist and as a Bible-translator. In Nida (1964, 1969), almost every translation problem is discussed. He adapts transformational grammar by proposing eight model kernel sentences as transitional stages between source and target language structures. He applies componential analysis by using common, diagnostic and supplementary components as tools for comparing and contrasting items within a semantic field. He discusses the logical relations of words with each other, the difference between cultural and linguistic translation, the relevance of discourse analysis, the difficulties of translating between remote cultures, levels of usage, the psychological connotations of words and practical problems of translation. His reduction of propositions to objects, events, relationals and abstracts may be more fruitful to translators as a comprehension procedure than the kernel sentences. His distinction between dynamic and formal equivalence is too heavily weighted against the formal properties of language. Nida's recent books (1974a and 1975a) are specifically concerned with semantic grammar and componential analysis, but they can be profitably applied to the first stages of translation procedure. He has notably summarized the present state of translation theory (1974b).

Fedorov (1958, 1968) stresses that translation theory is an independent linguistic discipline, deriving from observations and providing the basis for practice. Like the Leipzig School, he believes that all experience is translatable, and rejects the view that language expresses a peculiar mental word-picture. However, the lack of a common outlook or ideology at present impairs the effectiveness of translation. Komissarov (1973) sees translation theory moving in three directions: the denotative (information translation), the semantic (precise equivalence) and the transformational (transposition of relevant structures). His theory of equivalence distinguishes five levels: (1) lexical units, (2) collocations, (3) information, (4) the situation, and (5) the communication aim. Jumpelt (1961) applies the Trier–Weisgerber field theory to technological texts, and effectively distinguishes superordinate and subordinate terms in the technical literature. The Leipzig School (Neubert, Kade, Wotjak, Jäger, Helbig, Ruzicka), much of whose work has been published in the periodical *Fremdsprachen*, in its six *Beihefte*, and in *Linguistische Arbeitsberichte*, distinguishes sharply between the invariant (cognitive) and the variant (pragmatic) elements in translation, and turns transformational grammar and semiotics to account. It is sometimes short on procedures and examples, and restricts itself to non-literary texts. Neubert's and Helbig's writing has been imaginative. Koller (1972) is particularly useful in distinguishing information from communication, and Reiss (1971) has categorized and illustrated the variety of text-types. Catford (1965) has applied Halliday's systemic grammar to translation theory, and has fruitfully categorized translation shifts between levels, structures, word-classes, units ('rank-shifts') and systems. He distinguishes between 'context' (of situation) and 'co-text' (of language). He sets greater limits to the possibilities of translation than other theorists. Firth (1968) points to contextual meaning as the basis of a translation theory and sees translation theory as the basis of a new theory of language and firmer foundations in philosophy. Mounin (1955, 1964, 1967) discusses translation theories and their relation to semantics and supports the 'linguistic' against the literary theory of translation. Levy (1969) and Winter (1969) apply linguistics to the translation of literary texts, including the phonological aspects of poetry. Wuthenow (1969), Kloepfer (1967) and Cary (1956) reject all but a literary approach to translation theory.

The above-mentioned literature is basically theoretical. Of the literature which applies linguistics to translation procedures, Vinay and Darbelnet (1976) are outstanding. They enumerate seven procedures—transliteration, loan translation, literal translation, transposition, modulation, equivalence, adaptation—and make perceptive distinctions between French and English. Friederich's work on English and German (1969) is also invaluable, whilst German and French have been compared by Truffaut (1968) and Malblanc (1961). Mention should also be made of Wandruszka's (1969) multilingual comparisons and Fuller's (1973) distinctions between French and English. Valuable essays are collected in Störig (1963), Brower (1966), Smith (1958) and Kapp (1974), whilst Garvin (1955) includes the Prague School's contributions to translation theory.

There is a considerable literature on machine translation (e.g. Booth, 1967) but at least since Bar-Hillel (1964) there is fairly general agreement that computers will not be much used for translation (except in restricted areas such as meteorology) in the foreseeable future; they are already of incalculable assistance to terminologists in compiling glossaries and bilingual dictionaries. Melčuk's work on MT (e.g. in Booth, 1967) has thrown light on translation procedure.

G. Steiner (1975) contains a variety of outstanding literary translation and summaries of translation theories, and emphasizes the importance of translation as a key to the understanding of thought, meaning, language, communication and comparative linguistics. He puts the case for 'poem to poem' against 'plain prose' translations (1966).

* * *

There is wide but not universal agreement that the main aim of the translator is to produce as nearly as possible the same effect on his readers as was produced on the readers of the original (see Rieu, 1953). The principle is variously referred to as the principle of similar or equivalent response or effect, or of functional or dynamic (Nida) equivalence. It bypasses and supersedes the nineteenth-century controversy about whether a translation should incline towards the source or the target language, and the consequent faithful versus beautiful, literal versus free, form versus content disputes. The principle demands a considerable imaginative or intuitive effect from the translator, since he must not identify himself with the reader of the original, but must empathize with him, recognizing that he may have reactions and sympathies alien to his own. The emphasis of this principle is rightly on communication, on the third term in the translation relationship, on the reader ('Who is the reader?' is the translation teacher's first question), who had been ignored previously, except in Bible translation. The translator should produce a different type of translation of the same text for a different type of audience. The principle emphasizes the importance of the psychological factor—it is mentalistic—its success can hardly be verified. One would want to know how each reader reacts—how he thinks, feels and behaves. The principle allows for a wide range of translation styles: if the writer of the original has deviated from the language norms of the type of text he has written, whether it is an advertisement, a report or a literary work, one would expect the translation to do likewise. A poem or a story in such a case would retain the flavour of the original, and might perhaps read like a translation.

Whilst the successful practitioner of equivalent effect appears to be achieving something like the crystallization stated by Stendhal to be the essence of love, there are some cases where the effect cannot be realized. If a non-literary text describes, qualifies or makes use of a peculiarity of the language it is written in, the reader of the translation will have to have it explained to him, unless it is so trivial that it can be omitted. This applies say to Freud's slips of the tongue and 'jokes', where a similar communicative effect might be obtained by fresh examples, but where the source language examples would still have to be retained. In fact, the sentence, 'Er behandelte mich wie seinesgleichen, ganz famillionär' (Freud, 1975) could be translated as, 'He treated me as an equal, quite like a famillionaire', but it has not the naturalness of the German. Similarly, in the case of Freud's puns on anec-dotage, alco-holidays, monument-arily, the German must be retained.

Secondly, a non-literary text relating to an aspect of the culture familiar to the first reader but not to the target language reader is unlikely to produce equivalent effect: particularly, if originally intended only for the first reader. The translator, therefore, say, in translating the laws of a source-language country, cannot 'bend' the text towards the second reader.

Thirdly, there is the artistic work with a strong local flavour which may also be rooted in a particular historical period. The themes will consist of comments on human character and behaviour—universals, applicable to the reader of the translation, and therefore subject to the equivalent-effect principle. On the other hand, the work may describe a culture remote from the second reader's experience, which the translator wants to introduce to him not as the original reader, who took or takes it for granted, but as something strange with its own special interest. In the case of the Bible, the translator decides on equivalent-effect—the nearer he can bring the human truth and the connotations to the reader, the more immediately he is likely to transmit its religious and moral message. But if the culture is as important as the message (the translator has to decide), he reproduces the form and content of the original as literally as possible (with some transliterations), without regard for equivalent-effect. If Homer's *οἰνώψ πόντος*, the 'wine-dark sea', were to be translated as the '(sky) blue sea' merely to achieve equivalent-effect, much would be lost. As Matthew Arnold (1928) pointed out, one cannot achieve equivalent-effect in translating Homer as one knows nothing about his audiences.

In fact, if the creative artist writes for his own relief (in Benjamin's words, 'No poem is written for its reader, nor is regard for those who receive a work of art useful for the purpose of understanding it' (1923)), then the equivalent-effect principle is irrelevant in the translation of a work of art; the translator's loyalty is to the artist, and he must concentrate on recreating as much of the work as he can. This is literal or maximal translation in Nabokov's sense (1964), 'rendering, as closely as the associative and syntactical capacities of another language allows, the exact contextual meaning of the original'. Syntax, word-order, rhythm, sound, all have semantic values. The priorities differ for each work, but there are three rules of thumb: (a) the translation should be as literal as possible and as free as is necessary (Cauer, 1896), i.e. the unit of translation should be as small as possible (Haas, 1962); (b) a source language word should not normally be translated into a target language word which has another primary one-to-one equivalent in the source language (*schwarz* should not be translated as 'dark' because 'dark' is *finster* or *dunkel*: established collocations like *schwarze Augen,* 'dark eyes', are the exception); (c) a translation is impermeable to interference—it never takes over a typical source language collocation, structure or word-order. These rules apply to 'literal' as to the much more common equivalent-effect translation. Interference, however plausible, is always mistranslation. The *European Communities Glossary* (1974) reads like a guide on how to avoid it.

Paradoxically, the 'literal' principle of translating works of art is 'scientific' and verifiable, whilst the equivalent-effect principle is intuitive. If the emphasis is on human nature rather than on local culture, a masterly translation such as Stefan George's of Shakespeare or Baudelaire may conform to both principles.

There are also other restricted methods of translation: information translation, ranging from brief abstracts through summaries to complete reproduction of content without form; plain prose translation (as in Penguins) to guide one to the original, whose language should always be a little familiar; interlinear translation, which shows the mechanics of the original; formal translation, for nonsense poetry (Morgenstern) and nursery rhymes, where the meaning and the scenario, but not the tone, can be ignored; academic translation, for converting a text to a standard literary style; a combination of transliteration, translation and paraphrase for texts concerned with the source language, where the metalingual (Jakobson, 1960) function predominates. Translation theory, however, is not concerned with restricted translation. Whilst principles have been, and will be, proposed for dealing with recurrent problems ('translation rules'), a general theory cannot propose a single method (e.g. dynamic equivalence), but must be concerned with the full range of text-types and their corresponding translation criteria, as well as the major variables involved.

* * *

Many theorists have divided texts according to subject-matter (literature, institutions, technology, etc.), but it is perhaps more profitable to begin with Bühler's statement (1934) of the functions of language which had a wide influence on the Prague School and has been used by some translation theorists (Reiss, 1971; Hartmann and Vernay, 1970). (Figure 1 is an extended version.)

In this scheme, the expressive function A is author-centred, the personal use the writer makes of his language; function B is the 'extralinguistic' information content of the text; function C is reader-centred (for this Bühler used the inadequate word *Appell*; he also used 'signal', a better term). In calling it the 'vocative' function I include all the resources with which the writer affects the reader, in particular the emotive, so that he 'gets the message'.

Figure 1. Text continuum (adapted from Bühler).

A	B	C
EXPRESSIVE FUNCTION (or self-expressive, creative, subjective)	INFORMATIVE FUNCTION (or cognitive, denotative, representational, intellectual, referential, descriptive, objective)	VOCATIVE FUNCTION (or social injunctive, emotive, rhetorical, affective, excitatory, conative, dynamic, directive, connotative, seductive, stimulative, operative, suggestive, imperative, persuasive, rhetorical)
(AUSDRUCK) – (pragmatic) (stylistic)	(DARSTELLUNG) –	(APPELL) – (pragmatic) (stylistic)

Figure 2. Translator's continuum (adapted from Frege).

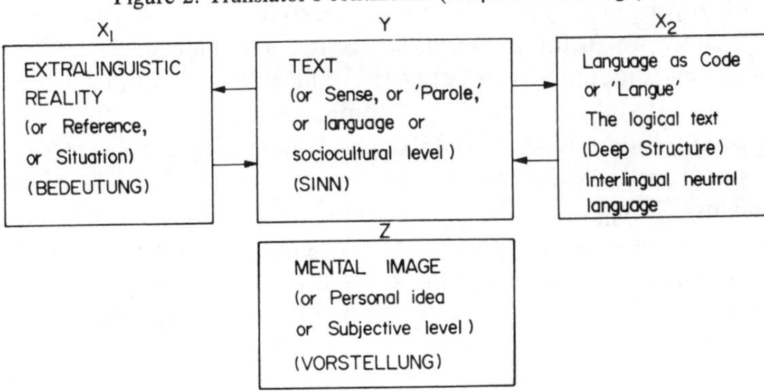

Looking at the text from the translator's angle, I adapt Frege's (1960) distinctions (Fig. 2). The translator works on level Y, which is the language of the text. He has two parallel sources of reference and comparison: X_1 is the situation in the real world, or its reflection in the text-writer's mind, when he (the translator) steps aside from the text, and asks himself: Now what is actually happening? Who is this? Where is this? Can I name it? Is this true?, etc. X_2 is the logical structure of the underlying clauses, the clauses in their simple uncluttered form, desirably with an animate subject and an inanimate object, and which may later have to be converted to corresponding syntactic structures in the target language. Level Z is the 'internal image . . . properly, differences in translation should only be at this level' (Frege).

Thus, for a part of a text Y, *le Président de la République*, X_1, may be Valéry Giscard d'Estaing, while X_2 is perhaps 'The man who presides over the Republic'. Level Z may suggest any subjectively coloured figure of authority, but as this is standardized language (see p. 16), it does not obtrude upon the translation ('the French President').

In Fig. 3 the scheme is simplified.

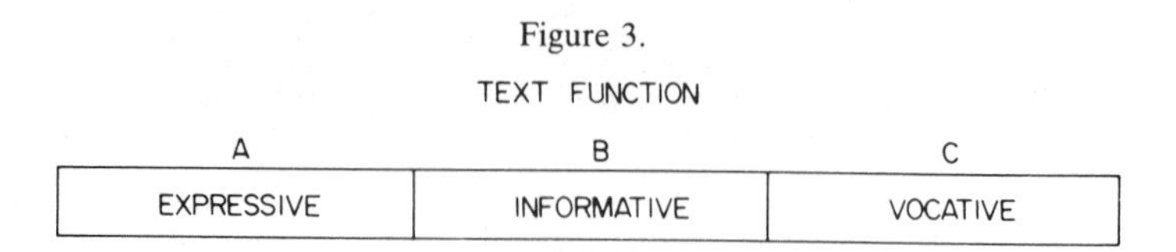

TRANSLATION LEVEL

X	REFERENTIAL
Y	TEXTUAL
Z	SUBJECTIVE

The translator has an instrument consisting of three levels XYZ—compare the tubes of a jointed telescope. With it he observes a text which exhibits the three functions of language ABC in varying degrees. He may have to deflect his instrument, which may be focused mainly at A for a poem, or B for a technical report, or C for an advertisement, but sometimes rests between A and B for a description of nature in the poem, or between B and C for the final recommendations of a report, as no text, and few sentences are undiluted A or B or C. Even names like 'Johnny' or 'Petrushka' may be C as well as B. Whilst the translator always works from X, he continuously checks Y against X. Level Z, the partly conscious and partly unconscious element corresponding to the text writer's A, is always present, but the translator has to reduce its influence to a minimum, until he is left with what appears to him to be an almost gratuitous choice between equally valid units of language, which may be lexical or grammatical; this then becomes a question of stylistics, and his version on this level of *quot homines, tot sententiae* may be as good as ten others. A difference between literary and non-literary translation is also clarified by the diagram. In non-literary translation, the informative function B, which is identical with the translator's referential X, is real; in the case of a realistic literary text, the function B is also treated factually, but even the details have typical and general implications. In any work of art of moral seriousness, the referential function is a comment on human behaviour and character and all passages are implicitly metaphorical and allegorical; whatever the content—abstract, symbolical, naturalistic—the expressive function A is most important in the text, and inevitably the translator's level Z is more influential than in other types of text.

Figure 4 shows tentatively how the three functions may affect the work of the translator.

All texts have an informative function, and the examples (1) merely illustrate the main emphasis. Style (2) for A is assessed by the translator according to its grammatical and lexical deviations from ordinary language; for B one would expect the appropriate register; whilst for C, where examples are sharply divided between official writing (laws and notices) and publicity and propaganda, styles are correspondingly formulaic or persuasive. In a scientific report, there would be considerable use of the third person, past tenses (present tenses in French), multi-noun compounds, passives. For notices, grammatical divergencies in each language: 'Wet paint' becomes 'Freshly painted' in German and 'Mind the paint' in French; 'Beware of the dog' is 'Biting dog' in German and 'Wicked dog' in French. The unit of translation (6) is always as small as possible and as large as is necessary (grammatically it is usually the group or phrase), but an advertiser is likely to ignore it, whilst a literary translator may try to bring it down to the word. The more the text uses the resources of language, and therefore the more important its form, the greater the losses of meaning (8); the greatest loss is in poetry, since it uses all resources of language. ('The poetry is the untranslatable element', Robert Frost said.) A technical translator has no right to create neologisms (9), unless he is a member of an interlingual glossary team, whilst an advertiser or propaganda writer can use any linguistic resources he requires. Conventional metaphors and sayings (10) should always be conventionally translated (the convention is shown in the dictionary), but unusual metaphors and comparisons should be reduced to their sense if the text has a mainly informative function (11). The appropriate equivalents for keywords (10) should be scrupulously repeated throughout a text in a philosophical text; theme words are the writer's main concepts and terms of art; in literary works, the stylistic markers are likely to be an author's characteristic words (Thomas Mann's *verworfen, mürbe, abnutzbar, überreizt* in *Death in Venice* or his leitmotivs, 'the gypsy in the green wagon' and 'the fair and blue-eyed ones' in *Tonio Kröger*); in an advertisement for wine, they may be the token-words, i.e. *mots-témoins* (Matoré, 1953), that are transferred to evoke a fact of civilization too snobbish to be translated: *cuvée, château, grand cru, appellation contrôlée.* In a non-literary text, there is a case for transcribing as well as translating any key-word of linguistic significance, e.g. Hitler's favourite political words in Maser's biography.

Figure 4.

	A EXPRESSIVE	B INFORMATIVE	C VOCATIVE
(1) Typical examples	Literature authoritative texts	Scientific and technical reports and textbooks	Polemical writing, publicity, notices, laws and regulations, propaganda, popular literature
(2) 'Ideal' style	Individual	Neutral, objective	Persuasive or imperative
(3) Text emphasis	Source language (SL)	Target language (TL)	Target language
(4) Focus	Writer (1st person)	Situation (3rd person)	Reader (2nd person)
(5) Method	'Literal' translation	Equivalent-effect translation	Equivalent-effect recreation
(6) Unit of translation	Small	Medium	Large
Maximum	Collocation	Sentence	Text
Minimum	Word	Collocation	Paragraph
(7) Type of language	Figurative	Factual	Compelling
(8) Loss of meaning	Considerable	Small	Dependent on cultural differences
(9) New words and meanings	Mandatory if in SL text	Not permitted unless reason given	Yes, except in formal texts
(10) Keywords (retain)	Leitmotivs Stylistic markers	Theme words	Token words
(11) Unusual metaphors	Reproduce	Give sense	Recreate
(12) Length in relation to original	Approximately the same	Slightly longer	No norm

Jakobson (1960) has added the metalingual, the phatic and the aesthetic to Bühler's language functions, and Fig. 4 could be expanded to include them.

* * *

All texts may be regarded by the translator as an amalgam of standardized and non-standardized language. The distinction between them is that for standardized language, when it is used as such (but technical terms often melt into ordinary language—e.g. 'fail-safe', 'parameter'), there should be only one correct equivalent, provided one exists, provided it is used in the same situations by the same kind of person, and that is the 'science' of translation. Whilst for non-standardized language, of whatever length, there is rarely only one correct equivalent, and that is the art or craft of translation.

Standardized language consists partly of terminology, and as Bachrach (1974) has stated, increased research and teaching is required here. The terms need attaching to pictures and diagrams (the Duden principle—processes as well as objects), collecting in lexical fields, as in a thesaurus, as well as in cognate groups, with frequency, formality etc., indicated. Whilst many terms are internationalisms, others, as Maillot (1969) has pointed out, are polysemous. *Résistance* means 'resistor' as well as 'resistance' *réacteur* 'resistance' and 'reactor', *capacité* 'capacitance' and 'capacity'. Larbaud (1946) stated that a translator must look up every word, especially the ones he knows best. Preferably, words should be looked up only to confirm knowledge, and every time one consults a bilingual dictionary the word should be checked in half-a-dozen source and target language monolingual dictionaries and reference books. Any target language word found in a bilingual, but not in a monolingual, dictionary must be rejected. Bilingual dictionaries often have obsolete, rare or one-off words invented through interference.

However, standardized language goes beyond technical terms. It includes any commonly used metaphor, idiom, proverb, public notice, social phrase, expletive, the usual ways of stating the date or time of day, giving dimensions, performatives expressed in accepted formulae. Thus one would expect only one valid translation for 'Keep Britain tidy', 'One man's meat is another's poison', 'c'est un con' and for phatic phrases such as 'Nice weather we're having'. There should be little choice in translating the restricted patter in the specialized uses of language mentioned in Halliday (1973)—weather reports, recipes, the language of games, as well as company reports and accounts, the format of agendas and minutes, medical reports. The stale language within each peer-group, the modish words instantly internationalized by the media, the predictable patter, the fill-in between stimulus and response—all often have their equally predictable equivalents in the detritus of the target language. The translator's invariant terms include not only the technical and scientific which may be supranational and the institutional, cultural and ecological which may be national, but also the characteristic expressions within a register, e.g. a patient's 'admission' (*accettazione*) or 'discharge' (*dimissione*) from hospital; the referring terms noted by Strawson (1970a) as 'quaint names, substantial phrases which grow capital letters' such as the 'Great War', 'The Annunciation', names of organizations and companies, titles of books, pictures, etc., which are transcribed unless there is already a generally accepted translation, which must then be used; quotations from authorized translations, which must be used and acknowledged; the jargon and 'in' words that cluster round social groups and occupations ('We call it "stint" and "snap"—what do you call it?'). Inevitably organization, bureaucracy, technology, the media continuously increase and congeal the area and extent of standardized language.

* * *

Which leaves non-standardized language, language creatively used, which is how language is daily used by everyone. Here, translation becomes a craft and an art—or simply art—where there are limited choices. Here, too, the scientific method operates, since the sense of the translation must be tested for each unit and stretch of language against the original, and vice versa, as well as against the reference, so that clear errors of language and fact are eliminated. Further, the translation has to be seen as natural language acceptably used in the context, if it is so in the original. The translator's craft lies first in his command of an exceptionally large vocabulary as well as all syntactic resources—his ability to use them elegantly, flexibly, succinctly. All translation problems finally resolve themselves into problems of how to write well in the target language. Benjamin (1923) stated that in a good work, language surrounds the content as a shell surrounds its fruit, whilst a translation is a coat hanging loosely round the content of the original in large folds. A translation is never finished, and one has to keep paring away at it, reducing the element of paraphrase, tightening the language. The shorter the translation, the better it is likely to be.

Secondly, the translator as craftsman has to know the foreign language so well that he can determine to what extent the text deviates from the language norms usually used in that topic on that occasion. He has to determine with an intuition backed by empirical knowledge the extent of the text's grammatical and semantic oddness, which he must account for in a well written 'expressive' text, and may decide to normalize in a badly written 'informative' or 'vocative' text. Moreover, he requires a degree of creative tension between fantasy and common sense. He has the fantasy for making hypotheses about apparently unintelligible passages, and the common sense for dismissing any unrealistic hypothesis—it is pointless to pursue an idea (unlike an ideal) that cannot be real or realized. More practically, he needs the common sense for eliminating interference and spotting strange acronyms. (What are *K opératoires* but *cas opératoires*?)

The translator has to acquire the technique of transferring smoothly between the two basic translation processes: comprehension, which may involve interpretation, and formulation, which may involve recreation (Fig. 5).

He has to have a sharp eye for oppositions, contrasts and emphases (foregrounding, see Garvin, 1955) in the original, and, if it is a non-literary text, he has to know how to accentuate these in his own version. He has to distinguish synonyms used to give additional or complementary information from synonyms used simply to refer to a previously mentioned object or concept. In literary translation (see Nietzsche, 1962) his hardest task is to catch the pace of the original.

Figure 5.

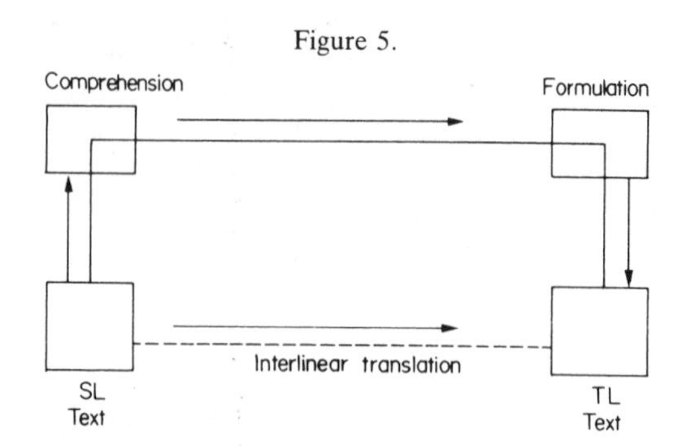

Translation shares with the arts and other crafts the feature that its standards of excellence can be determined only through the informed discussion of experts or exceptionally intelligent laymen; no popular acclaim can stamp the value of a translation any more than of a vase or a new piece of music. After mistakes have been 'proved' by reference to encyclopaedias and dictionaries, experts have to rely on their intuition and taste in preferring one of two or three good translations of a sentence or paragraph. Their final choice at this level is as subjective as the translator's choice of words, but they must be ready to give reasons for their choice. The main matters under dispute may be whether the translator has understood the tone, the writer's attitude towards the information presented, which is often indicated in the syntax—say, the use of modal verb forms, subjunctives—rather than the words.

Further, the experts, the third readers, have to decide intuitively whether the text is natural ('Would one actually see that on the printed page?'), with the proviso that they first agree what kind of printed page they are talking about. In the case of 'expressive' writing the criterion is: 'Would *he* write that?'

* * *

Goethe (1813) stated that translation is impossible, essential and important. The words of all languages overlap and leave gaps of meaning: there are unnamed, and perhaps unnamable, parts of a hand or a cloud. Benjamin (1923) stated that translation goes beyond enriching the language and culture of a country which it contributes to, beyond renewing and maturing the life of the original text, beyond expressing and analysing the most intimate relationships of languages with each other and becomes a way of entry into a universal language. Words that according to the conventional wisdom are peculiar to national character (say, *nichevo* for Russian, *magari* for Italian, *hinnehmen* for German, *sympathique* for French, *schlampig* for Austrian German (many more come to mind)) may perhaps fill in the gaps in general and universal experience, which will remain.

2. What translation theory is about

Instance, O instance
(*Troilus and Cressida* V. ii. 155.)

Translation theory is a misnomer, a blanket term, a possible translation, therefore a translation label, for *Übersetzungswissenschaft.* In fact translation theory is neither a theory nor a science, but the body of knowledge that we have and have still to have about the process of translating: it is therefore an -ology, but I prefer not to call it 'translatology' (Harris, 1977) or 'traductology' (Vasquez, 1977), because the terms sound too pretentious—I do not wish to add to any -ologies or -isms. Besides, since, as Gombrich (1978) has pointed out, *Kunstwissenschaft* translates 'art theory', 'translation theory' will do.

Translation theory's main concern is to determine appropriate translation methods for the widest possible range of texts or text-categories. Further, it provides a framework of principles, restricted rules and hints for translating texts and criticizing translations, a background for problem-solving. Thus, an institutional term ('MP') or a metaphor ('the stone died' (see Levin, 1977)) or synonyms in collocation or metalingual terms may each be translated in many ways, if it is out of context; in these areas, the theory demonstrates the possible translation procedures and the various arguments for and against the use of one translation rather than another in a particular context. Note that translation theory is concerned with choices and decisions, not with the mechanics of either the source language (SL) or the target language (TL). When Catford (1965) gives a list of words that are grammatically singular in one language and plural in another, he may be helping the student to translate, he is illustrating contrastive linguistics, but he is not contributing to translation theory.

Lastly, translation theory attempts to give some insight into the relation between thought, meaning and language; the universal, cultural and individual aspects of language and behaviour, the understanding of cultures; the interpretation of texts that may be clarified and even supplemented by way of translation.

Thus translation theory covers a wide range of pursuits, attempts always to be useful, to assist the individual translator both by stimulating him to write better and to suggest points of agreement on common translation problems. Assumptions and propositions about translation normally arise only from practice, and should not be offered without examples of originals and their translations. As with much literature *à thèse*, the examples are often more interesting than the thesis itself. Further, translation theory alternates between the smallest detail, the significance (translation) of dashes and hyphens, and the most abstract themes, the symbolic power of a metaphor or the interpretation of a multivalent myth.

Consider the problem: a text to be translated is like a particle in an electric field attracted by the opposing forces of the two cultures and the norms of two languages, the idiosyncrasies of one writer (who may infringe all the norms of his own language), and the different requirements of its readers, the prejudices of the translator and possibly of its publisher. Further, the text is at the mercy of a translator who may be deficient in several essential qualifications: accuracy, resourcefulness, flexibility, elegance and sensitivity in the use of his own language, which may save him from failings in two other respects: knowledge of the text's subject matter and knowledge of the SL.

* * *

Let us look first at the practical problems. The translator's first task is to understand the text, often to analyse, or at least make some generalizations about his text before he selects an appropriate translation method, so it is the business of translation theory to suggest some criteria and priorities for this analysis.

First, *the intention of a text.* An article on 'Personnel management of multinational companies' may really be a defence of multinational companies, written in innocuous internationalese, with contrasting formal to informal sentences emphasizing innocence: 'problème trop complexe pour être abordé globalement . . . critique qui a tendance à effacer nuances et détails et n'a donc presque plus rien à voir avec la réalité.' The defensive style speaks for itself.

Phrases such as these show that the writer is concealing his propaganda purpose behind a mass of statistics and facts about multinational companies. The translator, who has to be faithful to the author and not to his own view of multinational companies, has to bear the intention of the original in mind throughout his work.

Or again, note the two more or less equivalent versions of a Chinese text quoted by Achilles Fang (in Wright, 1976): 'You may say that they didn't go the right way about their business, but you must know that it is equally the fault of the times' and 'You may blame them for their misguided intelligence, yet you will have to agree with me that their obscurity was due to a lack of opportunity'.

Fang comments that the point, which is the first thing the translator is concerned with, comes out more clearly (?) in the second sentence (which might be clarified as 'they remained obscure as they had no chance of shining').

Secondly, *the intention of the translator.* Is he trying to ensure that the translation has the same emotional and persuasive charge as the original, and affects the reader in the same way as the original? Or is he trying to convey the cultural flavour of the SL text, a combination of idiosyncratic language and untranslated regional terms? Or is he addressing a different uninformed reader, who has to have the SL text made more explicit and any cultural or institutional term explained? (cf. Neubert, 1968).

Thirdly, *the reader and the setting of the text.* The translator asks himself: Who is the reader? What education, class, age, sex? Informed or ignorant, layman or expert? Where would the text be found, viz. what is the TL equivalent of the SL periodical, newspaper, textbook, etc.? All this would help the translator to decide on the degree of formality (officialese, administrative, formal, informal, colloquial, slang), emotiveness (intense, warm, neutral, cool, impassive, factual) and simplicity (universally comprehensible, media level, graduate level, fairly technical, technical, opaquely technical) he must pursue when he works on the text. He finds it useful, moreover, to distinguish between texts that are 'dramatic' or narrative ('verb' emphasis) and those that are 'static' or descriptive (nouns, noun-compounds, adjectives, adverbs).

Fourthly, *the quality of the writing and the authority of the text.* If the text is well written (i.e. the manner is as important as the matter, and all the words a vital component of the ideas), and/or if the SL writer is an acknowledged authority on his subject, the translator has to regard every nuance of the author's meaning (particularly, if it is subtle and difficult) as having precedence over the response of the reader—assuming that the reader is not required to act or react promptly. And again, if the SL text is entirely bound up with the culture of the SL community—a novel or a historical piece or a description attempting to characterize a place or custom or local character—the translator has to decide whether or not the reader requires, or is entitled to, supplementary information and explanation.

In any event, the author wants to 'communicate' but not at any price.

Before deciding on his translation method, the translator may assign his text to the three general categories previously mentioned, each of which is dominated by a particular function of language. The most satisfactory basis here is Jakobson's (1960) modification of Bühler (1934): the main functions of language are the expressive (the subjective or 'I' form), the descriptive or informative (the 'it' form) and the vocative or directive or persuasive (the 'you' form), the minor functions being the phatic, the metalingual and the aesthetic. All texts have aspects of the expressive, the informative and the vocative function: the sentence 'I love you' tells you something about the transmitter of the utterance, the depth of his feelings and his manner of expressing himself; it gives you a piece of straight information; and it illustrates the means he is using to produce a certain effect (action, emotion, reflection) upon his reader. That particular sentence, which also illustrates the most logical, common, and neutral sequence of arguments, viz. SVO, more particularly, animate subject–verb–inanimate object (the object of a sentence is 'inanimate', whether it be a person or a thing, because it has a passive role), with no emphasis on any of the three components, must be translated literally, since literal translation is always best provided it has the same communicative and semantic effect.

Very approximately, the translation theorist can assign such text-categories as serious literature (belles-lettres), authoritative statements (speeches or declarations) and personal or intimate writing to the expressive function; journalism, reporting, scientific and technical papers, general textbooks, most non-literary work where the facts are more important than the style, to the informative function; and advertising, propaganda, polemical works ('thesis literature'), popular literature (*Trivialliteratur*, best sellers)—all these, to *persuade* the reader—plus notices, instructions, rules and regulations—these to *direct* the reader—to the vocative function. The translation theorist then applies the following criteria to the translation of each text category: language bias (SL or TL); focus (author, reader or 'content', extra-linguistic reality);

type of language (figurative, factual or persuasive); unit of translation, which is always as short as possible, as long as is necessary (Haas, 1962) (word, collocation/group, clause sentence, paragraph, text); loss of meaning (large, small, nil); treatment of stock or original metaphors, and of recent or *ad hoc* neologisms; length in relation to the original, which depends on the languages concerned (German is one-third longer than English; English is longer than Latin) as well as the language function; purpose of translation (to convince or to inform); legitimacy of improving on the original; treatment of theme words (main concepts) and token-words (words that illustrate the scene of the text). There may well be other criteria. On the basis of these criteria the theorist decides whether to translate 'communicatively' or 'semantically'.

The minor functions of language are diverse. The translator is concerned only with phatic language where phrases such as 'of course', 'naturally', 'as is well known' (Stalin's phrase for what was not), 'it need hardly be mentioned', 'it is worth noting', 'interesting to note', 'important', etc. (usually 'it' is not so)—German has many more (*ja, eben, gewiss, usw*)—are used to keep the reader happy or in touch. The metalingual function of language has peculiar problems (see Chapter 5) when non-institutional words are used (e.g. 'ergative', 'optative', or deliberately polysemous expressions, words used in special sense or alternative expressions) and language describing the SL or exemplifying its properties, which do not exist in the TL—and may have to be transferred or monosemized in the TL translation. The aesthetic function, where the words and/or their sound-effects are more important than their meaning, covers 'pure' poetry, a lot of nonsense rhymes and children's poetry. The translator may decide to ignore meanings and reproduce sound-effects. This function is also intimately connected, but not, in my view, identical with the expressive function. In any purportedly 'art for art's sake', 'significant form' or 'abstract' work, the translator has to weigh the claims of 'meaning' against 'form'. In my own view, all 'abstract' work or art has a meaning (albeit general and usually emotive) which is sometimes more powerful than any of the more conventional versions of meaning, and one has to make sense of an 'abstraction' (say, Mallarmé's *Un coup de dés* or a Mondrian), if one is to appreciate it.

* * *

The theorist's main concern, then, is to select an appropriate general method of translation, always bearing in mind that 'standardized language', viz. technical terms, terms of art, formulae, the set language of institutions, procedures, games, phatic language, etc., must be translated by the equivalent TL standard term, if one exists. I have proposed only two methods of translation that are appropriate to any text: (a) *communicative* translation, where the translator attempts to produce the same effect on the TL readers as was produced by the original on the SL readers, and (b) *semantic* translation, where the translator attempts, within the bare syntactic and semantic constraints of the TL, to reproduce the precise contextual meaning of the author. All other translation methods serve special purposes: interlinear, literal (lexically context-free); information (facts only); service (*from* the translator's language of habitual use); plain prose (as a bridge to the original). The concepts of communicative and semantic translation are based on a narrowing of the ancient and old distinction between 'free' and 'literal' translation; with the proviso that the two methods may overlap in whole or in part within a text, provided that the text is virtually culture-free and is efficiently written; and on the assumption that in both methods, the translator must scrupulously turn his attention both to the ideas and the words and their arrangement (syntax and stress) before he operates his techniques and undertakes 'compromises' (e.g. overtranslating; undertranslating, by giving less detail than the original; compensating for semantic loss by replacing, say, a metaphor in one place with another in another part of the same sentence or paragraph).

Inevitably, most texts, particularly those rich in metaphor and polysemy (which cannot be adequately compensated), will be rather clearer, simpler and 'poorer' in translation, and will serve as one (of several possible) interpretations of the original. Many readers, for instance, who find German philosophers such as Kant or Hegel difficult, will find them easier in French or English.

The basic difference between communicative and semantic language is the stress on 'message' and 'meaning'; 'reader' and 'author', 'utterance' and 'thought-processes'; 'like' or 'as'—and 'how'; 'performative' and 'constative', but this is a matter of difference in emphasis rather than kind.

* * *

The translation theorist is concerned from start to finish with meaning. He is, however, not concerned with the theoretical problems and solutions of semantics, linguistics, logic and philosophy, but only with their applications in as far as they can help the translator solve his problems.

First, the translator must assess whether the whole or a part of the text is 'straight' (means what it says), ironical (slightly or entirely opposite in meaning), or nonsensical. The SL use of inverted commas (e.g. *Die Welt*'s "DDR") will assist him, if they exist; but irony often remains intended but not understood, or unintended but imagined.

Secondly, the theorist has to decide which of the countless varieties of general meaning he has to take account of. In my opinion, these are the linguistic, the referential, the subjective, the 'force' or 'intention' of the utterance, the 'performative', the inferential, the cultural, the code meaning, the connotative, the pragmatic and the semiotic. I illustrate:

Text extract: 'Mon ami l'a embrassée dans le hall de l'hôtel.'

Linguistic: 'My friend kissed her in the hotel hall.'
(Note that a translation is the only direct statement of linguistic meaning. To render linguistic meaning within the same language, one has recourse to convolutions such as 'The man I like (and who likes me) and have known for some time embraced the woman in the public room in the front of the large house where people pay to stay' or 'synonymy' such as 'My mate kissed her in the front room of the inn'.)

Referential: Jean Dubois kissed Mrs. Veronica Smith in the hall of the Grand Hotel, Dijon, at 3 pm on 5 January 1979.

(*Ami, l'* and *hôtel* are referential synonyms, and may have to be replaced in the translation to avoid ambiguity or clumsy repetition).

Intention: Possibly, to show that JD and VS are close friends. (Intention can normally only be determined by the context of the extract.)

Performative: (perhaps) JD kissed VS to declare his love for her. ('Performative' meaning is here distinguished from an illocutionary statement such as 'It's getting dark, isn't it?' meaning 'Why don't you put the light on?')

Subjective: (perhaps) My personal *bête noire* kissed her in the hotel hall.

Inferential: 'My friend' not 'I', etc.,
'Her', not 'him', etc.,
'In the hall', not 'the dining room', etc.

Cultural: '*Embrassée*' signifies a casual greeting only. *L'hôtel* is a large mansion, hotel, sales-room, etc.

Code: (perhaps) JD indicated to VS that she should go ahead. (This refers to the action, not the sentence.)

Connotative: JD's boldness, audacity or impertinence. (Connotative meaning is more or less potential, and is not obvious here. Descriptive words like *jaune, lion, présence, farfelu,* etc., have more obvious connotative meaning, which may be universal as well as cultural or subjective.)

Semiotic: This is the complete contextual meaning of the text extract, taking account of all the varieties of meaning mentioned above, as well as the 'pragmatic' meaning which may render any component of the text peculiarly significant to the reader or to the social, regional, or political group of readers addressed. In this case, the word *hôtel* may (it is unlikely) rouse hostile, pejorative or attractive feelings in the readers, which the translator may have to account for.

All varieties of meaning may or may not assist the translator. He is always expected to know the referential ('encyclopaedic') as well as the linguistic ('dictionary') meanings, whether he makes use of them or not. Whatever the text, and particularly if it is institutional, scientific or technological, he must understand the principal terms (objects, devices, laws, etc.) involved, and briefly verify the definitions of peripheral terms.

* * *

For the translation theorist, the obverse sides of the varieties of meaning, which are all interrelated (Firth defined meaning as a 'network of relations'), are the various categories of obscurity and ambiguity in the SL text with which he is concerned. Thus on the first most general point, 'Er ist ein feiner Kerl!' may mean 'He is a decent bloke' or 'He's not a decent bloke' or 'He's a questionable bloke'.

Linguistic obscurity may be grammatical or lexical: grammatical ambiguity may tend to be confined to one language, as in '*Considering* his weakness, he decided not to take the test' or to be virtually universal, as in *le livre de Jean* (most common prepositions have multiple functions in most languages), or fairly widespread. 'Ils se félicitèrent de ce succès.' Note also the tendency for most grammars not to indicate whether an action is deliberate or involuntary, as in 'She *obscured* my vision'. Lexical ambiguity may be due to polysemy, 'The painting is nice!' or to homonymy, 'He crossed the pole'. In all cases of linguistic ambiguity, the translator has to bear in mind that the ambiguity may be deliberate, in which case it is his job to reproduce it, even if it means expanding the original; if it is not (the decision is his), he normally disambiguates according to the situational or the linguistic context, appending the less likely meaning if there is the slightest possibility of it being the correct one. Note that all live metaphor is polysemous, and has an element of ambiguity at its periphery; therefore, if a translator is unable to reproduce the metaphorical element in, say, *coudoyer les gens* (for English, 'rub shoulders with', 'mix with'), he may, in another TL, have to decide on the degree of familiarity, frequency, even rudeness to add as the secondary component of his componential analysis of the phrase.

Referential ambiguity, which is often due to erratic use of deictics or poor technical writing, is usually best cleared up by consulting the macrocontext or the 'encyclopaedia', respectively.

The performative, intentional, inferential and connotational meaning of texts may all be ambiguous, but here the translator has no resource except to reconsider the linguistic and situational context.

However, instances of cultural and pragmatic ambiguity may be the most difficult of all, in cases of fluctuating customs and attitudes respectively, since the text itself may give little clue to the meaning. I take 'cultural' meaning to refer to a SL community's customs, and here the 'meaning' of a meal, a kiss, a gesture, a drink, etc., may be ambiguous unless the translator has a deep knowledge of the community's social habits, including those relating to class, sex, occupation, region, etc. Secondly, if pragmatic meaning is taken to refer primarily to the SL community's attitudes and ideology, words like *parteilich* and *fortschrittlich*, statements like 'Was des Volkes Hände schaffen, ist des Volkes eigen' (in particular, the word *Volk*) cannot be interpreted through the linguistic or situational context, but only through an understanding of the GDR's prevailing political philosophy.

In literary texts, lexical ambiguities, particularly for theme-words, can sometimes be cleared up by consulting the author's other works—here the computer's assistance with the increasing number of concordances comes into its own. Further, a study of symbols, rites, taboos, etc., has to be made to disambiguate anthropological texts.

* * *

The translator having to handle grammar and emphasis often notes a tension between a natural (unmarked) and an 'emphatic' (marked) construction, often evidenced by different word order which he has to resolve:

Meinen Freund hat er begrüßt!
He actually greeted my *friend*!

Er hat meinen Freund begrüßt.
He greeted my friend.

He has to interpret grammatical meaning, both on a general level, and in relation to the distinction between SL and TL constructions.

Grammatical meaning is more significant (the 'tone' or 'flavour' of the text, its primary aspect, is perhaps dictated by its syntax), less precise, more general and sometimes more elusive than lexical meaning. It can sometimes be identified at text level (a comedy, a dialectical argument, a farce, a dialogue, a sonnet, a ballad, a formal agenda, the minutes of a meeting, etc., viz. the accepted term for a formal utterance) or at paragraph level (a declaration as thesis, antithesis or synthesis, followed by two or three supporting statements). But more commonly, grammatical meaning is identified only as (a) a sentence, which may be a declaration in the form of a (rhetorical) question, an order, a wish or an exclamation, or (b) a clause consisting of the topic ('theme'), the previously mentioned information, introduced perhaps by a definite deictic ('the', 'this', 'that'), and the comment ('rheme'), introduced by an indefinite deictic ('a', 'some', 'many', etc.), the new information. The translator can handle the topic using referential synonyms more freely than the comment, which must be faithfully rendered. Topic and comment must not be confused with subject and predicate. The meaning of a clause is that an entity acts, exists or equates with an entity or quality. Grammatical meaning can also be identified as (c) a word-group, which may comprise Nida's (1975a) entities, events, abstracts (or qualities) or relations. Note that a collocation cuts across a word-group, if it consists of an 'empty' verb plus verbal noun (e.g. 'pay a visit', etc.) and may be turned into a single TL verb ('visit').

Grammatical meaning may also be rendered by more or less standard transpositions from the SL to the TL. Thus a German encapsulated nominal phrase (*die vom Ingenieur gebaute Brücke*) may be rendered by noun plus adjectival clause; a Romance language noun with an adjectival clause or past participle, plus preposition and noun or a present participle plus noun-object, may become an English double noun compound ('family situation') or noun plus preposition plus noun ('the house on the hill'). There are many such standard procedures, well documented in the literature, e.g. in Vinay and Darbelnet (1976), Malblanc (1961), Friederich (1969), Truffaut (1968), Diller and Kornelius (1978) and various articles in *Lebende Sprachen.*

* * *

Lexical meaning starts where grammatical meaning finishes: it is referential and precise, and has to be considered both outside and within the context. Further, all lexical units have elements of grammar. Nouns may have gender, number, case; are 'count', or 'mass'; are plus or minus animate, abstract, human, etc. Verbs may be finite or infinitive, have person, gender and number, indicate time, mood, voice, aspect, transitivity. *In toto*, lexigrammatical meaning seen through nouns and verbs is, or is a variation on: 'An agent (implicitly animate) acts *or* affects an object (implicitly inanimate) with an instrument, at a certain time, at a certain place, in a certain manner, to the advantage and/or disadvantage of a second object (implicitly animate), causing the first object to be a new object (or have a new quality).' Within the context, agents and objects may each be personified, hypostasized or reified (for 'person' read 'institution', for 'intelligence'—(*pace* Ryle, 1963)—read 'spirit', etc.). This is, I believe, the basic neutral unmarked natural reference—string of any statement, but only the first two *or* three components are essential. In cases of (a) ambiguity, and (b) complicated syntactic structures, employed either for making particular emphasis or owing to the clumsiness, pomposity, incompetence, etc., of the writer, the translator may find it useful to refer to the above 'model', which boils down to 'Who does what to whom where, when, how, with what result?' and, where appropriate, 'Why?'

Secondly, and again out of context, the translator can look at lexical items (words, phrasal verbs, nouns, etc.) in three different ways as dictionary items: (a) having four types of senses: concrete, figurative (or mental), technical, colloquial (note that colloquial sense, often referred to as an 'idiom', is frequently difficult to relate to the other three types of senses (e.g. *maison*: house; family; home-made; that's the goods)); (b) having four degrees of frequency: primary (based on frequency in the modern language only and having nothing to do with 'true' meaning or etymology); secondary, collocational, nonce (e.g. *brechen*; break; infringe, vomit, crush, etc.; crack (nuts), infringe (law), commit (adultery)—the 'nonce' sense would be only in one utterance, and necessarily idiolectal; (c) core and peripheral; the core meaning includes all the essential senses (thus, for *assurer*, 'provide', 'secure', 'insure', 'guarantee', 'ensure', etc., make up the core meaning; 'verify', 'stabilize', 'settle' perhaps comprise the peripheral meaning).

Thus far the discussion of lexical meaning has been general. Lexical translation is more complicated. Any bilingual dictionary appears to imply that most SL words have precise TL equivalents. The translator knows that this is not so, even before words are related to their contexts, first through their collocation, then through clauses, sentences, etc., related to reference and their idiolectal concepts. On the contrary, most SL words have a variety of separate, contiguous, overlapping, inclusive or complementary senses (Nida, 1975a) (sememes), each of which consists of sense-components. Since both the equivalent words and their senses are differently arranged in the TL, translation may be said to consist lexically of a transfer not of senses (sememes), but of sense-components (semes). The various techniques and procedures of componential analysis can at least show the translator how to redistribute SL sense-components in the TL, thus showing him where to avoid a one (word)-to-one (word) translation. (When and when not to translate word for word, clause for clause, sequence for sequence is one of the main concerns of translation theory.) The translator has no stake in the question of semantic universals or the distinction between markers and distinguishers (Katz, 1964), classemes and semes (Pottier, 1974) which upset the linguists (e.g. Bolinger, 1965), but only in the procedures for splitting words or word series into components before transferring them and then relating them to context in the TL. Take the word 'bawdy'. Some typical dictionaries give the following definitions: 'lewd' (*Chambers's Twentieth Century*); 'obscene, indecent' (*Hamlyn's*); 'humorously indecent' (*COD*); '(1) relating to bawd, (2) 'obscene, lewd, indecent, smutty' (*Webster*); 'obscene' (*Penguin*); '(1) related to sex, (2) humorous' (*Collins Concise*). In bilingual dictionaries, it is '*obscène, paillard, impudique*' (*Harrap New Standard*); '*obscène, impudique*' (*Harrap*

Shorter); '*unzüchtig, unflätig*' (*Cassell's, Langenscheidt*); '*osceno, sporco*' (*Cassell's Italian*).

As I see it, a componential analysis of 'bawdy' will bring the translator much closer than this, on the whole, inadequate and frequently deficient series of synonyms.

The basic defect of synonymy is that the synonyms project, overlap, straddle in relation to the second language, that so many verbs (*stürzen, sich auseinandersetzen, constater, rayonner, cerner*) and adjectives (*schmachtig, décharné*) can have only about half their meaning conveyed by a single word in the second language. Componential analysis, however, concentrates on the nucleus of the meaning. I suggest that the components of 'bawdy' are:

A. *Essential (functional)*
   1. Shocking (emotive).
   2. Related to the sex act (factual).
   3. Humorous (emotive/factual).
B. *Secondary (descriptive)*
   1. Loud.
   2. 'Vulgar' (in relation to social class).

The translator should also note that the word is 'unmarked' or 'neutral' for dialect, sociolect and for degree of formality, emotiveness, generality and intensity.

How many of these components the translator will require to use will depend on (a) the importance of the word in the context, and (b) the requirement for brevity. If the concept ('bawdy') is a key-word in the SL text, he may translate all five, and at least the three essential components—A.1, A.2 and A.3—usually can still be combined. If 'bawdy' is peripheral to the content, one 'synonym', as in the dictionaries, may be sufficient, but two adjectives or an adjective qualified by an adverb will usually be preferable.

The ordering of emotive before factual and of functional before descriptive meaning is, as I have maintained elsewhere, generally valid in translation. Further, it is as important that the translator get the features of register right as the semantic components themselves.

I am suggesting that, as a translation procedure, componential analysis is both more accurate and profitable than the use of synonymy, that it is likely to bypass the all too common 'one-to-one' translation, and that normally my above-mentioned proposal may be the most economical method of carrying it out. The more conventional matrix method, variations of which are recommended by Nida, Pottier, Coseriu, Leech, Wotjak, Mounin, Beckele, etc., using synonyms and possibly a generic or superordinate term to determine common, diagnostic, potential (connotative) and supplementary components, is more useful when two or more of the synonyms appear and have to be distinguished in the SL text. Thus,

	Shocking	*Sex*	*Humour*	*Loudness*	*Vulgarity (class)*	*Intensity (order of)*
bawdy	+	+	+	+	+	3
ribald	?	+	+	+	+	4
smutty	+	+	+	−	+	8
lewd	+	+	−	−	−	2
coarse	±	−	−	−	+	6
vulgar	+	−	−	−	+	7
indecent	+	±	−	−	−	5
obscene	+	±	−	−	−	1

Note that the above is an 'open' series of words (the number of 'closed' series of words, such as those for cattle, furniture, ranks and colours, is small relative to the total vocabulary) and the use and choice of such words is determined as often by appropriate collocation as by intrinsic meaning (i.e. componential analysis): this particularly applies to generic terms or head-words such as 'big' and 'large', which are difficult to analyse. A further problem in translating any of this word-series arises from its primary component 'shocking', since it is so closely linked to any SL and TL culture in period of time and social class, and is subject, like any slang word, to rapid change in both respects: 'bloody' in *Pygmalion* (1912) becomes 'bloomin' arse' in *My Fair Lady* (1956). Note also that the obsolete 'bawd' cherished by modern dictionaries is merely a red herring.

Componential analysis is often set in the context of a semantic field or domain. The translation theorist has to be versed in field theory, bearing in mind that except in a narrow area or a series such as military ranks (Trier's *List–Kunst–Wissen* (1973) may or may not be another example) a field is not a structure or a 'mosaic' system (Trier's term), but a loose conglomeration of words of senses centred in one topic.

Componential analysis is normally seen as an extracontextual procedure, where the translator takes a lexical unit, looks into it as widely and deeply (in its historical resonance) as a monolingual dictionary will permit, and decides on its limits—its meaning can stretch so far, but no further. (*Une page cruelle* cannot quite be rendered by 'very cool remarks'). However, there is no reason why a different componential analysis should not also be made contextually, by detecting the semantic features 'imposed' on a word by its linguistic and situational context. 'Qu'il en avait été tout près, tout à l'heure, lorsqu'il avait découvert les étoiles' (A. Malraux, *La Condition humaine*). The translation by A. Macdonald has: 'How much nearer he had been to it a moment before, when he had first seen the stars.' The translation of *découvert* as 'first seen', which may or may not be justified, can only be visualized in the situation by a decomposition in relation to Chen's situation, when 'discovered', 'found out' is reduced to 'first seen' as its basic features.

It should be added that whilst componential analysis is basically and beneficially an extracontextual procedure, from a translator's point of view it can be operated at three stages. The conventional procedure:

man: male/adult	boy: male/child
woman: female/adult	girl: female/child

is of little use to him unless at least two of the items (say 'boys' and 'girls') were juxtaposed in the SL text, and the TL language had no one-to-one equivalents. If only one item, say 'girl', appeared in the SL text, an extracontextual CA might give as essential components: (1) female, (2) aged perhaps 3 to perhaps 35, (3) probably unmarried. At the third microcontextual stage, a sentence 'She was merely a girl' might give (a) female, (b) aged perhaps 14 to perhaps 35, (c) physically weak, hesitant, dilatory, unpunctual, indecisive, etc. Only the macrocontext could then assist the translator to decide the sense of the third component.

The following are the main uses of componential analysis for the translator:

1. To translate an SL word into two or more TL words by distributing its semantic components over a larger TL area.
2. To distinguish the meanings of two collocated SL synonyms, if the distinction is emphasized in the SL text (therefore 'din and clamour' may be *vacarme et clameur* but may be *grand brouhaha*, and *sauvage et farouche* could only be extricated from the context).
3. To analyse the content of one or more SL words within a series (e.g. of meals, clothes, etc.).
4. To expose and fill in gaps in the TL lexis, due to cultural distance between SL and TL, in the same semantic field (e.g. *carafon, Generaloberst, bourgade, bourg, Ordinarius* or any French term for bread).
5. To analyse neologisms (e.g. 'zonked'—exhausted, slang).
6. To explain cultural differences between one word with one common main component, but different secondary components, in SL and TL.
7. To analyse theme words that require extended definitions in TL (e.g. 'esprit').
8. To reduce metaphor, which always has two or more sense-components, to sense (e.g. in 'Le soleil a mangé la couleur bleue du papier', *mangé* may be 'impair' and 'remove').

* * *

The translation theorist is concerned with every type of translation procedure:

(a) *Transcription* ('loan words', adoption, transfer), which may or may not be required for SL institutional or cultural words to provide authenticity or local colour respectively. Some of these remain in the TL permanently—*détente, démarche* ('adopted words'); others are 'loans'—*kolkhoz, komsomol, sputnik*—they will not stay.

(b) *One-to-one translation*, e.g. *la maison*, 'the house'.

(c) *Through-translation* ('loan-translation'), e.g. 'People's Chamber' for *Volkskammer*, 'Committee on Trade and Development' for *Comité du Commerce et du Développement*, a common procedure for international institutional terms.

(d) *Lexical synonymy*, translation by a close TL equivalent. It is often possible to achieve closer interlingual than intralingual synonymy, particularly in reference to objects and actions. 'To die, to sleep, to dream' can be translated literally into any language, and therefore is hardly synonymy. Objects with identical functions, e.g. 'a house'' 'a window', 'a bath', can usually be translated literally provided there is cultural overlap, although the objects may have a different shape, size and/or composition in and within the SL and the TL culture. Similarly, general (non-specific) qualities can often be translated. There are, however, many specific objects, actions and qualities, often defined by inadequate and inaccurate synonyms both in mono- and bilingual dictionaries, where a neat componential analysis will give the translator a somewhat more satisfactory version, e.g. *ein Greis*: a very old (aged) man (secondary components: greyness, senility).

(e) *Componential analysis* (already discussed). Some form of componential analysis should always be preferred to synonymy as a provisional translation procedure, particularly if the lexical unit is a key-word or is important in the context. Synonymy is more acceptable for 'peripheral' words not directly related to the main argument of the text. But, in general, the use of synonymy, the kind of synonymy one finds *ab lib* and *ad nauseam* in *Cassell's German Dictionary* (e.g. *Ende* is 'end; conclusion; close, finish; result, issue, goal, aim, object, purpose; extremity'), is the ruin of accurate translation, and paraphrase is even worse.

(f) *Transposition*, the replacement of one grammatical unit by another. 'According to my friend', *mein Freund meinte.*

(g) *Modulation* (see Vinay and Darbelnet, 1976)—variation in point of view: e.g. *Lebensgefahr, danger de mort*, 'mortally dangerous' (i.e. *no* English equivalent); *assurance-maladie*, health insurance.

(h) *Compensation*, when loss of meaning or sound effect or metaphor in one part of a sentence is compensated in another part.

(i) *Cultural equivalence*, e.g. (*baccalauréat*, 'A-level').

(j) *Translation label*, i.e. an approximate equivalent, sometimes proposed as a collocation in inverted commas, which may later be accepted: e.g. *promotion sociale*, 'social advancement'; *autogestion*, 'worker management' or 'self-management at all levels'.

(k) *Definition*, usually recast as a descriptive noun-phrase or adjectival clause.

(l) *Paraphrase*, an amplification or free rendering of the meaning of a sentence: the translator's last resort.

(m) *Expansion* (*étoffement*)—grammatical expansion: e.g. 'taste of', *avoir le goût de.*

(n) *Contraction*—grammatical reduction: (F) *science anatomique*, 'anatomy'; (E) 'empty phrases', *des phrases.*

(o) *Recasting sentences.* French complex sentences are sometimes recast as English co-ordinate sentences. German complex sentences are sometimes rendered as two or more TL sentences.

(p) *Rearrangement, improvements* (jargon, mistakes, misprints, idiolect, clumsy writing, etc.). Only justified if (a) the SL text is concerned mainly with facts, or (b) the writing is defective.

(q) *Translation couplet*, literal translation *or* translation label *plus* transcription.

All translation procedures vary between *constraint* (mandatory) and *option* (optional). Other procedures such as over- and under-translation have already been discussed.

* * *

The area of text-linguistics, cohesion or discourse analysis, i.e. linguistic analysis beyond the sentence, has evident application in translation theory. The connections between sentences range from punctuation (which may differ in SL and TL), demonstrative deictics, referential synonyms, comparatives, superlatives, enumerations (which are 'dashes' in French) to contrastive or accumulative conjunctions. If the connections are explicit, there is no problem. The translator is more interested in the logical gaps, the missing verbs or noun-case implications which can be discovered only by considering the previous or the subsequent sentences. 'What are the needs and requirements?' may be a mystifying sentence until the translator has discovered who needs and requires what, for what or for whom, of whom, where, and when. Thus, again, translation theory makes a connection between discourse analysis, on the one hand, and the variations of valency theory, case-grammar and Tesnière's dependency grammar, on the other—Tesnière (1959) himself produced forty pages of valuable translation theory which he called *métataxe*. Further aspects of discourse analysis that may assist the translator are all the devices of emphasis (italics, marked word-order, emphatic pronouns or suppletive verbs, superlative, *it's, who*, 'cleft sentences', etc.), which may contrast with unmarked parallel elements in the preceding or succeeding sentence. Nevertheless, discourse analysis may be only a marginal aspect of translation theory, since the sentence is usually the basic translation unit, and often has a coherent appropriate meaning. Discourse analysis may be mainly an essential point of reference for (a) establishing the significance of all connectives including pronouns, and (b) clarifying semantically undetermined expressions.

* * *

Lastly, the translation theorist is concerned with certain particular problems: metaphor, synonyms; proper names; institutional and cultural terms, grammatical, lexical and referential ambiguity, cliché, quotations; cultural focus, overlap and distance, idiolect; neologisms; poetry; jargon, the four categories of key terms.

Of these problems, metaphor is the most important. I have suggested elsewhere that there are four types of metaphor: fossilized, stock, recently created and original; that one has to consider the metaphor, the object it relates to, the image (vehicle) and the sense (tenor, ground) before one translates; that there are five methods of translating metaphor: transferring the image, finding an equivalent image, converting the metaphor to a simile or sense plus the simile; finally, most frequently, converting the image to sense, which may involve analysis into several components, including figurative and concrete elements. Further, the translator has to consider cultural, universal and personal elements in the metaphor, and whether communicative or semantic translation is to be used. C. Brooke-Rose's distinction (1958) between metaphor and symbol combined with literal meaning has to be respected in the sense that the latter, if seriously conceived, may have to be culturally adapted. Again, since all colloquial language is metaphorical, recent and usually ephemeral, it often requires consistent recreation, particularly in typical specialized topics such as sport, finance, pop music, etc. Lastly, the translator has to consider when, if ever, he is justified in translating flat 'literal' (i.e. fossilized metaphor) language by stock metaphor, either as a compensation procedure or to enliven flat language in an 'information' text.

The last subject I propose to deal with in any kind of detail is neologisms, which may be either recently coined by others or original. They can be categorized as:

(a) *Formal*—completely new words. These are rare—the *locus classicus* is the seventeenth-century word 'gas' (from 'chaos')—in semantic translation. If they are original, they should be transcribed, and recreated, if recently coined. In communicative translation, they should be 'reduced' to their sense. Brand names should be transcribed or given their TL brand names.

(b) *Eponyms*—recently based on proper names, including inventors and names of firms and towns. (For the purposes of translation theory at any rate, I am extending the meaning and area of 'eponym' to include all instances of transferred use of proper names, e.g. 'macadamize', 'Stalingrad', 'academic'. The secondary meaning of antonomasia (use of a proper name to express a general idea) is also included within my definition of 'eponym', but the primary meaning of antonomasia (substitution of epithet, description, etc., for proper name) is included within my 'referential synonym'.) The translator often has to be careful not to transcribe these (*boycotter*, but not *limoger*) and in particular beware of the Western nations' chauvinism about their medical vocabulary (Röntgen, Graves, Hodgkin, Wilson, etc.).

(c) *Derived*—formed with productive prefixes (i.e. 'de-', 'mis-', 'non-', 'pre-', 'pro-') and suffixes (e.g. '-ism', '-ize', '-ization'), e.g. misdefine, non-event, encyclopaedism, taxon, *paraclinique*, etc. If such neologisms are transparently comprehensible, the translator can cautiously 'naturalize' them, assuming that Latin and Greek roots are acceptable in the TL—particularly in technological texts.

(d) *New collocations*, e.g. 'urban guerrilla', 'unsocial hours', *route fleurie*, *ouvrier spécialisé* ('skilled worker'). Normally it is unwise to attempt a loan or 'through translation' unless the translator is officially authorized to do so, otherwise he has to 'normalize'. Is 'scenic route' acceptable for *route fleurie*?

(e) *Phrasal* (nouns or verbs)—'trade-off', 'zero-in', etc. The translator has to normalize these in the TL usually by translating into two or three words.

(f) *Acronyms* (now a translation label for any combination of initial letters or syllables, and apparently the most productive element in European languages). International acronyms are usually translated (e.g. EEC, CEE, EG)—national acronyms are usually retained with, if necessary, a 'translation' of their function, rather than their meaning, e.g. 'CNAA—CNAA, degree-awarding body for higher education colleges (non-university) in the United Kingdom'; 'EDF, the French

Electricity Authority', 'ZUP, areas for priority housing development'. Words derived from acronyms have to be normalized (e.g. *cégétiste*, 'member of CGT, the French TUC'; *onusien* (related to UNO); *smicard*, 'minimum wage earner'.

(g) *Blends* (' "portmanteau" words'), i.e. combinations of two words, highly productive. These either become internationalisms for at least European languages if they have Latin/Greek roots (e.g. 'meritocracy', 'tachygraph', 'eurocrat', 'bionics', many medical terms) *or* they are 'borrowed' (e.g. *sovkhoz, sovnarkom, sovpreme, enarch*) or adopted (e.g. 'motel'). If no recognized equivalent exists they should be translated (e.g. *Abküfi*, 'mania for abbreviations', *écotage*, 'environment cult', but 'workaholic', *ergomane*(?)). Opaque blends such as 'ruckus' should, where possible, have both components (ruction, rumpus) translated.

(h) *Semantic*, old words with new meanings, e.g. 'sophisticated', 'viable', 'credible', 'gay', *base* (F), *Base* (G). These should be 'normalized' (i.e. translated by a 'normal' word) but 'base' should perhaps replace the patronizing 'rank and file' and the excruciating 'grassroots', as an old word with a new meaning (cf. 'chalk face').

(i) *Abbreviations* (shortened form of word). These are commoner in French and German than English: e.g. *Uni*, *Philo*, 'Beeb', 'vibes', *bac*, *Huma*; they are normalized (i.e. translated unabbreviated), unless there is a recognized equivalent (e.g. bus, metro, plus sci–tech terms).

* * *

The process of decoding a linguistically difficult text has been described as 'decentring' (Brislin, 1976). Nida (1964), following Chomsky, has proposed several 'kernel sentences' as the basis of a neutral or intermediate language, logically constructed, with metaphors converted to sense, between SL and TL. For European languages, the main problem is one of abstract 'jargon', i.e. words that contain three or four parts of speech within themselves. Take the following sentence from Sartre's *Critique de la raison dialectique* (p. 209): 'L'unité négative de la rareté intériorisée dans la réification de la réciprocité se réexteriorise pour nous tous en unité du monde, comme lieu commun de nos oppositions.' The translator has to force this sentence into some kind of neutral language: 'Since we have not enough goods (*rareté*, scarcity), we live together (*unité*) unhappily (*négative*) and therefore in our minds (*intériorisée*) our links with each other (*réciprocité*) are purely material (*réification*); in our public life again (*réexteriorise*), we appear to be all together in the world, where we all meet in a common place manner though we oppose each other!' (I take *lieu commun* in two senses). This 'interpretation' can be compared with J. Starr and J. B. Atkinson's 'translation': 'The negative unity of scarcity, interiorized in the reification of reciprocity, re-exteriorizes itself for us all in the unity of the world as the common ground of our oppositions' (Cumming, 1968).

In the pre-translation process we reduce texts to simple language before we reconvert them to the corresponding jargon, if it is appropriate. The most important stage in this process is usually the splitting up of words into components that each represent a part of speech; a phrase such as 'the growthful actualizing of potential' would usually be converted to 'teachers gradually bring out the promise their pupils have shown', again showing that the translator is often compelled to supply verb nouns with subjects and objects. This process presupposes the notorious *tertium comparationis*, the existence of a universal logic embedded in each language without which translation and communication would not be possible.

* * *

When a part of a text is important to the writer's intention, but insufficiently determined semantically, the translator has to interpret. In fact the cultural history of translation is full of examples of such interpretation, misinterpretation and distortion (Voltaire 'misunderstood' Shakespeare), which may be due to the translator's incompetence as much as to the contemporary cultural climate. Translation is normally written in modern language, which is in itself a form of interpretation, and lexically at least (i.e. not grammatically, except in the distant past) a reflection of the TL culture. Most good translations are stamped by the translator's personality more or less as firmly as, say, Menuhin's interpretation of 'the Beethoven or the Elgar', if I may use a semantically determined but intellectually pretentious phrase (unless addressed to professional musicians).

Interpretation presents the translator with a challenge. In particular, when he is faced with documents of a past age or of a geographically remote culture, he has to probe layers of lexical development: words as spirits, as myths, as people, as objects, as objects and symbols, as metaphors, as idioms; further, abstractions may be personified or reified. Only a precise ethnological and linguistic knowledge can assist the translator in making the 'cut' at the appropriate place, and many general key-terms, the Greek καλός κἀγαθός, the Latin *virtus*, the French *gentilhomme* may have to be continually redefined. 'The act of translation places alien utterances in our mould', as Crick (1976) has stated in his brilliant book. Evans-Pritchard (1975) has written of the hasty 'adoption' and generalization (transcription) of words like 'taboo' (from Polynesia), 'mana' (from Melanesia) and 'totem' (from N. American Indians), 'baraka' (from N. African Arabs), so that they quickly lost their cultural meaning; of the difference in meaning of words such as 'god', 'spirit', 'soul' or 'ghost' to the native and the translator, with its 'partial overlap' of meaning. 'The translation is the interpretation', he stated, warning that most influential late-nineteenth-century thinkers were agnostics or atheists when they wrote and tended to look for function or role or theory rather than the richness of meaning.

Interpretative translation, if one can use the term, requires a semantic method of translation combined with a high explanatory power, mainly in terms of the SL culture, with only a side glance at the TL reader. In fact the greater the explanatory power, the more the reader is likely to understand, but the translation must not 'compromise' in his direction. I refer to interpretative translation of texts about the SL culture. But other texts which have important semantically undetermined passages or words, e.g. mathematical texts or newspaper reports, may require interpretation and be communicatively translated.

Except in the GDR, where translators are trained to show socialist consciousness in their versions, translators now have to strive to be 'objective' and 'scientific' through a paradoxical procedure: first, thinking themselves into the minds of their authors; then, 'reconciling' their author's *language* with their own; working through a second kind of 'double articulation' (cf. Martinet, 1960), that of word and proposition, concept and idea, respectively, which are different but inseparable, because the neural processes that precede and produce words are not likely to give up their secrets; finally, taking account of their own interests and prejudices by reminding themselves that they too will learn more from their opponents than from their friends, and therefore will preserve 'alien' thought rather than try to convert or adapt it. This I think is the modern translator's spirit that, say, Evans-Pritchard advocated: how successfully it can be practised is moot, but I think it will be a little better than previously.

* * *

I conclude by attempting to suggest what translation theory cannot and can do. It cannot make a bad translator into a good one. It cannot make a student intelligent or sensitive—two qualities of a good translator. In fact, if someone is sensitive to language as well as his own language and pursues facts as well as words, he can do without translation theory, just as an actor sensitive to his art can do without training. Translation is an art as well as a skill and a science, and translation theory cannot teach anyone to write well, although it can expose bad writing as effectively as translation itself. (Bad writing is bad writing in any language, and is harder to disguise and is more exposed, when translated.) It barely touches the 'art' of translation, but it should provide a training in scrupulous and meticulous *accuracy*.

What translation theory can do is to show the student all that is or may be involved in the translation process (and certainly that is far more than what he is usually aware of) and to offer principles and guidelines (some of which, like those relating to the translation of institutional terms, are contradictory), after considering which, he makes his choices and decisions. Further, translation theory can stop him making howlers like translating the title of a periodical or mistakes of usages like translating a layman's term by a technical term. Mainly, the translation theorist is concerned to see that no linguistic or cultural factor is ignored when one is translating. Provided that all the theorist's generalizations arise from practice and are continually illustrated by examples and their proposed translations, there is much to be done.

Finally, translation theory has an excitement and pleasure of its own, which parallels translation itself. It is concerned with mundane and practical things like the use and significance of inverted commas or variations on the Cloze procedure of dealing with misprints, at one moment, and questions like the relation between thought, language and behaviour at another. It is relatively uncharted; in many areas of knowledge, there appear to have been original thinkers who have, albeit briefly, reflected on the problems of translating their subject. Further, one has the consolation of knowing that however mistaken the generalizations one is setting up, the illustrations are normally natural and interesting. Incidentally, any terms translation theory (unlike linguistics) invents should be 'transparent', i.e. self-explanatory, and since it helps the translator to reduce jargon to simple language, it should avoid this type of jargon itself. (Up to now, its leading practitioners have not done so.)

Translation theory, like translation, has no particular bounds. All the more reason for it to be concerned with precise concrete instances.

* * *

Translation theory goes hand in hand with translation methodology at every stage, so that it acts as a body of reference both for the translation process procedure and for translation criticism. Since translation theory is applied to a variety of texts, and is not basically concerned with comparing language systems, its theorizing function consists of identifying a general or particular problem (say) how to translate *oikeuskansleri, eduskunta, nimismies* (Finnish), enumerating the various options, relating them to the TL text and reader, proposing a solution and then discussing the generality of the problem for future use. It is an applied and interrelated discipline, even if it is far from being wholly applied linguistics. Certain theoretical problems, such as what constitutes translation equivalence, variance or invariance, the ideal unit of translation, or even the process of translation accompanied by diagrams and logical symbols, appear to me now to be not very profitable unless they are related to one language function informing a group of text-types. As I see it, any talk of a single translation theory, or of one semantic theory for that matter, is a waste of time. Translation theory is eclectic; it draws its material from many sources. Like meaning or translation, it embraces a whole network of relations. At the same time, translation theory, precisely because it is bound up with methodology (a plan either for translation practice or for translation criticism runs through the entire preceding paper), goes into areas beyond any linguistics: the decision on the quality of a SL text; the arguments in favour of *or* against various procedures for translating institutional or cultural terms; the translator's use of punctuation: question marks, colons, inverted commas and italics; the criteria for misprints; the grey area between evidence and intuition and taste; and particularly, the training in a sense of priority, of what is important and unimportant in the sense and sounds of a text—I doubt whether this has anything much to do with linguistics. On the other hand, Wandruzska (1978) has maintained that a sound linguistics depends on a sound translation theory, whilst Vincent (1976) says precisely the opposite, and maintains that translation theory will depend on developing a working model for discourse analysis. But I think our main problems are more immediate than these. Translation theory precipitates a methodology concerned with making the translator pause and think, with producing a natural text or a conscious deviation from a natural text or a closest natural equivalent, with sensitizing him against howlers and false cognates, but not being afraid to recognize true cognates.

The translation theorist or teacher picks up instances as he meets them in a text. But he will also profit by relating them to the type of translation theory syllabus I have attempted to sketch here, beginning with the large questions of text analysis, meaning and translation methods, passing through points or word or punctuation detail to symbolism and interpretation. It is clear that some sections of the syllabus are, as they stand, a little peripheral. Much has still to be done to relate types of meaning, discourse analysis, valency theory and metaphor study to translation theory. The work is only at a start.

3. Communicative and semantic translation (I)

1. A translation must give the words of the original.
2. A translation must give the ideas of the original.
3. A translation should read like an original work.
4. A translation should read like a translation.
5. A translation should reflect the style of the original.
6. A translation should possess the style of the translation.
7. A translation should read as a contemporary of the original.
8. A translation should read as a contemporary of the translation.
9. A translation may add to or omit from the original.
10. A translation may never add to or omit from the original.
11. A translation of verse should be in prose.
12. A translation of verse should be in verse.

(*The Art of Translation,* T. H. Savory, Cape, 1968, p. 54.)

In the pre-linguistics period of writing on translation, which may be said to date from Cicero through St. Jerome, Luther, Dryden, Tytler, Herder, Goethe, Schleiermacher, Buber, Ortega y Gasset, not to say Savory, opinion swung between literal and free, faithful and beautiful, exact and natural translation, depending on whether the bias was to be in favour of the author or the reader, the source or the target language of the text. Up to the nineteenth century, literal translation represented a philological academic exercise from which the cultural reformers were trying to rescue literature. In the nineteenth century, a more scientific approach was brought to bear on translation, suggesting that certain types of texts must be accurately translated, whilst others should and could not be translated at all! Since the rise of modern linguistics (philology was becoming linguistics here in the late fifties), and anticipated by Tytler in 1790, Larbaud, Belloc, Knox and Rieu, the general emphasis, supported by communication-theorists as well as by non-literary translators, has been placed on the *reader*—on informing the reader effectively and appropriately, notably in Nida, Firth, Koller and the Leipzig School. In contrast, the brilliant essays of Benjamin, Valéry and Nabokov (anticipated by Croce and Ortega y Gasset) advocating literal translation have appeared as isolated, paradoxical phenomena, relevant only to translating works of high literary culture. Koller (1972) has stated that the equivalent-effect principle of translation is tending to rule out all others, particularly the predominance of any formal elements such as word or structure.

The apparent triumph of the 'consumer' is, I think, illusory. The conflict of loyalties, the gap between emphasis on source and target language will always remain as the overriding problem in translation theory and practice.

However, the gap could perhaps be narrowed if the previous terms were replaced as follows:

Figure 6.

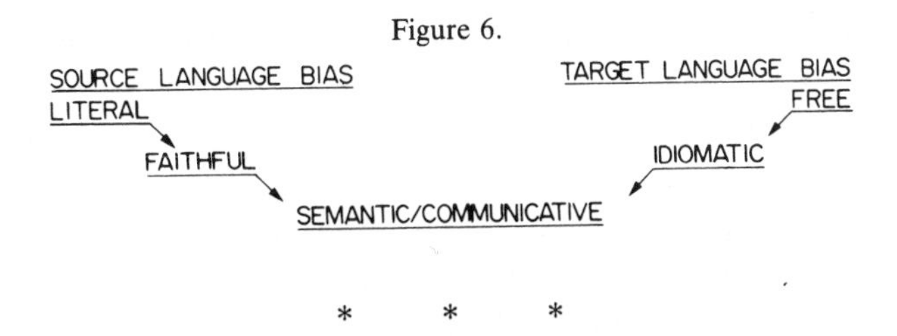

* * *

Communicative translation attempts to produce on its readers an effect as close as possible to that obtained on the readers of the original. Semantic translation attempts to render, as closely as the semantic and syntactic structures of the second language allow, the exact contextual meaning of the original.

In theory, there are wide differences between the two methods. Communicative translation addresses itself solely to the second reader, who does not anticipate difficulties or obscurities, and would expect a generous transfer of foreign elements into his own culture as well as his language where necessary. But even here the translator still has to respect and work on the form of the source language text as the only material basis for his work. Semantic translation remains within the original culture and assists the reader only in its connotations if they constitute the essential human (non-ethnic) message of the text. One basic difference between the two methods is that where there is a conflict, the communicative must emphasize the 'force' rather than the content of the message. Thus for *Bissiger Hund* or *Chien méchant,* the communicative translation *Beware of the dog!* is mandatory; the semantic translations ('dog that bites', 'savage dog') would be more informative but less effective. Generally, a communicative translation is likely to be smoother, simpler, clearer, more direct, more conventional, conforming to a particular register of language, tending to undertranslate, i.e. to use more generic, hold-all terms in difficult passages. A semantic translation tends to be more complex, more awkward, more detailed, more concentrated, and pursues the thought-processes rather than the intention of the transmitter. It tends to overtranslate, to be more specific than the original, to include more meanings in its search for one nuance of meaning.

However, in communicative as in semantic translation, provided that equivalent-effect is secured, the literal word-for-word translation is not only the best, it is the only valid method of translation. There is no excuse for unnecessary 'synonyms', let alone paraphrases, in any type of translation.

Conversely, both semantic and communicative translation comply with the usually accepted syntactic equivalents (Vinay and Darbelnet's 'transpositions') for the two languages in question. Thus, by both methods, a sentence such as '*Il traversa la Manche en nageant*' would normally be translated as 'He swam across the Channel'. In semantic, but not communicative translation, any deviation from SL stylistic norms would be reflected in an equally wide deviation from the TL norms, but where such norms clash, the deviations are not easy to formulate, and the translator has to show a certain tension between the writer's manner and the compulsions of the target language. Thus when the writer uses long complex sentences in a language where the sentence in a 'literary' (carefully worked) style is usually complex and longer than in the TL, the translator may reduce the sentences somewhat, compromising between the norms of the two languages and the writer. If in doubt, however, he should trust the writer, not the 'language', which is a sum of abstractions. A semantic translation is concrete. Thus when faced with:

> 'Der Gesichtspunkt der Nützlichkeit ist gerade in Bezug auf ein solches heißes Herausquellen oberster rang-ordnender, rang-abhebender Werturteile so fremd und unangemessen wie möglich; hier ist eben das Gefühl bei einem Gegensatze jenes niedrigen Wärmegrades angelangt, den jede berechnende Klugheit, jeder Nützlichkeit-Kalkul voraussetzt'
>
> (*Zur Genealogie der Moral,* (2) Nietzsche)

the translator has to cling to words, collocations, structures, emphases:

> 'The utilitarian point of view is as alien and inappropriate as it possibly could be precisely to such an intense eruption of supreme rank-classifying, rank-discriminating value-judgements: here in fact feeling has reached the antithesis of the low degree of fervour presumed in every type of calculating cleverness, every assessment of utility.' (My version.)

Thus a translation is always closer to the original than any intralingual rendering or paraphrase misnamed 'translation' by George Steiner (1975), and therefore it is an indispensable tool for a semantician and now a philosopher. Communicative and semantic translation may well coincide—in particular, where the text conveys a general rather than a culturally (temporally and spatially) bound message and where the matter is as important as the manner—notably then in the translation of the most important religious, philosophical, artistic and scientific texts, assuming second readers as informed and interested as the first. Further, there are often sections in one text that must be translated communicatively (e.g. *non-lieu*—'nonsuit'), and others semantically (e.g. a quotation from a speech). There is no one communicative nor one semantic method of translating a text—these are in fact widely overlapping bands of methods. A translation can be more, or less, semantic—more, or less, communicative—even a particular section or sentence can be treated more communicatively or less semantically. Thus in some passages, Q. Hoare and G. Nowell Smith (1971) state that: 'we feel it preferable to choose fidelity over good English, despite its awkwardness, in view of the importance of some concepts in Gramsci's work.' Each method has a common basis in analytical or cognitive translation which is built up both proposition by proposition and word by word, denoting the empirical factual knowledge of the text, but finally respecting the convention of the target language provided that the thought-content of the text has been reproduced. The translation emerges in such a way that the exact meaning or function of the words only become apparent as they are used. The translator may have to make interim decisions without being able at the time to visualize the relation of the words with the end product. Communicative and semantic translation bifurcate at a later stage of analytical or cognitive translation, which is a pre-translation procedure which may be performed on the source-language text to convert it into the source or the target language—the resultant versions will be closer to each other than the original text and the final translation.

* * *

In principle, cognitive translation transposes the SL text grammatically to plain 'animate subject + verb + non-animate object' clauses, or, in the extended version, to sequences of: 'an agent (subject) does (active verb) something (direct object) to or for someone (indirect object) with something (instrumental) somewhere (locative) sometime (temporal) to make something (resultant)'—additionally, an agent/object may be in a variety of relationships with another agent/object (possessive, equative, dependency, source, partitive, genitive, characteristic, etc.)—(relationships often covered or concealed by the English preposition 'of'), which must be spelt out in a clause. Thus the grammatical meaning of the SL text becomes explicit. Further, cognitive translation splits up the word-class derivatives, i.e. adverbs (= preposition + adjective + noun), adjectival nouns (e.g. 'whiteness'), qualifying prefix-verb-nouns (e.g. 'contribution'), noun-verbs (e.g. 'to ration'), noun-adjective-verb-nouns (e.g. 'rationalization'), etc., into their components and explicates the relations of all multiple noun compounds (e.g. 'data acquisition control system': system to control the acquiring of data). Further, it replaces figurative and colloquial language, idioms and phrasal verbs with denotative terms; clears up lexical and grammatical ambiguities; interpolates relevant encyclopaedic information for ecological, cultural and institutional terms; replaces pronouns with nouns and identifies referential synonyms; reduces cultural terms to their functional definitions; and analyses the semantic features of any words that are likely to be split into two or three words when translated. Thus as far as is possible (the process is artificial) the text is removed from its natural cultural and linguistic axis to an artificial neutral universal plane of language.

Nida in his admirable analysis of grammatical meaning (1974a, pp. 47–49) approaches cognitive translation somewhat differently, preferring to split surface structures into separate underlying (previously concealed) sentences. Thus he analyses: 'their former director thought their journey was a deception' into: (a) he directed them formerly, (b) he thought X (the entire following expression), (c) they journeyed, (d) they deceived Y (without specifying who Y is), adding an analysis of the relationship between (c) and (d)—e.g. means-result: by journeying they deceived', means-purpose (they journeyed in order to deceive), additive events (they journeyed and they deceived).

For cognitive translation, I think: 'The man who used to be their director (to direct them) thought they had travelled to deceive (by travelling they had deceived, they had travelled and deceived)' is adequate. Another (more likely?) alternative missed by Nida must be added: 'The man who used to be their director thought they had merely pretended to travel, in order to deceive others.' (Most verbal nouns may be active or passive in meaning.)

It is not usually necessary to make a full cognitive translation, a procedure similar to Brislin's (1976) 'decentring'. Where the cultures of two languages have been in contact for centuries, the translator normally resorts to cognitive translation only for obscure, ambiguous or complex passages. A cognitive translation may serve as a *tertium comparationis* between texts with distant cultures and radically different language structures.

*   *   *

Where cognitive translation results in a poorly written and/or repetitive text, communicative translation requires a bold attempt to clarify and reorganize it. A text such as the following would require considerable rewriting before it is translated:

> 'If industrialists are so keen for Britain to join why does not the Government make it possible for those who want to get into Europe without the sacrifice to British sovereignty . . . which must be the inevitable result of our joining if we are to rely on M. Debré's words recently that the Common Market is unworkable without the Treaty of Rome.'

(*The Times,* 18 July 1961, quoted in *The Use of English,* R. Quirk, Longmans, 1964.)

Proposed rewrite:

> 'As industrialists are so keen, why does not the Government make it possible for Britain to get into Europe without sacrificing her sovereignty? According to M. Debré's recent statement, this would first require amendments to the Treaty of Rome, which is the legal instrument governing the Common Market.'

I am assuming that whilst a semantic translation is always inferior to its original, since it involves loss of meaning, a communicative translation may be better, since it may gain in force and clarity what it loses in semantic content. In communicative translation the translator is trying in his own language to write a little better than the original, unless he is reproducing the well-established formulae of notices or correspondence. I assume that in communicative translation one has the right to correct or improve the logic; to replace clumsy with elegant, or at least functional, syntactic structures; to remove obscurities; to eliminate repetition and tautology; to exclude the less likely interpretations of an ambiguity; to modify and clarify jargon (i.e. reduce loose generic terms to rather more concrete components), and to normalize bizarreries of idiolect, i.e. wayward uses of language. Further, one has the right to correct mistakes of fact and slips, normally stating what one has done in a footnote. (All such corrections and improvements are usually inadmissible in semantic translation.)

In theory a communicative translation is *ipso facto* a subjective procedure, since it is intended primarily to achieve a certain effect on its readers' minds, which effect could only be verified by a survey of their mental and/or physical reactions. In fact, it is initially as constrained by the form, the structures and words of the original as a semantic translation (the pre-translation process) until the version is gradually skewed to the reader's point of view. Then the translator starts to ask himself whether his version is 'happy', i.e. a successful 'act', rather than whether it is true, i.e. an exact statement (cf. Austin, 1962). He begins to extend the unit of translation, having secured the referential basis, i.e. the truth of the information; he views words and phrases in expanding waves in their linguistic context, restructuring or rearranging clauses, reinforcing emphases. Nevertheless, each lexical and grammatical unit has to remain accounted for—that is his Antaean link with the text.

* * *

In one sense, communicative translation, by adapting and making the thought and cultural content of the original more accessible to the reader, gives semantic translation another dimension. The Leipzig School, notably Neubert and Kade, have referred to this as the 'pragmatic' element, but I think this is a little misleading. To begin with, Peirce and notably Morris defined 'pragmatics' as the branch of semiotics that deals with the relation between signs or linguistic expressions and their users (transmitters and receptors). Communicative translation, however, is concerned mainly with the receptors, usually in the context of a language and cultural variety, whilst semantic translation is concerned with the transmitter usually as an individual, and often in contradistinction both to his culture and to the norms of his language. Moreover 'pragmatic' is a confusing term, since even in the context of translation (let alone its abundant senses in philosophy) it is also used in the sense of 'nonliterary', 'technical' and 'practical'. Neubert and Kade have maintained that the pragmatic (in the semiotic sense) is the variant, difficult and often 'untranslatable' element in translation, whilst the cognitive (the material basis and environment) is invariant, relatively easy and always translatable. Whilst this view obviously has some truth (the objective, physical and concrete being on the whole easier to translate than the subjective, mental and figurative), it ignores the indisputable proportion of truth in the Humboldt thesis (the weak thesis) that each language has its own distinctive structure, reflecting and conditioning the ways of thought and expression of the people using it, but for which translation would be an easy business. Further, this view hardly comes to terms with the fact that most material objects derive their names from the result of mental analogies and comparisons, that is, from metaphor, not from any scientific made-to-measure neologisms, and that all languages are wilful and different in their naming of some of the commonest physical objects. Lyons (1976) and Weightman (1967) have independently shown how inadequate or overloaded would be any translation into French of the apparently simple, observational, objective, non-'pragmatic' sentence 'The cat sat on the mat'. Both the French version (possibly, 'Le chat était accroupi sur le paillasson') and the rather better German version ('Die Katze hockte auf der Fußdecke') are overtranslations, illustrating French and German's lack of words of sufficient generality and consequently of equivalent frequency. On the other hand, there are many cases where the 'pragmatic' element can be translated without difficulty, provided the viewpoint represented in the SL culture is well understood by the reader of the translation: thus words like 'revisionist', 'terrorist', 'patriotic', 'proletarian', 'formalistic', etc., can be 'agreed' according to the national culture in the educated writing of many world-languages. A GDR term such as *Abgrenzen* (refusal to compromise with non-socialist policies), though it is a pragmatic 'hot potato', can usually be safely translated without any of the three points of view (the transmitter's, the receptor's, the translator's) obtruding on the message. For Jäger (1975), the 'pragmatic element' is what transforms a 'semantic' (i.e. cognitive) into a 'functional' (i.e. communicative) translation—like most of the linguistic theorists, he only accepts the validity of communicative (his 'functional') translation and implicitly downgrades semantic translation.

* * *

I would prefer to avoid the use of the term 'pragmatic' and to regard both communicative and semantic as divergent refinements or revisions of cognitive translation. In both cases, the cognitive element may soon have to be abandoned, since the TL view of the same referent (object or message) may differ from the SL (cf. *château d'eau*—'water tower'; *pas de danger*—'not likely!'). The transition to semantic translation normally reduces the unit of translation, and brings the text closer to the figurative and formal elements of the original, including where possible its sound effects. Therefore the text becomes more idiosyncratic and 'sensitive'. Length of sentences, however long or short, position and integrity of clauses, word-position for emphasis, are preserved, unless the divergence between the relevant norms of the source and target languages (which also have to be considered, although the individual writer's 'style' finally prevails) is extensive. The transition to communicative translation normally makes the text smoother, lighter, more idiomatic and easier to read. Syntax is remodelled, commoner collocations and more usual words are found. Semantic translation is basically addressed to one 'reader' only, namely, the writer of the SL text, with the assumption that he can read the TL and will be the best arbiter of the translation's quality.

* * *

Since the overriding factor in deciding how to translate is the intrinsic importance of every semantic unit in the text, it follows that the vast majority of texts require communicative rather than semantic translation. Most non-literary writing, journalism, informative articles and books, textbooks, reports, scientific and technological writing, non-personal correspondence, propaganda, publicity, public notices, standardized writing, popular fiction—the run-of-the-mill texts which have to be translated today but were not translated and in most cases did not exist a hundred years ago—comprise typical material suitable for communicative translation. On the other hand, original expression, where the specific language of the speaker or writer is as important as the content, whether it is philosophical, religious, political, scientific, technical or literary, needs to be translated semantically. Any important statement requires a version as close to the original lexical and grammatical structures as is obtainable. Thus Spears' (1966) translation of the following passages of De Gaulle's 18 June 1940 broadcast is unacceptable:

> 'Infiniment plus que leur nombre, ce sont les chars, les avions, la tactique des Allemands qui nous font reculer. Ce sont les chars, les avions, la tactique des Allemands qui ont surpris nos chefs au point de les amener là où ils en sont aujourd'hui. . . .'

> 'It was the tanks, the planes and the tactics of the Germans, far more than the fact that we were outnumbered, that forced our armies to retreat. It was the German tanks, planes and tactics that provided the element of surprise which brought our leaders to their present plight.'

(Suggested version:

> 'Far, far more than their numbers, it was the tanks, the planes and the tactics of the Germans that caused us to retreat. It was the tanks, the planes and the tactics

of the Germans that took our leaders by surprise and thus brought them to the state they are in today.')

'Car la France n'est pas seule! Elle n'est pas seule! Elle n'est pas seule!'

'For remember this, France does not stand alone. She is not isolated.'

(Suggested version:

'For France is not alone! She is not alone! She is not alone!')

In these and other passages, Spears has attempted to modify the starkness, simplicity and rawness of De Gaulle's speech. (As a communicative translation of a narrative, Spears's first paragraph is valid, but the translation of quotations, however unimportant, is normally semantic rather than communicative, since the translator is not responsible for their effect on the second reader.)

Autobiography, private correspondence, any personal effusion requires semantic treatment, since the 'intimate' flavour of the original is more important than its effect on the reader.

One would normally expect to translate serious literature (high art) semantically, but one has to bear in mind that all art is to a greater or lesser extent allegorical, figurative, metaphorical and a parable, and therefore has a communicative purpose. Figurative language only becomes meaningful, if it is recreated in the metaphors of the target language and its culture, or, if this is not possible, reduced to its sense. In the case of minor literature that is closely bound to its period and its culture (short stories in particular), semantic translation will attempt to preserve its local flavour—dialect, slang and cultural terms (*mots-témoins*) will present their own problems. In the case of works with universal themes (e.g. love lyrics) and a background that is similar for SL and TL (say, in ecology and living conditions), there is no reason why a basically semantic translation should not also be strongly communicative. Bible translation should be both semantic and communicative, although the 'modern' preference (Schwarz, 1970) for 'philological' as opposed to 'inspirational' translation has for long moved away from studies which regarded the text as inspired and untouchable. Nida has shown in his many books that the TL reader can only accept the geographical and historical remoteness of the cultural background being presented to him, if that behaviour itself and all imagery connected with it is recast in his own (modern) culture. In fact, as the myths recede and less knowledge can be expected from modern man, each new translation of the Bible becomes more communicative, with the omission of technical terms, dialect and slang, and directed at increasing numbers of less-well-read people. Again, the immediate communicative importance of drama is usually greater than that of poetry or of serious fiction, and for this reason adaptations (where characters and milieu are transferred) are sometimes made, whilst they are almost unknown in the novel. However, in the most concentrated drama (Shakespeare, Chekhov) the essence of which is that words are packed or charged with meaning, semantic takes precedence over communicative equivalence, since the translator assumes that the dramatist has made use of his inventive resources to give his language communicative potential; it is now the translator's task to extract the utmost semantic equivalence from the original. Again, where the medium (i.e. the form) is as important as the message, and the peoples of the two language cultures can normally say the same things using different words, the two elements fuse.

It is not always possible to state which is the better method to use for a particular text. In a mainly informative text, the section containing recommendations, instructions, value-judgements, etc. may be translated more communicatively than the descriptive passages. Where language is used to accompany action or as its symbol (speech-acts), it is treated communicatively, whilst definitions, explanations, etc. are semantic. 'Standardized language' must always be translated communicatively, whether a standardized equivalent exists or not, even if it appears in a novel or a quotation, unless the term is used descriptively rather than operatively in the original text.

Normally in communicative translation it is assumed that the readers of the translation identify with those of the original. However, this is unlikely when elements of the source language culture or of the source language itself are discussed in the text. Nevertheless, 'communication' is as important here as in a text where the subject-matter is of general interest. Where, say, an institution of the SL community is being described, a special meaning of a SL word is used or the double meaning of a homophone or homonym is being exploited, the translator, if he thinks the point sufficiently important, has to render the author's message communicatively and also address himself independently to the TL reader; in short, he has to 'make' the pun as well as explain it. He has to assess (a) the extent of his reader's knowledge of and interest in the relevant aspect of the source language or culture, (b) the text's level of specialism. If he is writing for the general reader, he may be able to achieve his purpose by transcribing the appropriate new SL terms unlikely to be familiar to his reader and adding their approximate cultural equivalents (e.g. *Fachhochschule* or 'polytechnic'). If the terms are not likely to recur, he may decide not to transcribe them. If the text is specialized, the translator may wish to give his reader all possible information, including the transcription, the cultural equivalent, the encyclopaedic definition within the source culture and the literal translation of any new term on the first occasion of its use. He may even propose a 'translation label', i.e. a word used in a new sense, provided he states that he is doing so, and he believes the object or concept is likely to recur in the TL usage. (Thus *Volksrat*, second chamber, regional assembly in GDR, cf. *Bundesrat* in FRG, People's Council, National Council.) Or again, if 'Flying planes can be dangerous' is to be translated, the double meaning has to be explained in the TL with SL illustrations. All that is lost is vividness. Finally, whilst ambiguity, polysemy, word-play, etc. in literary works have to be reproduced as best they can in the TL only (in poetry and plays it is a 'hit or miss' procedure—in prose fiction there is room for brief expansion), such facts of language when discussed in non-literary works (e.g. on language, criticism, psychology) must be fully reproduced in the SL and explained in the TL. This has been superbly done by James Strachey in his translation of Freud's *Jokes and their Relation to the Unconscious* (1975) (his introduction contains valuable comments). The book had been previously translated by A. A. Brill as *Wit and Its Relation to the Unconscious* and many examples of word-play replaced by analogous English 'equivalents', a spurious procedure, since the translator gave no evidence of any patient ever having made such word-slips or puns in English.

In the following passage on therapeutic methods in rheumatology, 'La mobilisation active est une des bases fondamentales du traitement des maladies ostéo-articulaires. On parle aussi de kinésithérapie active ou de cinésithérapie, ou de gymnastique thérapeutique; ce sont des synonymes', the translator may give the two or more English equivalents, possibly 'active kinesitherapy' and 'remedial exercises', adding, if he wishes, that 'in French the following three terms are used'. In all the above cases the normal flow of communicative translation is interrupted for his own readers by the translator's glosses, which are a combination of transcription and semantic translation.

Legal documents also require a special type of translation, basically because the translator is more restricted than in any other form. Every word has to be rendered, differences in terminology and function noted, and as much attention paid to the content as to the intention and all possible interpretations and misinterpretations of the text—all legal texts are definitions, Adorno noted—thus the semantic aspect; nevertheless, the standard format, syntax, archaisms, as well as the formal register of the TL, must be respected in dealing with documents that are to be concurrently valid in the TL community (EEC law, contracts, international agreements, patents)—hence the communicative aspect. Legal documents translated for information purposes only (foreign laws, wills, conveyancing) have to be semantically translated.

A semantic translation attempts to recreate the precise flavour and tone of the original: the words are 'sacred', not because they are more important than the content, but because form and content are one. The thought-processes in the words are as significant as the intention behind the words in a communicative translation. Thus a semantic translation is out of time and local space (but has to be done again every generation, if still 'valid'), where a communicative translation is ephemeral and rooted in its context. A semantic translation attempts to preserve its author's idiolect, his peculiar form of expression, in preference to the 'spirit' of the source or the target language. It relates to Bühler's 'expressive' function of language, where communicative translation responds to the representational (*Darstellung*) and vocative (*Appell*) functions. In semantic translation, every word translated represents some loss of meaning (e.g. the loss of sound and rhythm in the word-for-word translation of the De Gaulle speech previously quoted), where in communicative translation the same words similarly translated lose no meaning at all. The syntax in semantic translation which gives the text its stresses and rhythm—the 'foregrounding' as the Prague School calls it—is as sacred as the words, being basically subject only to the standard transpositions (Vinay and Darbelnet) or shifts (Catford) from one language to another. There is a constant temptation, which should be resisted, to transcribe the terms for key-concepts or theme words.

The closer the cultural overlap between the two languages—this overlap being more important than the structural affinity or the geographical propinquity of the two languages, but the translator's empathy being the most important factor of all—the closer, therefore better, the translation is likely to be. This applies particularly to legal and administrative texts, where the names of institutions peculiar to one national community are frequently not translated, unless they are also important in the TL's culture or are transparently translatable, whilst the names of institutions with easily identifiable TL cultural equivalents form part of each language's readily 'convertible' 'translation stock' (Rabin, 1966). In communicative translation, however, the 'message' is all important, and the essential thing is to make the reader think, feel and/or act. There should be no loss of meaning, and the aim, which is often realized, is to make the translation more effective as well as more elegant than the original. A communicative translation works on a narrow basis. It is 'tailor-made' for one category of readership, does one job, fulfils a particular function. A semantic translation is wide and universal. In attempting to respond to the author, living or dead, it addresses itself to all readers, all who have ears to hear, or just to Stendhal's 'happy few'.

* * *

My last comparison will take metaphor as its touchstone.

I here propose to abandon the conventional clumsy I. A. Richards's terminology of vehicle/tenor and to use my own, viz. metaphor/object/image/sense. Thus in a 'sunny smile' the metaphor is 'sunny', the object is 'smile', the image (vehicle) is the 'sun', the sense (tenor) is perhaps 'cheerful', 'happy', 'bright', 'warm' ('warm' is also a metaphor, but more fossilized). Note this is a stock metaphor which normally has a narrow band of 'object' (e.g. look–mood–disposition).

Metaphor, as Dagut (1976) has pointed out in a brilliant article, has been much neglected in the literature. I propose to discuss three types of metaphor: dead (fossilized), standard (stock) and original (creative). (The types are clearly distinguishable at their centres, but they merge with each other at the periphery.) All languages consist of a stock of more or less fossilized metaphors. Many new words are metaphors. One has only to compare the collocations for the main parts of the body (say *Fuß, pied,* foot) to see that even in their commonest uses they are not all inter-translatable. (Further, their precise physical areas do not coincide.) In some cases the translator has to convert from a dead metaphor (F: *front*) to a transparent one ('forehead') or to a concrete word (G: *Stirne*). Though there is often an area of choice, there is not usually a distinction here between communicative and semantic translation, although one could for instance maintain that *figure* is a more semantic translation of 'face' than *visage* or *face.* Normally dead metaphors, being furthest removed from their source, are the easiest metaphors to translate, and their figurative aspect is ignored in SL and TL (e.g. *erwägen* = ponder) unless it is revived by an extended image (e.g. 'weigh up in my personal scale').

There are five possible procedures in translating standard, i.e. more or less common, metaphors, which may be simple (one word) or extended (idioms). In making a decision, the translator has to weigh each option against the relative frequency (and, therefore, naturalness) and currency of the TL equivalent within the appropriate language variety. The first solution is to translate by a metaphor using the same or a similar image (vehicle) ('a ray of hope'; *ein Hoffnungsstrahl*); the second is to translate with a different image that has the same sense (*avoir d'autres chats à fouetter:* 'to have other fish to fry'); the third is to convert the metaphor into a simile; the fourth is to qualify the simile with the sense (*c'est un lion* = 'he is as brave as a lion'), which in communicative translation may be advisable, if the metaphor is obscure; the fifth is to translate as much as possible of the sense behind the image, the sense being the common area between the metaphor's object and the image, as seen by the writer and interpreted by the translator. The question of whether to use semantic or communicative translation will arise only when the translator is in doubt about which solution to adopt. Thus (*pace* Reiss) a 'storm in a tea-cup' will normally be translated as *une tempête dans un verre d'eau* or *ein Sturm im Wasserglas*, whatever the context, as long as the three idioms remain equally current within that context. Communicative translation may prefer 'a lot of fuss about nothing' etc., a semantic translation 'a mountain out of a molehill' when the 'storm in a tea-cup' becomes too well-worn. There is also a case for eliminating a few clichés masquerading as metaphor or idioms in a poorly written text requiring communicative treatment. Further, the decision whether to translate 'as cool as a cucumber' by *tranquille comme Baptiste* (pejorative) or *avec un sang-froid parfait* (*imperturbable, superbe,* etc.) may depend on whether a semantic or communicative translation respectively is more appropriate.

Creative metaphor, as Dagut, quoting Richards (1965), points out, is 'the constitutive form of language'. Further, it is a much commoner phenomenon than those who think of it as the preserve of poets might imagine, and it is often the most accurate and concise descriptive instrument in language, as opposed to mathematics. Notoriously, translators know that it is found most commonly in the financial columns of newspapers: 'Milton Keynes's commercial beacon. . . . The ticket on which the town sells itself . . . the start of the slow clamber back, or a brief holiday window between two years? . . . no check in the push to sell long gilts . . . the new long tap less attractive. . . . Mercifully (cf. hopefully, thankfully, gratefully)' (*Guardian*, 30 Dec. 1976). Dagut also quotes from a recent issue of *Time* magazine: 'Mrs Thatcher shacks off her gloves and barrels into battle.' Whether one translates the images or the sense of these phrases will depend first on whether this figurative language is equally appropriate in the TL, and, secondly, on how important and expressive, in the translator's opinion, the image is semantically (if it is not important, he will translate it communicatively).

Assuming that a creative metaphor is worth translating, there is no question that the more original and surprising it is (and therefore the more remote from the national culture), the easier it will be to translate, since in its essence it will be remote from common semantic as well as cultural associations. For this reason, Kloepfer's (1967) dictum so disapprovingly quoted by Dagut, 'Je kühner und freier erfunden, je einmaliger eine Metapher ist, desto leichter läßt sie sich in andern Sprachen wiederholen', is perfectly valid. The difficulties arise when the metaphors are not so inventive (Dagut quotes 'she *killed off* the free milk programme', which is not a metaphor in his exclusively creative sense at all, and which could perhaps be translated by a polysemous word such as *achever* or *tuer*), and here Dagut rightly states that 'the translatability of a metaphor is determined by the extent to which the cultural (i.e. referential) experience and semantic (linguistic) associations on which it draws are shared by speakers of the particular TL'. The examples he gives (literal and semantic translation from Hebrew into English) are telling. However, he strangely fails to mention the third factor of universal or extracultural experience, which makes translation of metaphor relatively easy, provided the semantic range of the relevant words are fairly congruent. Thus, in the following lines from E. E. Cummings (1963) (from 'if I have made, my lady intricate'), 'the sweet small clumsy feet of April came into the ragged meadow of my soul', 'feet' is virtually extracultural, in contrast with 'April' whose connotations (freshness, sweetness, showers, unfolding of buds and blossoms, etc.) are restricted to the temperate regions of the Northern Hemisphere, and 'meadow' whose existence (and therefore connotations) is also (differently) geographically circumscribed. Of these three metaphors, 'feet' could be translated into any language, but 'April' and 'meadow' would be subject to cultural (i.e. ecological) constraints. (I believe that certain physical and natural objects—and certain mathematical, physical and moral laws—are *a priori* and therefore extracultural, and they are at least less acculturated than other objects and laws. The meanings of objects and concepts are apprehended partly in as far as they are universal or common to all cultures, partly in as far as they form part of a particular culture, and partly through individual perception.) Note that a creative metaphor is normally difficult enough to translate without the translator being able to account for sound-effect (as in the above-mentioned *Time* quotation) unless the sound-effect 'is more important than' (i.e. is) the sense. If the metaphor includes a neologism (but 'shack' and 'barrel' are American English), the translator must create his own neologism in semantic, but not normally in communicative translation.

Neubert has suggested that 'Shall I compare thee to a summer's day?' (sonnet no. XVIII, W. Shakespeare) could not be semantically translated into a language spoken in a country where summers are unpleasant. This is not so, since the reader should get a vivid impression from the content of the sonnet of the beauty of summer in England, and reading the poem should exercise his imagination as well as introduce him to English culture. A communicative translation into a Middle East language would certainly require a different imagery and a new poem. However, one could assume that all serious poems should be semantically translated and that the more original the metaphor, the more disconnected it is from its culture and therefore the more its originality can be preserved by a literal translation.

The translation of a metaphor may be a four-fold process: the source language term (e.g. *fermé*) collocated with *visage* leads to the image 'closed' which leads to 'wood' which leads to 'wooden face'. The four elements (SL term; SL image; TL image; TL term) depict the sense and quality of lifelessness and hardness. These are the conventional processes of communicative translation.

Language has verbs, adjectives and adverbs that refer naturally to persons, but may be transferred in some cases to objects (e.g. 'it's killing'; 'the price is famously high'; 'stunned surprise'). Similarly, most languages have ambiguous words such as 'fruit, stock, harvest' which in some contexts may be either concrete or figurative or even both. At times a sentence may even be on three levels, viz. specific, generic and figurative, e.g.

'Le devenir du médicament conditionne l'action pharmacologique.'
'The rate of absorption of drugs determines their action.'
'The development of drugs determines their action.'
'The future of drugs will determine the scope and importance of pharmacology.'

In all these cases, a communicative translation will tend to be the easiest version that is consonant with the function of the utterance, whilst a semantic translation will attempt to embrace the total meaning. To sum up, metaphors are not affected by the semantic–communicative argument when they have standardized TL equivalents: in other cases they are translated semantically, but with some allowance for different cultures, if they are original and important; communicatively, emphasizing or explicating their sense, in most other cases.

* * *

It may be objected that communicative translation should always be semantic and that semantic translation should always be communicative. I do not think this is possible. There is a contradiction, an opposition, at best an overlapping between meaning and message—when both are equally pursued. If, like Darbelnet, one believes that 'la traduction est l'opération qui consiste à faire passer d'une langue dans une autre tous les éléments de sens d'un passage et rien que ses éléments, en s'assurant qu'ils conservent dans la langue d'arrivée leur importance relative, ainsi que leur tonalité, et en tenant compte des différences que présentent entre elles les cultures auxquelles correspondent respectivement la langue de départ et la langue d'arrivée'—communication appears to have no place. On the other hand, following Nida's 'Translating is communicating' with its emphasis on a readable (instantly?), understandable text (although Nida also insists on accuracy and fidelity), one notices inevitably a great loss of meaning in the dropping of so many Biblical metaphors which, Nida insists, the reader cannot understand.

The translation theorist has to raise the question, in considering Nida's dynamic equivalence, not only of the nature (education, class, occupation, age, etc.) of the readers, but of what is to be expected of them. Are they to be handed everything on a plate? Are they to make any effort? Are they ever expected to look a word up in a dictionary or an encyclopaedia? I have no wish to question the appropriateness of the *Good News Bible* translation, and obviously the translation of any performatives (public notices, etc.) must also be instantly intelligible. However, I am writing against the increasing assumption that *all* translating is (nothing but) communicating, where the less effort expected of the reader, the better.

The fact is, as any translator knows, meaning is complicated, many-levelled, a 'network of relations' as devious as the channels of thought in the brain. The more communication, the more generalization, the more simplification—the less meaning. One is most aware of meaning when one is thinking, or, to be more precise, when one is silently talking to oneself, that process of internalized or interiorized language one engages in when one thinks, but for which no language appears to have a word. (It is supplemented by the formation of images.) But as soon as one writes or speaks, one starts losing meaning—the images disappear, the words are constructed into clauses—and when one channels and points one's communication, in order to make it effective, towards one or a group of receptors, one confines one's meaning even more. When the third stage is reached—translating, the communication into another language—there is even further loss of meaning. The clash between communication and meaning can be illustrated by the difference between say *affectant les fonctions amnésiques* and 'affecting the functions of memory', *trains réguliers et facultatifs,* 'normal and special trains', *ça le regarde* and 'that's his lookout'—in all cases, the message is the same (perhaps?) but there is a difference in meaning such as Darbelnet would perhaps refuse to recognize. Again, it has been pointed out too often that the terms *Brot, pain, bread* may have different meanings in the three languages if one is thinking of the savour, the shape, the composition, the importance of this food, but if one asks a supplier to send a hundred loaves of bread, the message is an effective act of communication, and connotations are likely to be neglected. The contrast can be made most strongly and paradoxically, if I say that the more I savour the meaning of a word in all its richness, relating it to its object and its connotations, the less I am inclined to communicate, being absorbed—whilst if I want to communicate, I deal with meaning at its narrowest, sharpest, most concise—in fact, ideally, meaning is just a reflex or an automatism to me.

A message, therefore, is only a part of a complete meaning, just as a word, say, 'table', only covers a small part, is a mere label (a 'flat slab or board', a metaphor for a tavern?) for the whole object. Communication has a similar relation to language as functions has to structure. Language, like structure, like 'global' meaning, is rich, diverse, many-layered: once one thinks of a message, a communication, a function, the utterance becomes sharp, thin, direct. Chomsky (1976) denies that language is primarily communicative, and emphasizes that in 'contemplation, inquiry, normal social interchange, planning and guiding one's own actions, creative writing, honest self-expression, and numerous other activities with language, expressions are used with their strict linguistic meaning irrespective of the intentions of the "utterer" with regard to an audience' (p. 69). Transferring this distinction, I suggest that for most of the linguistic activities mentioned above (I except "normal social interchange" which has to be converted to "standardized language" equivalents) a semantic translation is indicated. Semantic translation is subtler, more comprehensive, more penetrating than communicative translation, and does not require cultural adoptation. House (1977b) in a paper, confusingly distinguishes 'overt' (i.e. semantic) from 'covert' (i.e. communicative) translation—shades of 'co-text' and 'context' (Catford, 1965)—but usefully points out that a 'covert' translation 'enjoys or enjoyed (*sic*) the status of an original source text in the target culture', i.e. one of its main characteristics is that no one should suspect that it is a translation. Unfortunately she does not distinguish stylistically between the two types of translation, and in her '"textual" profile', she omits such important dimensions as degree of generality and of emotiveness.

The distinction between semantic and communicative translation, which a behaviourist might well deny, shows how closely translation theory relates not only to the philosophy of language, but even to philosophy in an older sense of the term, when it meant perhaps 'interpretation of the meaning of life'. Thus an affirmative attitude to translation would perhaps stem from a belief in rationalism, in the communicability and renewal of common experience, in 'innate' human nature and even in natural law.

Normally, one assumes that a semantic translation is briefer and 'more literal' than a communicative translation. This is usually, but not always, so. If the original is rich in metaphor, has simultaneously abstract as well as physical meanings and is concerned with say religion, ritual magic, witchcraft or other domains of discourse which have covert categories, a prose translation with explanatory power (the interpretation must be within the translation, not follow it) is likely to be longer than the original. It has to reproduce the full meaning of the original, not simply one of its functions.

Semantic translation is sometimes both linguistic and encyclopaedic, whilst communicative translation is strictly functional. 'Adam's rib', as Crick (1976) has pointed out, has always been an inadequate translation.

If, as I believe, we are to use, in principle, semantic translation for works of philosophy, religion, anthropology, even politics, in texts where the manner and the matter are fused, which are therefore well written, then the translation must be more explicit and usually fuller than for works of literature, particularly poetry. In poetry symbol is retained or transferred; in anthropology, it is retained and explained within the text. As Evans-Pritchard has said 'The translation is the interpretation', and therefore, the full meaning must be in the text, not in a string of notes.

A sentence such as 'Mary was a virgin mother' must be explicated in accordance with precisely what the translator believes the writer to have intended, normally retaining both the literal and the symbolical/figurative interpretation.

Crick has stated that in anthropology, Evans-Pritchard led the general shift from function to meaning: in meaning, the significance of symbols and rites in the culture, as well as their effect on spectators and participants, are uncovered. In a period where bare communication (functionalism) is overvalued, I think there has to be a corresponding shift to semantic translation of all texts that merit it (they are not that many).

* * *

All translation remains a craft requiring a trained skill, continually renewed linguistic and non-linguistic knowledge and a deal of flair and imagination, as well as intelligence and above all common sense. Semantic translation, basically the work of one translator, is an art. Communicative translation, sometimes the product of a translator's team, is a craft. (Those who can, translate. Those who cannot, teach translation theory, learning hopefully from their mistakes.)

The above is an attempt to narrow the range and definition of valid translation, and to suggest that Savory's clever and notorious definitions, which form the superscript of this paper, since they rest on incorrect assumptions, can be reconciled. However, not for a moment am I trying to minimize the difficulties of many aspects (too long overlooked) as well as instances of the translator's task, whether it be 'communicative', 'semantic' or a combination of both. Moreover, I believe that there are also many texts that present few or no difficulties to a translator, and that an effective, if approximate, translation of any text into any language is always possible.

Note: The best twentieth-century comment I know on this type of remark is in Thomas Mann's Introduction to *Der Zauberberg* (Princeton University, 1939): 'An outstanding Swedish critic declared openly and decisively that no one would ever dare to translate this book into a foreign language, as it was absolutely unsuitable for translation. This was a false prophecy. *The Magic Mountain* has been translated into almost all European languages, and, as far as I can judge, none of my books has aroused such interest in the world.' Cf. various remarks about Racine's untranslatability into English. (He has recently been successfully translated.) A successful translation is probably more dependent on the translator's empathy with the writer's thought than on affinity of language and culture.

Appendix

The basic difference between communicative and semantic translation could be illustrated as follows:

1

Examples where communicative translation is correct:

(a) *Défense de marcher sur le gazon*
C. Keep off the grass
S. Walking on the turf is forbidden
OR
It is forbidden to walk on the turf.

(b) *Frisch angestrichen!*
C. Wet paint!
S. Recently painted!

2

'Die Geschichte Hans Castorps, die wir erzählen wollen—nicht um seinetwillen (denn der Leser wird einen einfachen, wenn auch ansprechenden jungen Menschen in ihm kennenlernen) sondern um der Geschichte willen, die uns in hohem Grade erzählenswert scheint (wobei zu Hans Castorps Gunsten denn doch erinnert werden sollte, daß es seine Geschichte ist und daß nicht jedem jede Geschichte passiert): diese Geschichte ist sehr lange her, sie ist sozusagen schon ganz mit historischem Edelrost überzogen und unbedingt in der Zeitform der tiefsten Vergangenheit vorzutragen.' (*Der Zauberberg,* Thomas Mann.)

Semantic:

'Hans Castorp's story, which we propose to tell—not on his own account (for in him the reader will make the acquaintance of a simple though attractive young man) but for the sake of the story, which seems to us to be highly worth telling (it should however be remembered to Hans Castorp's credit that it is his story, and that not every story happens to everybody): this story took place a very long time ago, it is already so to speak covered with the patina of history, and it must in any event be presented in a tense corresponding to the remotest past.' (My translation.)

Communicative:

'We propose to tell Hans Castorp's story not for his sake, but for the story's. The reader will discover that in fact he is rather a simple but attractive young man. But the story seems to us to be well worth telling, even though it took place a long time ago, and is already covered in the dust of history. It is essential to show that it took place in the remote past. Further we must bear in mind in Hans Castorp's favour that this is his own story, and a story like this one does not happen to everyone.' (My translation.)

N.B.

There are cases where for (1), the semantic translation is required (to show the 'thought-processes' of the utterance), and where for (2), the communicative translation may be preferable to make the utterance on first reading more comprehensible and attractive.

3

'Samedi 10 juillet s'est terminée une session dite extraordinaire qui était plutôt la continuation d'une session qui, elle, fut loin d'être ordinaire.

'Alors que les députés s'offraient en juin le luxe de débattre pendant vingt séances du projet sur les plus-values, les sénateurs, eux, se morfondaient, le gouvernement n'ayant pas suffisamment utilisé le possibilité de déposer des textes en première lecture devant cette Assemblée. Ainsi le Sénat enregistrait-il, au terme de la session ordinaire, un déficit de 30% par rapport à la durée pendant laquelle il avait siégé au printemps de 1975.'

Semantic:

'On Saturday 10 July a so-called extraordinary session which was rather the continuation of a session which itself was far from being ordinary came to an end.

'Whilst in June the deputies offered themselves the luxury of debating the capital gains bill for 20 sessions, the senators for their part were becoming sadly bored, the government not having sufficiently utilized the possibility of introducing drafts for first reading for that assembly. Thus at the end of the ordinary session, the Senate recorded a deficit of 30% compared with the length of time it had sat in spring 1975.'

Communicative:

'Saturday 10 July saw the close of an "extraordinary" session; it was in fact the continuation of a session which was itself far from ordinary.

'Whilst in June the deputies could afford the luxury of debating the capital gains bill for 20 sessions, the senators kicked their heels in despair, as the government had not made enough use of the opportunity of passing bills on to them for a first reading. So at the end of the ordinary session, the Senate had sat for only 70% of the corresponding period in spring 1975.'

Cognitive translation:

'On Saturday 10 July "they" closed a session which "they" called extraordinary; the session in fact continued a session which was itself far from being ordinary.

'Whilst the nationally elected members of parliament (deputies) in June offered themselves the luxury of debating for 20 sessions the bill which related to the profits which people made on capital, the members elected by councillors to represent departments (senators) (second house) did nothing themselves and were bored and gloomy whilst they waited, as the government had not sufficiently used the possibility of passing bills on to their own house for a first reading. Thus the Senate recorded at the end of the ordinary session that they had sat 30% less than the time they had sat in the spring of 1975.'

4. Thought, speech and translation

A postscript to 'Communicative and semantic translation'.

The first section of this chapter is a brief attempt to underpin theoretically my tentative distinction between communicative and semantic translation. I have neither the pretension nor the qualification to make a contribution to the nature of thought (except in as far as I have attempted to analyse my own thought processes), and I have deliberately avoided any reference to its origin and development. It will however soon become obvious that I am closer in my own thinking to Vygotsky and to Chomsky than to Piaget or to Labov, let alone to Whorf or any behaviourist view. When Vygotsky writes, 'Inner speech is not the interior aspect of external speech—it is a function in itself. It is to a large extent thinking in pure meanings' he provides me with a source of reference for my definition of 'semantic translation' in contrast to 'communicative translation'. (All references in Adams, 1972.)

* * *

I believe that the primary activity, application and purpose of language in the mature adult is *thinking*, not speech or writing or communication or (self-)expression.* It is not possible to prove or disprove this assertion, but merely to produce some evidence. First, one cannot think for long without having words in one's mind. The effort not to 'think', that is, to keep one's mind blank or to concentrate on a mental pictorial image (or on a sensation of smell, taste, sound or touch) rather than pursuing one's normal internal monologue is like holding one's breath; one can't keep it up for long. Language therefore informs but does not comprise thinking. One can, however, use words without sound, without thinking, if one (a) repeats short sentences, phrases or words, (b) counts numbers, (c) tells oneself nonsense stories—the remedy for insomnia. Secondly, even the most loquacious person spends most of her time thinking; I doubt whether most people spend more than five hours a day speaking. (The most loquacious, the most lonely, usually spend most time alone, thinking.) Moreover, whilst thought and writing are concurrent activities (it is not possible to write without continuous inner speech), the relation between thought and speech is intermittent—thought sparks off speech, and speech is frequently an automatism, a reflex action, the response to a stimulus and only 'weakly' the product of thought. Therefore, thought is closer to writing than to speaking, and in this sense, writing, arising from and controlled by thought, has primacy over speaking. Further, when

* Thought saturated in language is one of the two prefaces to behaviour, speech acts, writing or speaking—the other is a more or less physical stimulus.

one listens to a person, one normally 'thinks' only in the interstices of his conversation—otherwise one 'comprehends' wordlessly. When one listens to natural sounds or music, the proportion of internal monologue (thought) is much higher—over 80% of the total time, perhaps. Sleep on the other hand appears to be concurrently and continuously occupied by mental pictorial images and interior monologue. When one is translating orally (simultaneous interpretation), one only starts thinking, in the sense of inner speech, when one is lost for a word or meets some difficulty; when one writes a translation one is thinking all the time.

If one accepts the proposition that thinking precedes speech and writing and therefore that the main purpose of language is *not* to communicate (since thought is by definition private and non-communicative although it is partially, but never wholly, communicable) one has to review the now generally accepted arguments in favour of the 'primacy of speech' (Pit Corder, 1973) or 'the priority of the spoken language' (Lyons, 1968, 1972) and reject the proposition that writing is merely a poor substitute for an imitation of speech.

No one would question that speech is older and more widespread than writing, nor that a child speaks before it writes. Having knowledge of a language, however,* often precedes speaking, which requires additional accessory capacities. Lenneberg's (1967) report of the child who could babble and read but not speak is well known. The argument that all systems of writing are demonstrably based upon units of spoken language is moreover questionable. Sounds, syllables and words are as vivid in the mind as they are when they are spoken aloud and I believe that writing systems (like speech systems) are originated in thought, moderated, socialized, made more 'communicative', etc., in speech, and then again mediated through thought. However, the most important reason for challenging the primacy of speech over writing is that writing is much more closely related physically and mentally to thought than is speech. Writing is permanent, it is used not necessarily because the addressee is inaccessible to speech, but because one wants to make a strong and durable impression on him. All the world's most important thoughts and statements, including Lincoln's, Churchill's, De Gaulle's and doubtless Pericles' speeches, were probably written before they were spoken. Even the material transmitted by TV and radio is written to be spoken. Speech, however, is often a response to a stimulus and though it is often preceded by thought, it is frequently thoughtless while it lasts. I do not, however, accept the "classical" (Lyons, 1968) principle of the priority of the written language, which was based on the superiority of Sanskrit, Ancient Greek, Latin, Byzantine Greek, Old Church Slavonic (compare the superiority of Classical Arabic and Mandarin—'civil servant language'—Chinese over the vernaculars and dialects), etc., over the spoken language—all these are instances of Gramscian 'hegemony', the intellectual exploitation of the uneducated by the so-called educated, in other words an élitist racket, not as materially profitable as commercial exploitation, but exceedingly comfortable and fraudulent.

* * *

* Note that there are many unwritten languages.

I now turn to further consideration of my distinction between the 'semantic' and 'communicative' methods of translation. Where writing is closest to thought, where the reader is 'listening in' rather than being consciously addressed, the method of translation is normally 'semantic'. In my previous article, I wrote that of all forms of literature, the drama, since it is addressed to a spectator, might have to make most 'concessions' to communicative translation. However, I excepted Chekhov and Shakespeare, as being the greatest drama. Now I suggest that Shakespeare's most important thoughts are expressed either in his 'monologues' (in both senses of the word) or in long speeches where he appears to be addressing posterity rather than anyone on the stage or the spectator.

I take it as axiomatic that in thought or in monologue, the expressive function of language is predominant, the informative is incidental, the social and the phatic inoperative. Moreover in a Shakespearean monologue the expressive and aesthetic functions are fused. A glance even at the old Schlegel translation of Hamlet (I. 2) will show that the dialogue is treated fairly 'communicatively':

Q: I pray thee, stay with us; go not to Wittenberg.
Ich bitte, bleib bei uns geh nicht nach Wittenberg.
H: I shall in all my best obey your madam.
Ich will Euch gern gehorchen gnädige Frau.
K: Why, 'tis a loving and a fair reply.
Wohl, das ist eine liebe, schöne Antwort.

whilst in the subsequent monologue the translator wrestles with concentrated thought and the semantic loss is considerable and inevitable:

H: O, that this too too solid flesh would melt,
Oh, schmölze doch dies allzu feste Fleisch,
Thaw, and resolve itself into a dew!
Zerging! und löst in einen Tau sich auf!
Or that the Everlasting had not fixt
Oder hätte nicht der Ew'ge sein Gebot
His canon gainst self-slaughter! O God, God,
Gerichtet gegen Selbstmord! O Gott! Gott!
How weary, stale, flat and unprofitable
Wie ekel, schal und flach und unersprießlich
Seem to me all the uses of this world!
Scheint mir das ganze Treiben dieser Welt!
Fie on't! O, fie! 'tis an unweeded garden
Pfui, Pfui darüber! 's ist ein wüster Garten
That grows to seed: things rank and gross in nature
Der auf in Samen schießt; verworfnes Unkraut
Possess it merely. That it should come to this!
Erfällt ihn gänzlich. Dazu müßt es kommen?

Schlegel's fine version is a continuous undertranslation, a generalization, missing the physical sense of 'thaw', 'possess', 'unweeded', 'fixt', 'rank and gross'. Nevertheless, the syntactic scaffolding of the monologue is splendidly reproduced, permeated in the

German as in the English by the timeless rhythms of speech or thought, without concessions to 'communicativeness'. Certainly it will be a pity if ever, in the name of the 'message' or 'communication', this speech has to be remodelled or retranslated, omitting Hyperion (already reduced to Apollo by Schlegel), the satyr, Niobe, Hercules, etc.—consciously directed to the mind of the living spectator rather than to the fullest possible explication of Shakespeare's thought.

Dichten = condensare, as Ezra Pound (1934), a wayward, suggestive and frequently inaccurate translator, rightly stated, although apparently unaware that he was punning, and that *dichten* has nothing, even etymologically, to do with *dicht.* As a poet, the translator is constrained by metre and genre. If he is translating prose, he has a little more space to bring out connotation as well as denotation, symbol as well as sign; harsh alternatives are fewer. Reading a page of Paul Valéry (1946) it seems to me that a translator cannot retain the pregnant brevity of *la niaise manie . . . taché d'une erreur . . . se rendre perceptible.* A componential analysis of key-words will show that they 'work' physically as well as figuratively, and where possible both levels have to be retained.* Semantic translation, like thought, relates to the word or the word-group; communicative translation, like speech, relates to the sentence. Semantic translation of difficult texts, however, is inevitably selective and therefore interpretative and evaluative, since the translator expresses his values by rejecting or excluding the components of meaning which he regards as less pertinent or peripheral.

I conclude this postscript with a few words on 'communicative' translation, the more common method, since 'semantic' translation is used only where texts run close to thought-processes and every stage of the thought-process is significant. I am not attempting to devalue communication or communicative translation, merely to contest their present dominance. The primary purpose of speech is to communicate, and communicative translation is related to speech as semantic translation is to thought. Just as one learns a foreign language mainly to communicate (unless one is learning only to read and translate it), not to think in it, so one is right in assuming that most translation is communicative translation which is close to 'social speech' in the sense I have described. Usually, one translates a text to meet the reader's demands—to inform him, to persuade him, to give him advice. All this is communicative translation, as is any performative or direction or instruction, any use of 'standardized' language such as 'no trumps', 'lovely weather, isn't it?', 'critical path analysis', 'micro-incineration', etc. Again communicative translation is required when the original has to be rearranged or improved in any way as Wilss (1978) unconsciously does in his recent useful manual: 'This time tomorrow I shall have been on my way to Berlin for a long time', which he translates as 'Morgen um

* Note the richness of the word *shrug*, which may mean to 'raise' or to 'draw in' the shoulders, always as an expression of indifference, aloofness or aversion.

diese Zeit bin ich schon längst auf dem Weg nach Berlin', which is much better (i.e. 'This time tomorrow I'll be well on my way to Berlin'). Further, if the original is reasonably well written and is either extracultural or overlaps with the target language culture, there is no reason why it should not be translated communicatively and semantically at the same time—the 'ideal' solution, not because it will be a unique ideal translation (this idea, still fostered by Koller, the Leipzig School and others, but not by Wilss, is preposterous),* but because it is designed to satisfy both the author of the text and the reader of the translation in equal measure.

* The absence of an 'ideal' translation (except for short, not source language—or culture—specific sentences), i.e. of the type of single correct answer that one strives to find in a mathematical or a scientific problem, is a reflection of the fact that language like translation is far from being a science, though both are subject to all scientific procedures such as making hypotheses, observing, verifying, collecting data, testing against and reexamining hypotheses, etc.

5. Communicative and semantic translation (II)

The concepts of communicative and semantic translation represent my main contribution to general translation theory, and I return to them as I have to modify and clarify both concepts.

The two concepts were formulated in opposition to the monistic theory that translation is basically a means of communication or a manner of addressing one or more persons in the speaker's presence; that translation, like language, is purely a social phenomenon.

In view of the fact that translation rests on at least three dichotomies—the foreign and native cultures, the two languages, the writer and the translator respectively, with the translation readership looming over the whole process*—it seems unlikely that it can be incorporated in one theory. Further, all the writers of the past have defined two or three methods of translation, sometimes only recommending one and disparaging the remainder (e.g. Nida and Nabokov), at other times, as in Schleiermacher's classical definition, leaving the translator free to lean either on the writer's or the reader's shoulder. Lastly, behind this translation argument there is a philosophical conflict. This is said to be the age of reproduction, of the media, of mass-communication and I am suggesting that the social factor is only a part of the truth, continuously overemphasized by technology and the present political advance to democracy. Thus the 'expressive' text represents an individual, not wholly socialized nor conditioned, voice.

Admittedly, all translation must be in some degree both communicative and semantic, social and individual. It is a matter of difference of emphasis. In communicative translation, however, the only part of the meaning of the original which is rendered is the part (which may even be the 'opposite' of the original, as in *objets trouvés*, 'lost property') which corresponds to the TL reader's understanding of the identical message. If the translator is dealing in standardized terms for both languages, there may be no problems. Otherwise, the translator has to bear in mind a composite identikit reader, following appropriate TL usage, modifying, correcting and improving the latest versions of the fair copy of his translation often without any reference to the original. Clearly, there is a danger here of capturing too small a part of the original message, as for instance in the following example taken from Seleskovitch (1979): 'Il n'y a pas de mal à prendre de temps en temps un verre de trop quand on sort' rendered as 'It's all right to get a bit drunk at a party.' One of the many problems of communicative translation is to decide to what extent one should simplify and therefore emphasize the basic message. A second is to strike a mean, to decide on the highest common factor of intelligence, knowledge and sensitivity possessed by the

* The facts of the matter—the extra-linguistic reality—is an additional powerful factor.

total readership—inevitably one thinks of communicative translation as mass communication. A third is precisely not to insult the intelligence of the readership, as the media often do. But the most important problem is the intuitive nature of communicative translation—the fact that its success can be measured only by investigating the reaction of the readers to whom it is addressed.

* * *

In reconsidering semantic translation, I begin by distinguishing it from literal translation.

In previous articles I have adapted Nabokov in defining semantic translation as an attempt to render, as closely as the semantic and syntactic structures of the target language allow, the exact contextual meaning of the original ('only this is true translation', Nabokov wrote); I contrasted this method of translation with communicative translation, which is also true translation, and much more in demand.

I now propose two further definitions:
(1) Interlinear translation (Nabokov's lexical or constructional translation): the primary senses of all words in the original are translated as though out of context, and the word-order of the original is retained. The main purpose is either to understand the mechanics of the source language or to constitute a pre-translation procedure for a complicated SL text.

(2) Literal translation: the primary senses of the lexical words of the original are translated as though out of context, but the syntactic structures of the target language are respected.

The basic difference between semantic and literal translation is that the former respects context, the latter does not. Semantic translation sometimes has to interpret, even explain a metaphor, if it is meaningless in the target language (nevertheless, only as a last resource, only if the translator is convinced that the relevant background knowledge is inaccessible to his reader). In semantic translation, the translator's first loyalty is to his author; in literal translation, his loyalty is, on the whole, to the norms of the source language.

It is ironical that Nabokov (1964) himself often translated literally, not semantically: 'She, to look back not daring, accelerates her hasty step' (*Eugene Onegin*, 5, p. 1311, 1.1–2), many times relying on the reader referring to the copious notes as well as having access to the original. Further, in stating 'To my ideal of literalism I sacrificed everything (elegance, euphony, clarity, good taste, modern usage, and even grammar) that the dainty mimic prizes higher than the truth', he is violating his own principles ('as closely as the syntactical capacities of another language allow') by sacrificing 'even grammar'.

Nabokov's contribution to translation theory, his attack on the 'paraphrasts', his scorn of the communication racket, etc., was tremendous, but his own practice was not as close to his principles as, say, Andreas Mayor's version of *Le Temps retrouvé*.

If the 'semantic' translator is asked whether his (agreed) first duty to his author is not to communicate the meaning of the text to the reader, his answer is perhaps Yes and No. Certainly, if the text is not modern, the translation has to be put into modern language, which in itself moves it nearer to the reader. Further, if the language contains symbolism and expressive elements which are likely to be completely inaccessible to the reader, then it is the translator's duty at least to make their comprehension possible. Moreover, in translating a philosophical text, he may be tempted to write what Alan Bass (see Derrida, 1978) has called a 'compound English', 'a compromise of English as we know it and as he would like it to be in order to capture as much of the original text as possible'. Bass rejects this in favour of a natural syntax combined with a detailed explication of theme—words by way of commentaries in brackets, which forces him to write three times as much as the original for one short passage. Bass believes that the translator's position resembles that of the psychoanalyst who attempts to translate the manifest language of dreams into a latent language, which is no more helpful than the other clichés about translation. In general, philosophical texts have a stronger communicative element than artistic texts, dealing with generalities rather than particularities, with explanations and definitions rather than images and symbols, and the translator would orientate his purpose accordingly.

On the other hand, the original author does not 'communicate' with the reader any more than the translator, in an artistic text. The translator only goes as far as making it possible for the modern reader to understand, to listen, to eavesdrop like Polonius behind the arras. Why? Because the translator has to be jealous of the form of the original, the form which, adapting Gombrich's (1972) words, 'modifies, refines and articulates thought'; which, if it were distorted (it inevitably is partially distorted), distorts the thought. That is why the translator of a great work of literature, or any important utterance, is on a tightrope, has to work so carefully. His first loyalty is to his author, his second is to the target language, his last to the reader.

Further, in poetry in particular and imaginative writing in general, all common and general concrete words have connotations, and therefore have some of the force of a metaphor without its image or vehicle. Sooner or later, they themselves are used as images or vehicles, and become metaphors (every year, common or vogue words in any semantic field become metaphors). When these words are translated, they lose their connotations or metaphorical sense, unless there is a cultural overlap between source and target language. Thus, a tree which may symbolize or faintly suggest development or life or strength in one language may, being rarer in another, have few connotations and the translator may have to attempt to replace the object with another with corresponding connotations in the TL (the commoner the word, the more abundant its connotations). Since the symbol and connotations are at least a part of the meaning of the text, the 'semantic' translator is entitled to account for it, not necessarily to satisfy this or that reader.

* * *

In previous papers, I have underestimated the importance of aesthetic value, or of poetic truth in semantic translation (whilst Nabokov ignored it). I take Keats's dictum as axiomatic:

> 'Beauty is truth, truth beauty—this is all
> Ye know on earth, and all ye need to know.'
>
> *(Ode on a Grecian Urn.)*

I take it that poetic truth has no intrinsic or independent meaning, but that it is correlative with the various types of meaning in a text, and that if the translator destroys poetic truth, he impairs and distorts meaning. Thus, delicacy or gentleness conveyed in word-order and sound, as well as in cognitive sense, would be ruined, if the translator introduced crude alliterations or a contrived word-order. Aesthetic value is dependent on the following factors:

(a) *structure*—for the translation, the plan of the text as a whole and the shape and balance of the individual sentences;
(b) *metaphor*—the visual images which may also evoke sound, touch (including temperature and climate), smell and taste;
(c) *sound*—including alliteration, assonance, rhythm, onomatopoeia, and, in poetry, metre and rhyme.

A translator cannot ignore any of the three factors in prose or poetry, although he may, for each text or in principle, order these factors, giving priority to cognitive meaning.

Nabokov in theory ignored poetic truth, although in fact it appeared in some of his earlier translations. Now, I am suggesting that the aesthetic factor, if it exists in the original, must remain in the translation. Take the opening of Valéry's *Introduction à la méthode de Léonard de Vinci:* 'Il reste d'un homme ce que donnent à songer son nom et les oeuvres qui font de ce nom un signe d'admiration, de haine ou d'indifférence. Nous pensons qu'il a pensé, et nous pouvons retrouver entre ses oeuvres cette pensée qui lui vient de nous: nous pouvons refaire cette pensée à l'image de la nôtre.'

The passage is marvellously articulated, mathematically arranged as a progression; basically the structure must be reproduced, whilst the ellipses can be modified so that they are not as gaunt as literal translation would make them. Malcolm Cowley and J. R. Lawler's translation is as follows: 'What a man leaves after him are the dreams that his name inspires and the works that make his name a symbol of admiration, hate or indifference. We think of how he thought and we are able to find within his works a kind of thinking derived from ourselves that we attribute to him; we can refashion this thought in the image of our own.'

The following is an attempt to go as close to the cognitive meaning as I can without prejudicing aesthetic value: 'There remains of a man the thoughts which his name and the works making his name a mark of admiration, hatred or indifference evoke. We think that he has thought and we can find within his work a thinking which reaches him from us; we can recreate this thinking in the image of our own.'

Aesthetic truth, like music, is perhaps a more general quality than meaning, and this has been beautifully preserved in Cowley and Lawler's version. I do not think it would have been impaired if in the first sentence 'remains of' had replaced 'leaves after' in the second place and 'mark' or 'sign' had replaced 'symbol'. 'Inspires' is in the right place, at a considerable semantic loss! Stark as it is, I see no alternative to translating 'Nous pensons qu'il a pensé' as anything but 'we think that he has thought'; a slip ('ce qu'il a pensé') can be excluded, as the essay was revised 35 years later. The sentence, I think, serves simply to identify Leonardo's thinking with (educated) mankind's. In many other cases, the translators could, in my opinion, have come closer to the original without reducing its aesthetic value: 'de simples souvenirs en ressuscitent les mobiles et les réactions élémentaires', translated as 'his motives and elementary reactions can be supplied quite simply from our own memories', where 'restored to life by', or 'revived by', could easily replace 'supplied from'. Later, the translators take *lieu* as *lien* without explanation. With all this, they have wrestled with the text, and produced a fine version, blemished by unnecessary concessions to their own idea of style.

* * *

A semantic translation is not a rigid procedure: it is admittedly more objective than communicative translation, since the SL words as well as the sentences (elsewhere I describe these as the two articulations of meaning) are operative as a form of control. However, the translator may be constantly exercised between the proportion of denotation and connotation in the original text, bearing in mind that in a literary text, the connotative and allegorical aspect is the most important.

Thus translation theory cannot be dogmatic, must allow for and make allowances for a sensitive and wayward translation, such as A. Macdonald's of Malraux's *La Condition humaine*: here *les hommes* become 'ordinary life', *découvrir* 'first notice', *regarder avec indifférence* 'just glance at', whilst topic and comment are often reversed, and *luisaient faiblement* is 'a faint gleam', *le ciel lumineux s'y reflétait* 'it was a reflection of the glow in the sky'. All this can be justified as connoting how Chen viewed the scene. Other translations of facts, *auto-mitrailleuses* as 'machine-guns', *devant lui, perpendiculaire* 'in front of him, rose up', are harder to justify. Nevertheless, this translation gets away with it, as do some of Stuart Gilbert's, because of their empathy: further, since connotations (for Chen) appear to be the main objective, it is difficult to assess the translation using this 'potential' criterion.

* * *

Nevertheless, nothing is now more obvious than that the criterion of a translation, whether communicative or semantic, must be its measure of accuracy, its ability to reproduce the greatest possible degree of the meaning of the original: the heart of the meaning being the message in communicative translation—the significance, the enduring value and importance in semantic translation. Admittedly, in communicative translation a certain embroidering, a stylistic synonymy, a discreet modulation is condoned by some translators, however unnecessary it is, provided the facts are straight and the reader is suitably impressed. In semantic translation, inaccuracy is always wrong. Hans Keller (1977) in showing up the inadequacies of the two English translations of Kafka's *The Trial* puts the point paradoxically: 'Indefinite stylistic sensitivity may be the next best thing to a definable recognition of the literary truth, but it is never more than a substitute.' Keller happened to choose as his examples the opening and end of *The Trial* where mainly one-to-one translations are appropriate and therefore mandatory, and the primary meanings (in a legal context) of words such as *verleumden, Entscheidung*, are required. Although Keller fails to point out that in the great majority of translation problems 'definable recognition of literary truth' (presumably he means a single correct one-to-one translation) does not exist and the translator requires here as elsewhere a not so 'undefinable stylistic sensitivity', he is right in his main point, which is that there is no excuse for inaccuracy where accuracy, particularly of 'standardized' language, is possible. Here translation must be in line with the contemporary cultural climate, which is rightly for openness, frankness and truthfulness, irrespective even of context.

Clearly much remains to be examined. The delicate relationship between aesthetic value and semantic truth requires a full-scale discussion when translation and the expressive function of language are considered. In a significant text, semantic truth is cardinal, whilst of the three aesthetic factors, sound (e.g. alliteration or rhyme) is likely to recede in importance—rhyme is perhaps the most likely factor to 'give'—rhyming is difficult and artificial enough in one language, reproducing rhyme is sometimes doubly so. Structure will always be important and has its own (dangerous) sense connotations, e.g. balance, orderliness, harmony, logic, opposition (or their reverse) which may not always be in line with the purpose of the passage or its main themes.

* * *

Whilst recent publications (e.g. Wilss, 1978) have continued to assume, implicitly or not, or to look for a general single translation theory, there have been two exceptions: Diller and Kornelius (1978) have proposed two types of translation:

(a) primary translation, which establishes communication between SL writer and TL reader;
(b) secondary translation, which informs the TL reader of a communication between SL writer and reader (and includes the translation of literary and scientific texts).

The names and definitions are neat, but to regard literary as 'secondary' translation is not satisfactory, nor is it, as I have suggested, a matter of communication with the SL any more than with the TL reader.

Whilst 'primary' and 'secondary' translation correspond in general terms to my 'communicative' and 'semantic' translation, Diller and Kornelius (in an excellent book) do not analyse the differences. Secondly, as mentioned in my first paper, House (1977a) in the book based on her thesis distinguishes source culture-linked 'overt' translation and source culture-free 'covert' translation; equivalent function (i.e. dynamic equivalence) can be achieved only in cases of covert translation. In spite of her distinction between 'linked-to' and 'free-from' the SL culture, she states that covert translation will also require the application of a 'cultural filter'.

I assume some correspondence between her overt and covert and my semantic and communicative translations respectively. She does not work out the distinction. 'In the absence of completed linguistic–cultural contrastive studies, the evaluation of these two types of translation inevitably contains a subjective hermeneutic element.' This is word-dropping, but again, she represents a challenge to the prevailing view that everything must always be done for the reader of a translation, that he must have everything served up to him, that he is therefore the unifying and generalizing factor for every text-type and translation procedure. Which I cannot accept.

* * *

There is a certain parallel between, on the one hand, communicative and semantic translation, and on the other the universalist and the relativist theses of language and the various gradations between them.

Taken to their extremes, the universalist thesis is that since men have common thoughts and feelings, they should have no difficulty in communicating with each other, whatever language they use. The relativist thesis is that men's thoughts and feelings are predetermined by the various languages hence cultures they are born into, and therefore communication is not possible.

Communicative translation assumes that exact translation may be possible and may be perfect. It always reads like an original and it must, as Nida stresses, sound 'natural'. If the original is a complex technical or institutional text, it may be as difficult as an 'expressive' text, but the difficulty will reside either in the obscurity (usually the bad writing) of the text or the lack of equivalent technical institutional terms in the target language. With all this, the translator has a *message* to convey, and a message always can be conveyed. Basically this is a 'universalist' position.

On the other hand, complete meaning or significance whether of word, sentence or text, can hardly ever be transferred. In approaching an 'expressive' text, the translator's position is relativist. I do not think it is 'ultra-Whorfian', as Steiner (1978) misleadingly suggests, since we are entering the separate individual 'language-world' of *one* person, not of a whole ethnic group. (Steiner confuses the two.) Nevertheless, here the form of the text is important, and presents its own difficulty. (Some writers have said that where the form of a text is part of the message, translation is 'impossible'.) This has the same rather banal and meaningless truth as the 'opposite' pronouncement that one should translate as the original writer would if he had all the means of the contemporary TL at his disposal—which, however, is a valid argument for playing Mozart's* piano concertos with a piano rather than a fortepiano! Since the form of the text is important, semantic translation may well not read like an original TL text, but given the 'bands' of semantic translation, this is far from being a prescription. In any event, semantic translation will read like original writing—whether in the source or target language is largely irrelevant.

* I make no apology for any analogies with this composer, since as far as I am concerned the mention of his name immediately makes any other subject irrelevant. I am not unique in this respect. See, for instance, the great Edgar Wind's Reith lectures on *Art and Anarchy* (1968).

Steiner (1978) has usefully drawn attention to a puzzling passage in Chomsky's *Aspects of the Theory of Syntax* (1965): 'The possibility of a reasonable procedure for translation between arbitrary languages depends on the sufficiency of substantive universals. In fact, although there is much reason to believe that languages are to a significant extent cast in the same mould, there is little reason to suppose that reasonable procedures of translation are in general possible.' The main reason offered by Chomsky is that there is no 'point to point correspondence between particular languages'—a significant remark, suggesting that Chomsky thinks all translation should be one-to-one. By a 'reasonable procedure' he means 'one that doesn't involve extralinguistic information' apparently unaware that linguistic translation procedures must be contextually supported and sometimes supplemented by 'the encyclopaedia'. In the case of missing information—the supplying of this information, say for ambiguous pronouns: *nach seiner Besetzung*, 'after France's occupation', is itself a reasonable procedure. It is strange that Chomsky, who so stridently represents a universalist against a relativist position, should be so sceptical in his attitude to translation, but to my knowledge he has never shown any interest in the subject and should not have pontificated about it.

* * *

Communicative translation is always concentrated on the reader, but the equivalent-effect element is inoperant if the text is out of TL space and time. Thus the translation of a medical text by Galen or Hippocrates would attempt to clarify all the facts of the text, as though the original text were being explained to a modern reader—any equivalent-effect is only in the imagination.

Lastly, I am not suggesting that 'expressive' texts, in particular great literature, have no 'message': on the contrary, I think their (moral) message is of their essence. But this message is not simple or direct (like most propaganda), but diffused through every part of the text, and this is precisely why semantic translation has to wrestle with words as well as clauses, with the author's inner meaning and is only *ultimately* addressed to anyone who is willing to (learn to) read or listen.

6. The translation of proper names and institutional and cultural terms

Since proper names and institutional and cultural terms shade into each other, I discuss this important, extensive and virtually undebated subject within one chapter, but I propose to split it into five parts: proper names; historical institutional terms; international institutional terms; national institutional terms; and cultural terms.

* * *

The basic distinction between **proper names** and cultural terms is that while both refer to persons, objects or processes peculiar to a single ethnic community, the former have singular references, while the latter refer to classes of entities. In theory, names of single persons or objects are 'outside' languages, belong, if at all, to the encyclopaedia not the dictionary, have, as Mill stated, no meaning or connotations, are, therefore, both untranslatable and not to be translated.

In fact, while the position is nothing like so simple, the principle stands that unless a single object's or a person's name already has an accepted translation it should not be translated but must be adhered to, unless the name is used as a metaphor. If the name becomes commonly used, it may be modified in pronunciation and spelling; but nowadays, when people have become as jealous of their names as of their national and linguistic independence, this is not likely.

The established practices for translating the names of HISTORICAL FIGURES are as follows. Where sovereigns had 'translatable' Christian names and they were well known, their names, together with titles (e.g. Richard Coeur de Lion) were and are still usually mutually translated in the main European countries. However, in English, Lewis has reverted to Louis and Francis to François, and in French *George* is now preferred to Georges. 'Christian' names referring to Biblical figures (e.g. all saints in Biblical times and later) remain translated. Surnames have usually been preserved, but the surnames, first names and appellative names of some Italian artists have been 'naturalized' in some European languages (e.g. *Titien*, Titian, *le Tintoret*, Raphael, *Michelange, le Caravage, Léonard*, as well as *Machiavel*). Names of classical writers are usually naturalized (*Aristote*), while the French translate the first names of some historical and literary figures (Jean Hus, Henri Heine, who died in Paris). The only living person whose name is always translated is the Pope.

In belles-lettres, names are normally translated only if, as in some plays, the characters and milieu are naturalized. Neubert (1972) has pointed out that in the best German translation of *Tom Jones* the characters' surnames are translated since they 'mean' as well as 'name', but I do not think they would be translated in a modern version, since this would suggest that they change their nationality.

While surnames in fiction often have deliberate connotations through sound and meaning, the translator should explain the connotations in a glossary and leave the names intact (except, of course, in allegories like *Pilgrim's Progress, Everyman,* etc., where the characters are not specifically English).

Proper names in fairy stories, folk tales and children's literature are often translated, on the ground that children and fairies are the same the world over. The names of heroes of folk tales are not translated if they represent national qualities.

A possible method of translating LITERARY PROPER NAMES that have connotations in the SL is first to translate the word that underlies the proper name into the TL, and then to naturalize it back into a new SL proper name. Thus in translating Wackford Squeers into German, 'whack' becomes *prügeln* becomes *Proogle*, and possibly Squeers (squint, queer?) could become *schielen* and the name in a German version might be translated as '*Proogle Squeers*' or '*Proogle Sheel*'. In other cases the connotations, both of word-images and general sound-echoes, are similar in German (e.g. Crummles, Wittiterby, Pecksniff (*picken, schnüffeln*), Glubb) and the names would, therefore, remain as they are in the German version, but should be appropriately changed in languages which have different sound connotations. The attempt must be to reproduce the connotations of the original in the TL, but to find a name consonant with SL nomenclature, thus preserving the character's nationality. The translator also has to consider whether a previous translation or transcription may already be generally accepted, making it inadvisable to introduce a new one. Further, in translating names of institutions, as opposed to personal names (e.g. 'Dotheboys Hall') he need perhaps be less constrained to reproduce the Englishness, and could try something like: *Internat Schwindeljunge* (i.e. 'Swindleboys School').

I have taken Dickens's names as an example, but his work (and, of course, Shakespeare's, e.g. Belch, Aguecheek) as well as Wilde's and Shaw's is now too well known in most languages for any retranslation of proper names. The procedure could be tried for Elizabethan, Jacobean and Restoration Comedy (Pinchwife, Tweekwife (*zwicken*) for German, Pinchfarm for French, though the pun on 'pinch' is lost). Sheridan, Thomas Mann, Günter Grass, J. B. Priestley, Anthony Powell, J. C. Powys could receive the same treatment in places, but only where the work is virtually unknown in the TL culture, and where the translator is convinced that the connotations of the proper name is at least as important as the nationality. (If the work is an allegory without national application, proper names are translated straight.) These coined names could not be as effective as the originals, and would have to be more cleverly contrived than my own examples. (Alpert (1979) has rightly pointed out that Squeers also has a 'squint' component.)

There are Elizabethan and Jacobean comedies where the message is more important than the culture, and it could also be said that the remoteness of the period justifies a translation of the proper names. Gläser (1976) has noted that names in the *Doctor's Dilemma* have remained unaltered in German, although G. B. S. may well have regarded German doctors then and now as no less fatuous than British ones. On the other hand, to translate the characters' names in *Tom Jones* into 'pure' German, however well, seems misplaced to me. I offer my own solution as the only theoretically correct one, if the culture and the message are approximately equally important, but I realize that its practice requires exceptional linguistic skill.

The only types of proper names applied to *categories of objects* are trademarks, brand-names and proprietary names. These must not be translated unless they have become eponyms and are used generically (e.g. refrigerator, countless medical terms), and many such terms become eponyms before the object goes out of patent—in which case they must be translated, often by a common noun (hoover = *aspirateur*, etc.). Numerous drugs are marketed under different proprietary names in various countries: many are listed in Martindale's *Pharmacopoeia*, but consultation with the makers is usually required. Thalidomide was Contergan in the Federal Republic of Germany.

GEOGRAPHICAL NAMES share, with the names of some people, the rare characteristic that some of them (usually the smaller and less important) denote only one object and have no connotations. In bilingual areas, geographical features usually have two names, each phonologically or morphologically at home in its language. Further in the past, nations have tended to naturalize names of towns and provinces they have occupied, visited frequently or considered important: thus, the features have been renamed partly, to facilitate pronunciation (Prague, Warsaw, etc.) and spelling (Vienna), or a new word created partly as an excuse for linguistic chauvinism (Rhodesia). Rhodes, a diamond millionaire, believed in 'British rule throughout the world' and referred contemptuously to 'Negrophiles'. South Africa will become Azania and many other European geographical names in Africa are likely to have a short life now. There is now a slight tendency to restore original spellings (Romania, Lyon, Marseille, Braunschweig—no longer British, royal—etc.) and respect is likely to be shown to any newly-independent country by scrupulously observing the spelling of its name, however difficult to pronounce. Other geographical names are likely to remain gallicized, anglicized, italianized, etc., provided that they are fairly commonly used and that their additional, translated name has no political (e.g. irredentist) significance. The translator must check on usage, particularly where a different name is used (e.g. Lake Geneva/*Lac Léman*, Lake Constance/*Bodensee, Bâle/Basilea/Basel* but English Basle) and good atlases which give all possible names may not be helpful. Italian names for German and Yugoslav towns are rather 'remote', e.g. *Magonza, Treviri, Agosta, Fiume, Spalato, Ragusa, Colonia.* National pride and independence are reflected in the 'pure' African names for the new African states, and western Poland's shedding of German town-names. In the GDR all formerly German-occupied towns, rivers, etc. (not provinces), are called by their national names except Prague, but Czechs keep their own names for German towns.

Where the connotations of a geographical name are implied in a historical or literary text (e.g. for Treblinka) the translator will have to bring them out in his version, if his readers are unlikely to know them. Where the denotation of the name is not known or obscure to the reader the translator often adds the appropriate generic name: 'the river Rehe', 'the town of Ratheim'.

Names of streets and squares are not usually translated—with the exception, ironically, of Red Square, Wenceslas Square (Prague), Constitution Square, Athens, which remain untranslated if they are written as addresses. Public buildings may be partially translated (e.g. St. Giles *Kirche*) if the generic term is common and transparent.

As for FORMS OF ADDRESS, in September 1939 *The Times*, having been pro-Hitler for 6 years, suddenly downgraded 'Herr Hitler' (and, similarly, his colleagues) to 'Hitler', and we knew we were at war. The present practice is either to address all and sundry as *Mr* or *Mrs* (with increasing use of first names, thereby omitting the 'handles') or to transcribe *M., Herr, Signore, Señor*, etc., for all western and central European ('civilized') languages, allowing all other *prominenti* a Mr. The first practice will prevail, but the TL house-style (newspapers, periodicals, etc.) must be respected. Aristocratic and professional titles are translated if there is a recognized equivalent (*Comte*, *Graf*, *Herzog*, *Marchese*, *Marquis*, *Professeur*, *Doktor*, etc.); otherwise they are either transcribed (*Dom*) or deleted (*Staatsanwalt*, *avvocato*, *ingeniere*), with the professional information added, if considered appropriate.

Names of FIRMS, PRIVATE INSTITUTIONS, SCHOOLS, UNIVERSITIES, HOSPITALS, etc., are in principle not translated since they are related to the SL culture. If they 'shine through', they may occasionally be translated (*Banca Nazionale d'Italia*, 'National Bank of Italy'; *Kantonspital, Basel*, 'Basle Canton Hospital'), particularly in an informal text. Multinational companies trade under various names which the translator may have to trace. In general, the purpose of these names is to identify rather than describe the firm or institution, and if the TL reader wants to refer to them, he requires the SL name in the address.

The names of NEWSPAPERS, JOURNALS and PERIODICALS are always transcribed. Famous WORKS OF ART are usually referred to by their established translated titles (including the authorized titles of literary works), if they are well known here; but attempts to translate *Così fan tutte* (even when sung in English) have been abandoned, and Verdi's and Wagner's titles are often transcribed. When a work is not already known, its title is transcribed. A translator makes his own translation of a title only when he is translating the whole work or when additional comment is made on the title by himself or in the original text. Titles of paintings, if they have no established translation, should be transcribed as well as translated, so that the reader can look for further references if he wishes. Titles of untranslated books must be transcribed, with a translation in parenthesis, particularly for non-literary books when the title describes the content. Some paintings such as the 'Mona Lisa' have 'different' titles in the original—*La Gioconda* or *La Joconde*. Titles of musical works have to be treated cautiously—neither the 'Emperor' nor the 'Elvira Madigan' concertos exist in other languages, and references to opus or Köchel numbers are recommended.

* * *

It can, I think, be accepted that all **obsolete institutional terms,** unless they have established translation equivalents, should be transcribed. These are token words (*mots-témoins*, as Matoré, 1953, calls them), which give the colour and flavour of a period, and when translated, as Richard Cobb (1969) has pointed out, they sound ridiculous.

Cobb instances recent translations of *gardes-scellés* as 'keepers of the seals', *sans-culottes* as 'poor citizens', *procureur-général-syndic* as 'attorney-general-syndic'. It seems to me equally misguided and confusing suddenly to convert the *Ancien Régime* into the 'Old Régime' (Avril, 1969), or the *bordereau* into the 'file' or the 'list'.

However, the English reader, both layman and expert, is entitled to assistance with obsolete institutional words. A scholarly book might handle them in a glossary when the terms can be explained in detail. Cobb himself includes a brief glossary, mainly of modern words, but leaves many modern words untranslated and unexplained, relying on his enormous zest to convey at least the relish of their meaning. A more popular book such as Cobban's *A History of Modern France* (1965) shows how loan-words can be casually explained within the text, thus: 'the *gabelle*, the hated salt tax'; 'the *aides*, excise tax on drinks, tobacco, etc.'; 'the *don gratuit* or free gift'; *la grande peur* is found in the index to explain the Great Fear. Other institutional terms can be explained neatly in brackets: '*le secret du roi* (the king's secret diplomacy)'; in adjectival clauses (or participial phrases): '*abbés commendataires*, abbés who exercised no religious functions'; or in parenthesis. Further, one can use notes at the bottom of the page (or at the end of chapter or the book), where the institutional term can be explained at greater length.

Translators of historical terms have to be careful both to transcribe and explain *Ancien Régime* terms such as *parlement* (a notoriously misleading cognate) and *intendant*; the *Directoire* is usually adopted, the 'Consulate' and 'Second Empire' translated owing to their 'transparency'; the 'Popular Front' is usually translated because of its transparency as well as its international applications; the *drôle de guerre* is the 'phoney war' since it was a binational event.

Bismarck's *Kulturkampf* had international repercussions, but it is not translated, partly because a literal translation would be misleading and a neat equivalent would be hard to find.

* * *

Most **international institutional terms** have official translations, made by translator teams, at the appropriate international organization. These are often through-translations (*calques*, 'loan-translations'), e.g. *Organisation internationale du Travail*, 'International Labour Organization', which are usually known by their relevant acronyms, e.g. *OIT*, 'ILO', *AID*, (IDA', *OIPC*, 'ICPO', *CIDST*, 'STIDC' (see *European Communities Glossary*, F–E, 5th edition). Other organizations have international acronyms, e.g. 'CERN', 'Interpol', 'ISO', 'OTA', 'OAU'. 'Comecon' (German RGW) is officially translated as CEMA since the Council considers that 'Comecon' has pejorative connotations. Institutional terms are increasingly known by the initial letters of their component words whether these form natural syllables or not, and only rarely, as initially after the Russian Revolution, by the first syllables of the words (e.g. *Komsomol*). Many institutions form themselves into acronyms or give themselves titles which can be turned into easily remembered acronyms.

Although some organizations are 'through-translated', many are reformulated in translation (and offer obvious traps): *Direction du contrôle de sécurité d'Euratom*, 'Directorate for Euratom Safeguards'; *Groupe 'harmonisation douanière'*, 'Working Party on Harmonization of Customs Rules'; *comité specialisé*, 'committee of experts'; *comité permanent*, 'standing committee'.

Positions and institutions in the Roman Catholic Church (and Vatican State) are always (a dangerous word in translation theory) intertranslatable (*Saint-Siège*, 'Holy See', *Päpstlicher Stuhl*), although *curé* is usually transferred (local colour). In the case of Communist Parties, the titles differ but are made up of internationally transparent Marxist collocations ('People's Democracy', 'Workers' and Peasants' State', etc.) whilst positions and hierarchies are intertranslatable. Certain words, most of them 'originally' French, tend to become associated with international institutions; harmonize, concurrent, concertation, conjunctural ('originally' German), convention, informatics, important, intervention, degressivity.

Others, such as *conjoint, collegialité, conversion* (retraining), *conjoncture, cotitulaire, engagement* (commitment, liability), *homologue, modalité, nuisance, régime, ventilation, action, cadre* (skeleton), *évolution, exploitation, organigramme* (only for patents), *organisme, orientation, Sozialpartner, patrimoine* (assets), *plafond* (ceiling, platform?), *possibilité* (option), *prestation* (a sociological term already), *sectoriel, subvention, valoriser, transformation, zone*, have still not penetrated official English in their usual 'European' senses, but the basically French inspiration of Common Market language is evident, although the lingua franca or *koine* is inevitably English and the English influence is becoming stronger in Brussels. (The influence of Russian is more apparent in Comecon.) However, an individual translator's main task is to find the authorized translation, not to make his own.

* * *

In considering how the translator handles **national institutional terms,** the mass of modern political, financial, administrative and social terms, I propose first to list the relevant translation procedures and then to offer some general criteria of reference.

(a) Translation procedures

(i) *Transcription* (adoption, transfer, 'loan-words'), e.g. (often) *Bundesrat, Conseil d'État.* This may be described as the basic procedure.

(ii) *Literal translation.* This is a 'coincidental' procedure, used when the SL term is transparent or semantically motivated and is in standardized language: e.g. 'Senate' (F), *Präsident*, 'president'—note also semi-institutional terms in the same lexical field: *agglomération*, 'conurbation'; *la Chambre*, 'the chamber'; *investir*, 'vote in'.

(iii) *Through-translation* ('loan-translation', *calque*), e.g. 'National Assembly' (F), *Chambre des Pairs*, 'People's Army' (GDR), 'People's Chamber' (GDR) (only for important institutions).

(iv) *Recognized translation.* The FRG Ministry for Education and Science has produced the following: *Bundestag*, 'Federal German Parliament'; *Bundesrat*, 'Council of Constituent States'; *Fachbereich*, 'university department'; *Richtergesetz*, 'Law on Judges'; *Zivilschutzkorps*, 'civil defence corps'. These translations should be used for administrative texts. *Länder* is transferred as a couplet with 'States'. Note also: *Schweizerische Eidgenossenschaft, Confederazione Svizzera.* When an official SL body produces a TL version of one of its own institutional terms, the TL translator should 'support' it unless he disagrees with the version. (Footnote then required.)

(v) *Cultural equivalent.* These are sometimes 'abused' (e.g. *Premier Ministre*, Prime Minister), depending on the degree of cultural correspondence. Examples are: *recteur, Rektor*, 'vice-chancellor'; *PDG*, 'chairman of board'; *conseil de fabrique*, 'church council'; *syndicat professionnel*, 'trade association'; *conseil de révision*, 'army medical board'. *Technische Hochschule,* 'Technological university' (e.g. Bath, Brunel); *Gesamtschule, école polyvalente*, 'comprehensive school'.

(vi) *Translation label.* A translation label is an approximate equivalent or a new term, usually a collocation, for a feature peculiar to the SL culture. A new collocation would normally be put in inverted commas, which could be dropped on later occasions, in the hope that the term is accepted. Examples: *promotion sociale*, 'social promotion'; *HLM*, 'social housing', *Gastarbeiter*, 'guest worker'; *autogestion*, 'self-management'; *cogestion*, 'codetermination'; *aménagement du territoire*, 'regional' or 'national planning'.

(vii) *Translation couplets.* The most common form of translation couplet consists of the transcription of an institutional term followed by its translation (which may be a literal translation, a cultural equivalent or a translation label) in brackets; here one would assume that the SL term would be retained for the remainder of the text and in the relevant TL literature. Examples: *Knesset* (the Israeli Parliament); *Folketing* (the Danish Parliament); *Conseil d'État* (Council of State); *Gemeinde* (German unit of local government). Occasionally the translation has precedence, followed by the original in brackets—the procedure may be referred to as a TL translation couplet. Here one assumes that the TL term is important for the TL literature, both now and in the future, but may not be sufficiently well known; for example, 'Parliamentary Commissioner for Administration' (*ombudsman*), or, in a bilingual area, such as Quebec, 'witness post' (*piquet indicateur*), 'legists' (*hommes de loi*), 'purchaser' (*adjudicataire*) (Russell, 1979).

(viii) *Translation triplets.* A politically coloured term such as *Schandmauer* may require a literal translation ('wall of shame'), a transcription and the denotation (Berlin Wall).

(ix) *Through-translation* (i.e loan-translation). Important national institutional terms that are 'transparent' may be translated literally: *Assemblée Nationale:* National Assembly; *Staatsrat*, State Council; *Volkskammer*, People's Chamber.

(x) *Deletion.* A term of little importance in the TL culture, e.g. *Staatsrat* or *Avvocato* in front of a surname, or *Jugendweihe* ceremony in the GDR or *Habilitation* may be deleted in translation, provided it is marginal to the text, and some indication of function given where required.

(xi) *Naturalization.* The process of 'anglicizing' foreign names, e.g. Aristotle, by supplying them with English suffixes is no longer current, although any SL term (e.g. names of towns), which is frequently used and/or considered important, is usually pronounced as an English word. Note difference in pronunciation between 'Hamburg' and 'Klagenfurt'.

(xii) *Acronyms.* It is common practice to retain the acronym of an SL institution (e.g. SPD, CDU, FNLA), where necessary adding the translation of the title (e.g. Christian Democrats, etc.—most but not all European political parties have 'transparent' titles) or the function, if the term is obscure and less important, e.g. CNAA, 'national body awarding degrees of colleges and polytechnics'. KG, Knight of the Order of the Garter, highest order of British knighthood. Where an institutional acronym already has a recognized translation equivalent, it must be used, due attention being paid to the official equivalent (e.g. GDR, CMEA) rather than the more 'popular' equivalent (*East Germany, Comecon*) where appropriate. When an acronym forms a derivative (*cégétiste, smicard, énarque, onusien*) the derivative is usually split into two or three words depending on context.

(xiii) *Metaphor.* Metaphor is not usually associated with institutional terms, but the name of an institution may be personified to refer to its leadership or director(s) whilst the building or street where it is accommodated may also denote the institution or its director(s) (e.g. the Pentagon). Proust was already satirizing this fashion in *A l'ombre des jeunes filles en fleur* (vol. 1, p. 45). *Un cri d'alarme partit de Montecitorio . . .*, Italian Parliament; *L'émotion fut grande au Pont aux Chantres . . .*, pre-war Russian Foreign Office, Leningrad; *Le double jeu dans la manière du Ballplatz* = *Ballhausplatz,* Habsburg Foreign Ministry. Note also *l'Elysée,* French President; *Hôtel Matignon*, Prime Minister; *Quai d'Orsay*, Foreign Ministry; *Rue de Rivoli*, Ministry of Finance; *Botteghe Oscure*, Italian Communist Party; *Piazza del Gesù*, Italian Christian Democrats.

(xiv) Lastly, I suggest that alternative or supplementary information can be supplied by the translator in three ways: (a) within the text, (b) as a footnote to the page, the chapter or the book, or (c) as a glossary. The first method is the best provided it can be supplied briefly and unobtrusively without holding up the flow of the narrative: as an alternative term, in brackets, as a one-word definition (i.e. *scilicet*, etc.), as a paraphrase, participial phrase, defining adjectival clause, etc.

(b) Reference criteria

Many considerations for translating national institutional terms oscillate between polar oppositions, and there are delicate stages between each of them, which have to be weighed against each other, as well as the other considerations.

(i) On the one extreme an expert readership requires the SL term, whilst at the other, a lay readership needs a TL explanation, as detailed as its interest will allow. In between, an educated non-specialized readership may need a translation label or cultural equivalent.

(ii) If the term is of great importance to the FL reader, it should be translated where possible, e.g. the names of the public corporations: *La Sécurité Sociale*, the French health service; *EDF*, the French electricity board; *PTT*, the postal service; *SNCF*, French railways; *Conseil de la Reserve Fédérale*, USA Federal Reserve. If it is of average importance, it should be transcribed, possibly as a translation couplet; if it is of little importance and does not contribute to local colour, and particularly if it is a third country institutional term, it could well be translated; thus, *la Galerie des Cerfs*, the Gallery of Stags; the *Daima*, Japanese pre-war parliament, etc.

(iii) Institutional terms may vary between transparency and opaqueness for Romance languages (e.g. *concession minière*, 'mining concession'; and *franco domicile*, 'free at destination'). Transparency may be defined as the SL term 'shining' through (as an *ami fidèle*) the corresponding TL term, thereby resembling it closely in form: e.g. *concours interne*, 'internal competition', but *concours du Fonds*, 'aid from the Fund'. Note that political parties' names are usually translated if they are made up of culturally overlapping political terms such as 'liberal', conservative, etc. 'Labour Party' is transcribed to *die Labour Party* (G) and *le Parti travailliste* (F), as 'Labour' is used in a nonce-sense (*travailliste* has no other meaning). Most European political parties are also referred to by their acronyms (see also Gläser, 1976).

In Germanic languages, institutional terms may be semantically motivated, and translate easily: e.g. *Staatsschatz, Staatskasse*, 'the public revenues', whilst others, such as *Geheimrat*, *Staatsrat* and *Regierungsrat*, are deceptive and cannot be translated as 'privy councillors' though all are translated as such in *Cassell's German Dictionary* (revised 1978 edition). Lastly, where a term invites straight primary to primary sense translation, such a translation is probably justified if the term is sufficiently important: e.g. *Volkspolizei*, 'People's Police'; *Bundesrat* (FRG), 'Federal Council'.

(iv) The various degrees of cultural equivalence have to be borne in mind and have to be related to the expectations of the readership. To what extent is a *Volkshochschule* 'adult evening classes', or a *Poliklinik* 'an outpatients' department'? On the other hand, the translator has to take into account true national pride and local culture (or colour), which is an argument for transcription: (e.g. 'Open University', *Maison de la Culture*, *Kombinat*, *kibbutz*, *círculos infantiles*). On the other hand, he has to recognize chauvinism, snobbery and commercialism (e.g. *management, engineering*, 'Public School'), where he normally has to conform with established TL practice, but should, like a reliable dictionary, indicate any prejudice implied.

(v) Concision, neatness, 'fit', euphony (therefore the difficulty of translating briefly into the TL)—these qualities predispose 'popular feeling' (i.e. the media) to adopt the SL term: e.g. *samizdat* (naturalizes well), *Berufsverbot, medici condotti, Ostsiedlung, Kulturkampf, numerus clausus, Anschluss* (Latin's *only* point of superiority over most other languages may be its concision); on the other hand, any institutional term that is ponderous and lengthy is likely to be translated, and usually, as is now the case, identified by an acronym.

(vi) Lewis's discussion (1979) of GDR language raises the question of how to translate institutional terms coloured by capitalist or communist ideology. If one assumes one is not translating purely for equivalent-effect (on the TL reader), one has to clarify the cognitive component of the pairs *Schandmauer* and *Schutzwall* (Berlin Wall) or *Pankower Regime* and *der erste deutsche Arbeiter—und Bauernstaat* (GDR).

Such terms can be analysed semiologically into semantic and pragmatic components, and a translation 'triplet' (e.g. *Menschenhändler*, traders in people, East German term for persons assisting GDR emigrants) may be required. Other institutional terms typical of the capitalist or socialist system rather than ideology, e.g. *Landtag, Listenmandat, Konzern, Betriebsrat, Personalchef* for the FRG, *Staatsrat, Politbüro, Mehrjahrespläne, Vereinigung Volkseigener Betriebe, Prämienfonds* for the GDR are translated according to the criteria I have listed, care being taken to attribute them to the appropriate German state.

Generally, if there is a high degree of cultural equivalence, there is a case for a literal translation (titles of ministries) or for translating by the equivalent term (e.g. *tribunal d'instance*, 'French magistrates' court', but a *membre de l'Institut* is not a 'Fellow of the Royal Society').

(vii) Here, again, function is more important than description or composition. Thus 'Black Rod', 'gentleman usher for House of Lords'; 'Yellow Pages', 'advertising section of telephone directory'; 'father of chapel', 'shop steward of printers' association'.

(viii) Some consistency in translating or transcribing institutional terms is desirable in proceeding similarly with sets of terms, e.g. translation for all names of ministries, transcription for all the *grandes écoles*; but this criterion may clash with that of 'transparency', as in *Bundesrat* which is transparent and *Bundestag* which is not. A typical inconsistency is in Avril (1969), where *départements, cantons* and communes are juxtaposed. One could translate departments and cantons: (a) departments at least recur frequently, (b) both are 'transparent', (c) in this context they would not be confused with other 'departments' or Swiss cantons, and (d) they should, if possible, be in line with 'commune', but in specialized texts, the tendency is the reverse. For Italy, however, regions, provinces and communes are perhaps acceptable. Generally, series or hierarchies of terms in one lexical field are handled consistently. Thus: *région, département, canton, arrondissement, commune*; *Land, Kreis, Gemeinde*; *conservateur du château, régisseur du domaine, surveillants, concierges, gardes* (for Loire *châteaux*); *directeur du cabinet, directeur adjoint, conseiller technique, chargé de mission*. However, the considerations of importance and transparence already mentioned may clash with a consistent treatment of the above series.

Glosses may have to be added to sets of transcribed terms. Again, they should describe in conformity with the text's intention the function—not the form or the composition—of the term as briefly as possible. Take, for example, the hierarchy *auditeur, maître des requêtes, Conseiller d'État*: the first two terms are in my opinion untranslatable, although Harrap's translates them as 'commissioner' and '*rapporteur*' of the *Conseil d'État*; the third can, but should not be translated. When the three terms are analysed componentially for the purpose of supplying essential features of the gloss, the translator has several options. The dimensions of the three terms include seniority, nature of work (job specification), salary differential, number of posts, required qualifications—in these respects the three terms are distinguished. But the gloss is also likely to include the factors common to the three terms: membership of the *Conseil d'État* (the highest French administrative court), membership of a *grand corps*, graduate of a *grand école*, etc. The make-up of the gloss will depend not only on the purpose and general content of the text, depending on which of the dimensions (e.g. work or salaries) referred to are emphasized, but also on the degree of specialization and difficulty of the text. The latter will determine the amount of detail in the gloss, in particular in relation to the reader of the translation who, though he may be an expert in the subject, is likely to be less well informed than the reader of the original.

(ix) In bilingual areas, most institutional terms, as well as the names of towns and streets, have equivalents in both languages. France and the Federal Republic of Germany, being neighbours, translate many of each other's administrative terms: *Forstamt/District des Eaux et des Forêts*; *Gewerbeaufsichtsamt/Inspection du Travail*; *Regierungshauptsekretär/Chef de groupe.* All these terms would normally be transcribed rather than translated into English. In translating from a text originating in a bilingual country, there is a strong argument for supplying both the appropriate institutional terms.

(x) The more one country has to use another's institutional terms, and the more important they are, the more one is justified in translating rather than transcribing them. Thus the names of ministries, some public institutions, important civil service parts and departments, may be translated. Further, a token-word illustrating a country's practices, which is not usually translated, may become a theme-word, usually translated, as it gains in TL circulation: e.g. *Fremdenpass,* 'foreigner's pass' or 'identity papers', *steuerlicher Wohnsitz*, 'domicile for tax purposes', and the tendency to translate the names of well-known churches, cathedrals, public buildings.

When transcription is initially required because the foreign term is not transparent, e.g. *Bundesanstalt für Arbeit*, it is useful to put the English equivalent first—'Federal Institute of Labour'—adding the transcription in brackets. Further reference in the article should be to the English term, shortened to the 'Federal Institute'. If the institution is important and is frequently mentioned in the TL literature, the translation is likely to become established and subsequent transcription unnecessary. Contrariwise, where the institutional term is unlikely to become current in the English literature, it is advisable to transcribe it (e.g. *Schwerbeschädigtengesetz*), giving the translation in brackets ('Seriously Disabled Persons Act'), and to make any further reference to it in the source language.

(xi) Sometimes a combination of national feeling, both partisanship and opposition (or commercial interest) as well as euphony and 'fit', play a part in the non-translation of certain key institutional terms: *Führer, Duce, Caudillo, Ayatollah* (also virtually regarded as proper names), *apartheid, soviet.*

(xii) When a translator is in doubt, he should transcribe rather than translate institutional terms. Nida (1975a) has written that literalness and the attempt to translate everything are the translator's worst faults. A translation should be attempted only if the new term adequately describes the function of the original work, e.g. 'Worker participation' for *Mitbestimmung*, and not the fairly meaningless 'co-determination'. A translation into a term peculiar to the country of the TL, e.g. GPO for PTT, War Office for *Ministère de la Guerre* (at the time of the Dreyfus affair), the 'Treasury' for *les Finances*, should be avoided. In such cases one usually looks for a 'neutral', international term that could apply to many countries—e.g. Ministry of Posts and Telecommunications, Minister of Finance (instead of Chancellor of the Exchequer).

(xiii) Whilst the translation of foreign institutional terms is subject to many sometimes evidently conflicting considerations, and still leaves a large area of choice, one has to guard against three common mistakes: (1) new translation of terms that already have recognized translations, (2) use of TL terms that have a strong local colour, (3) 'preposterous' word-for-word translations, i.e. translationese.

(xiv) Lastly, since this is an area of 'standardized language' that is likely to become increasingly significant, particularly in pluralist societies, it is desirable that translating teams employed by national governments should make official translations of their principal institutional terms so that foreign translators should at least be able to use the correct versions if they wish to respect the SL country's interests.

* * *

Non-institutional **cultural terms** usually present fewer problems, and the considerations I have listed also hold good for their translation. Nevertheless, there are many problems. It is, I think, the translator's duty not to let words like *nouveau riche* or *parvenu* (prej.)* into the language again, since there is nothing particularly French about their referents. Again, both historians and their translators have a problem in deciding whether to transcribe the names of products or classes of people that have very little specifically local about them but their origins. Thus, let us take as an illustration F. Braudel's great *Capitalism and Material Life* (translated by M. Kochan). Both Braudel and his translator provide numerous translation couplets such as *Randvölker*, the marginal people known to German geographers as the *geschichtlos* people—'people without history'—where the SL terms are retained purely to give local colour (*Randvölker* may connect with other evidence, but not *geschichtlos*), since there is nothing particularly German about either referent. In other cases, translation couplets are offered presumably for the sake of the seventeenth-century (modernized) terms: 'Health certificates', *Gesundheitspässe* in Germany, *cartas de salud* in Spain? Local diseases are reproduced without a gloss: the *bosse, dendo, tac* or *Harion*. Local ecological terms are preferred to their TL equivalents (cf. various words for 'desert' used in English, e.g. steppe, tundra). My impression is that Braudel in many cases simply savours the sounds of the foreign (German, French, Italian, Russian, Chinese, Dutch, English, etc.) words, as one would expect of a leading

* (Prej.) indicates a word of prejudice in terms of human rights. 'Offensive' and 'derogatory' are inadequate labels.

Annales historian. In many other cases the use of local terms for foods (e.g. four types of French bread in the fourteenth century)—composition, not shape—or for various types of cultivation is justified. The translator, however, slips up by failing to recognize metalingual language: 'foods that have changed in meaning several times: *entrées, entremets, ragoûts*'. The meanings have changed in French but not in English. Occasionally, words like *aiguière* (ewer) and *Kachelofen* (earthenware stove) are retained, possibly because as token-words, they have a period rather than a local flavour. It seems a pity that in other cases, Braudel and his translator quote, say, a Dante line: *come un molin che il vento gira*, where translation ('like a mill turned by the wind') could easily be interpolated into the text; and refer to *fortuna, ventura, ragione, sicurta* as the key-words of commercial life, apparently relying on their transparency to French and English readers. However, Miriam Kochan's enthusiasm for transcriptions is welcome, and her translation couplets are neatly and variously introduced. I should perhaps conclude by pointing out that it is the translator's, as it is the lexicographer's, duty to discriminate any cultural term whose sense flagrantly, explicitly or connotatively infringes the Universal Declaration of Human Rights: it is not a question of modifying the force of such words as 'dike', 'gook', 'kike', 'blog' (working class, now defunct?) or 'hun', nor of excluding them from dictionaries, nor of suppressing the connotative senses of words like 'queen', 'dame', 'queer', 'alienated' (far from it), but of alerting the TL reader to their antihuman, not just derogatory significance. (All such words should be labelled 'prej.' in dictionaries.) Contrary to even now fashionable opinion, objectivity, in as far as it can exist, can be based only on human decency and morality.

Turning to more general cultural terms, one notes first that local ecological terms are usually retained: areas have their own winds, lakes, moors, types of accommodation: further, their natural and prepared food products, inventions, appliances, customs, etc., keep their names, sometimes with an early change of meaning (e.g. sauna) as noted by Catford (1965) and a later change of function, e.g. *Stand* (noted by Dahrendorf).

These are token-words which first add local colour to any description of their countries of origin, and may have to be explained, depending on the readership and the type of text. Later, if the products are generally exported, neither they nor their names are any longer felt to be foreign, and they become the adopted words which are common in all languages. They will on the whole appear more often in non-literary texts (social history, etc.), where local colour is important, than in the type of fiction where the message, the didactic element, is more important than the cultural element: words such as *pneumatique, avocat, Manelle*, important enough in descriptions of French social life, could be rendered by labels such as 'express letter', 'lawyer' and 'card-game' in a short story. Names for clothing, vehicles, dishes, art forms may temporarily become vogue-words, but when the vogue is over they become historical terms like *fichu, brougham* and *Spiegel*.

Further, one may consider the strange case of transferred words which have no peculiar cultural characteristic; words like *détente, démarche, rapprochement, coup d'état* and *entente* are accounted for by the former supremacy of French in diplomatic language; 'fairplay', 'trend' and 'job' went into German during the Allied occupation.

At various times, foreign visitors have felt that certain words were peculiar to the character of a foreign culture, and have imported the words into their own language, often keeping the reference to the foreign culture (such as *Gemütlichkeit, Gründlichkeit, machismo*, as well as the French diplomatic terms previously mentioned).

In my opinion the words mentioned are not peculiar to the foreign culture but denote a concept that is missing in the 'home' language. They are often imported for snobbish or vogue reasons. In 1980 no conceptual or mental terms can be identified with one culture, and any new conceptual terms should be translated. I include not only new psychological, scientific, political, artistic, emotional and intellectual terms, but also vocabularies in the fields of any new activities and customs open to loan-words for all types of exportable products and inventions and for cultural and institutional terms, whose referents are likely to be replicated in other language communities.

Thus the French Government's attempt to 'ban' Americanisms is well-intentioned and represents a challenge to translators (rather than the French Academy which consists mainly of amateurs) who have for so long, not only in France, failed in one of their responsibilities, that is in dealing with foreign words (there is no good reason why, for instance, 'pipeline' should be transcribed in any language, unless pipelines are to remain alien to the culture). It is also a challenge to advertisers, public relations, intellectual snobs, etc. (brilliantly satirized by Shakespeare in *Much Ado about Nothing* and other works), who use foreign words to accumulate prestige and profit.

Normally a translator can treat cultural terms more freely than institutional terms. He is not called to account for faulty decisions, whether he is translating imaginative literature or general works (e.g. history). Since little can be explained to the spectator, cultural terms are rather more likely to be translated or given a cultural equivalent in a play than in fiction. But generally the most favoured procedure for a recently noted term peculiar to a foreign culture (given national pride, greater interests in other countries, increased communications, etc.) is likely to be transcription, coupled with discreet explanation within the text. If the term becomes widespread it may be adopted in the TL. This method is the appropriate sign of respect to foreign cultures.

7. The translation of metaphor

As I see it, the main and one serious purpose of metaphor is to describe an entity, event or quality more comprehensively and concisely and in a more complex way than is possible by using literal language. The process is initially emotive, since, by referring to one object in terms of another ('a wooden face', 'starry-eyed'), one appears to be telling a lie; original metaphors are often dramatic and shocking in effect, and, since they establish points of similarity between one object and another without explicitly stating what these resemblances are ('he leads a dog's life', but *elle a du chien*), they appear to be imprecise, if not inaccurate, since they have indeterminate and undeterminable frontiers. However, there is no question that good writers use metaphors to help the reader to gain a more accurate insight, both physical and emotional, into, say, a character or a situation. Further, it is not difficult to show that a one-word metaphor, once it is accepted as a technical term, so becoming a metonym (e.g. 'dog', *chien*, *cane*), as a 'truck', 'tub' or a 'mine car', and becomes a more or less dead metaphor, may be added to the technical terminology of a semantic field and therefore contributes to greater accuracy in the use of language.

I have never seen this purpose of metaphor stated in any textbook, dictionary or encyclopaedia. The issue is clouded by the idea of metaphor as an ornament, as a figure of speech, or trope, as the process of implying a resemblance between one object and another, as a poetic device. Further, linguists assume that scientific or technological texts will contain mainly literal language, illustrated by an occasional simile (a more cautious form of metaphor), whilst the purpose of metaphor is merely to liven up other types of texts, to make them more colourful, dramatic and witty, notoriously in journalism. All emotive expression depends on metaphor, being mainly figurative language tempered by psychological terms. If metaphor is used for the purpose of colouring language (rather than sharpening it in order to describe the life of the world or the mind more accurately), it cannot be taken all that seriously.

Words are not things, but symbols of things. On Martinet's model we may regard words as the first articulation of meaning, and since all symbols are metaphors or metonyms replacing their objects, all words are therefore metaphorical. However, as translators we know that words in context are neither things nor usually the same symbols as individual words, but components of a larger symbol which spans a collocation, a clause or a sentence, and is a different symbol than that of an isolated word. This is the second articulation of meaning and to this extent language itself is a metaphorical web. Lastly, as Gombrich has pointed out (1978), metaphor is literally translation, and dead metaphors, i.e. literal language, are the staple of accurate translation.

Metaphor is in fact based on a scientific observable procedure: the perception of a resemblance between two phenomena, i.e. objects or processes. Sometimes the image may be physical (e.g. a 'battery' of cameras), but often it is chosen for its connotations rather than its physical characteristics (e.g. in 'she is a cat'). Violence is exercised on reality when the objects or processes are identified with each other, which in the first instance produces a strong emotive effect. Gradually, when the metaphor is repeated in various contexts, the emotive effect subsides, and a new term that describes reality more closely has been created, e.g. *étonné* which in a seventeeth-century text might be translated as 'thunder-struck', but is now translated as 'astonished'.

The vast majority of metaphors are either anthropomorphic (personification), the first process, or reific (mental to physical), the converse process, both processes reinforcing the emotive effect.

* * *

This stated, in considering the translation of metaphor, I divide metaphor into five types: dead, cliché, stock, recent and original, and propose the following terms:

(a) *Object*—that is, the item which is described by the metaphor. (Referred to by Beekman and Callow (1974) as 'topic'.)
(b) *Image*—that is, the item in terms of which the object is described (Richards's 'vehicle').
(c) *Sense*—that is, Richards's 'tenor', Beekman and Callow's 'point of similarity', which shows in what particular aspects the object and the image are similar.
(d) *Metaphor*—the word(s) taken from the image.
(e) *Metonym*—a one-word image which replaces the object, which may later become a dead metaphor, e.g. the 'fin' of a motor cycle. In many cases, a metonym is 'figurative' but not metaphorical, since the image distinguishes an outstanding feature of the object, e.g. *Rue de Rivoli* for the French Financial Ministry or *Bonn* or *der Bund* for the Federal German Government. It may also be a synecdoche, *pars pro toto*, say, 'a sail' for a 'yacht', or a symbol ('the seven seas' is 'the whole world') which the translator may have to explain within the text, and would normalize ('sail' as *navire*).

Further I distinguish between one-word metaphors (a *sunny* girl) and complex metaphors, which range from two or more words or idioms, e.g. to 'catch a fish', through nearly all the proverbs to complete poems (notably *über allen Gipfeln ist Ruh*, where the wood, or sleep, or death may be the object) and perhaps allegories. Note, also, that I distinguish between the image and the metaphor, which is the figurative word used in the image; in 'rooting out the faults', the object is 'faults', the image is 'rooting up weeds', the metaphor is 'rooting out', the sense componentially is (a) eliminate, (b) with tremendous personal effort. Therefore, in the TL version, some such verb as *éliminer, entfernen* would not do, unless the phrase was of marginal importance in the text. Here, as elsewhere, a translator needs to have a discriminating sense of priority, to distinguish carefully major and minor factors/components/parameters in each text.

It has been said that three-quarters of the English language consists of *used* metaphors. In fact, the deadest metaphors in any language are the opaque words it has imported from other languages: e.g. for English 'consider', to look at the stars; 'examine', 'to assay with the tongue of a balance'; 'think' from Old English and Gothic, to 'make light'. In translation, the images are disregarded.

There are three types of transparent dead metaphors. First, words like 'reflect' as 'think' or 'shine' as 'excel' where, as it were coincidentally, the image as well as the sense is retained in some second languages: *réfléchir, briller.* Secondly, the thousands of words denoting objects which cannot 'normally' be converted to figurative meaning, if the denotative meaning is retained. These are one-word metaphors, or better, metonyms, since they replace their objects: examples from motor-cycle technology are: fin, frame, port, skirt, seal, clutch, worm, collar, fork, idler, nut, cradle. All these words presumably superseded generic words like 'cover, lock, connection, spiral, band', etc., previously used to describe the relevant objects. Now, dead metaphors are no part of translation theory, which is concerned with choices and decisions, not with the mechanics of languages, but I am bound to point out that these technical metonyms are an immemorial trap for the translator: consider technical terms such as *Mutter, Feder, Geist, Auge, Katze, Tisch*, or again the extensions of the word for 'dog' in five European languages:

English:	mechanical device for holding, gripping, fastening: clamp, drag, hammer of gunlock.
French:	pawl, latch, catch, hammer, trolley, towing block.
German:	truck, tub, mine car.
Italian:	catch, cramp, cock, hammer.
Spanish:	Nil for *perro*, but 'trigger, bracket, corbel' for *can.*
Russian:	Nil for *sobaka*, a dog, but the diminutive *sobachka* has 'pawl', 'trigger', 'catch', 'trip', 'arresting device', 'pawl of ratchet'.

Perhaps items in all mono- and bilingual dictionaries should be clearly marked off in four separate sections: physical, figurative, colloquial and technical, so that those who consult them are left in no doubt about the presence of technical and colloquial meanings for most of the commonest words.

The last enormous group of dead transparent metaphors are non-technical words such as 'head', 'foot', 'bottom', 'arm', 'circle', 'square', 'deep', 'broad', etc., which potentially have both concrete and figurative senses and which broadly appear to have universal applications or aspirations for all languages but which again offer the translator certain traps, often owing to collocational influence, e.g. 'to the letter', *au pied de la lettre*; 'depth of water', *hauteur d'eau*; 'be out of my depth', *n'être pas à la hauteur*, etc. Such dead metaphors are sometimes brought to varying degrees of life with a supplementary context, which produces polysemy: thus 'large-scale' but 'high on the social scale', 'he sifted the facts' but 'he scrupulously sifted the facts'. A dead metaphor brought to life ('weigh up', 'rub out', i.e. 'kill' instead of 'remove') immediately becomes a translation-theory problem; desirably, the polysemy is transferred, if the TL slang will take it; *ausreiben*, but the translator may have to monosemize with the sense *tilgen*, or 'split' the sense with *auslöschen*. How glaring is a 'glaring error'? *Offenbar*, *auffallend, grob* or *grell*?

Note that technical dead metaphors can also come 'nearer to life' when they become complex. Thus the sexual 'image' is enhanced when 'male or female' modifies 'screw thread', but the metaphor as such does not become a translation problem.

* * *

I next consider cliché, which is a murky area between dead and stock metaphor. Clichés usually consist of two types of stereotyped collocations; figurative adjective plus literal noun (simplex metaphor), e.g. 'filthy lucre'; or figurative verb plus figurative noun (complex metaphor), e.g. 'explore all avenues', 'leave no stone unturned', 'stick out a mile', etc. Further, some vogue words (e.g. 'parameter', 'strategy', 'infrastructure', 'model', 'profile', 'crucial', etc.—*ad nauseam*) become clichés through inappropriate use or overuse.

As I see it, a translator is entitled to get rid of cliché in any informative text where only facts (or theories) are sacred and, more riskily, in a 'socially operative'* or 'vocative' text (where the vocative function of language predominates) such as propaganda or publicity, where the translator might be considered to be justified in helping the author obtain the optimum reaction from the reader.

A translator is not entitled to touch clichés in expressive texts, authoritative statements, laws, regulations, notices, etc. However, in his rendering of less weighty texts, a translator shows his elegance, resourcefulness, ability to be brief, simple and clear, etc., and how better than reducing 'the long arm of coincidence' to *extremer Zufall* or 'throw up the sponge' to *sich besiegt erklären* or 'draw the net wider' to 'increase the catchment area' or perhaps *augmenter l'aire de recrutement*; or again, to translate 'parameter' by *Maßstab*, and 'profile' by 'brief description'.

* * *

In discussing the translation of stock metaphors, I propose to list the seven main procedures for translating metaphor. Obviously, many stock metaphors are clichés, but I am now assuming that the translator is attempting to render them as accurately as possible, not to pare them down. 'She wears the trousers and he plays second fiddle' may be absurd, but both metaphors still seem to do a good job. Further, in each case I distinguish between one-word and complex metaphors. Stock metaphors may have cultural (cultural distance or cultural overlap), universal (or at least widely spread) and subjective aspects.

It is possible that no metaphors are universal. One would expect 'birth' to be 'awakening', 'sickness' to be moral as well as physical, 'sleep' to be 'rest' or 'death'. But where 'a culture is driven mad' (Auden) or the scribes distort natural feelings, images may not have the senses suggested. Although even 'dirt' usually represents 'impurity' or some kind of 'taboo', in some abnormally poor African societies it is a protection against cold. I assume that when all societies reach a certain similar stage of physical health and well-being, there will be some basic universal metaphors,

* The term is derived from a combination of K. Reiss (1977) 'der operative Text' and Lyons's (1968) '"social" function of language'.

consequently easing the translator's task, since he will be able to retain the image—i.e. render them 'semantically', which is not the same as literally—thus, *boue, Kot, fango*, 'mud' will have the same connotations in every language.

The following are, I think, the procedures for translating metaphor, in order of preference:

(1) **Reproducing the same image in the TL** provided the image has comparable frequency and currency in the appropriate register. This procedure is common for one-word metaphors: 'ray of hope', *rayon d'espoir, Hoffnungsstrahl*; 'gleam', *lueur, Schimmer*; 'sunny smile', *sonniges Lächeln*, etc.; whilst in many cases (for 'field', 'province', 'area', 'side', for instance) the metaphor is hardly perceptible. Transfer of complex metaphors or idioms is much rarer, and depends on cultural overlap, e.g. 'His life hangs on a thread', *Sein Leben hängt an einem Faden, Sa vie ne tient qu'à un fil*, or on a universal experience, e.g. 'cast a shadow over', *jeter une ombre sur, einen Schatten über etwas werfen*. As Francescato (1977) has stated, universals like 'head' are cognitive rather than linguistic and languages use different words (e.g. head, chief, main, master) for metaphorical equivalences. Often the image can be only partially reproduced: *manger la laine sur le dos*, 'fleece'.

It is more difficult to reproduce one-word metaphors where the sense is an event or quality rather than entity. However, the more universal the sense, the more likely the transfer: 'golden hair', *cheveux d'or, goldenes Haar*; 'die', *mourir, sterben* (many figurative senses). But one cannot reproduce to 'elbow one's way' into any foreign language, unless the metaphor is literalized (*en jouant des coudes, mit dem Ellbogen*).

Providing there is 'strong' cultural overlap, metonyms such as the 'pen', the 'sword', 'guns', 'butter', etc., which are symbols of concepts, not objects (note that 'dove' is a metonym not in writing, but in art, and a complex symbol), can often be transferred. Similes, which are not emotive and are more prudent and cautious than metaphors, must normally be transferred in any type of text, but in sci–tech texts the simile should be culturally familar to the TL reader. Thus *Das Licht verhält sich wie ein Schwarm von Teilchen* must become 'Light behaves like a swarm'—not 'a lot' or 'a collection'—'of particles'. Since the whole point of a simile, like that of a metaphor, is to produce an accurate description it is futile to tone it down with a smoother collocation.

Lastly, I note the special case of animal abuse. Why, asked Leech (1966), is 'you son of a bitch' or 'you swine' abusive, whilst 'you son of a kangaroo' or 'you polar bear' is not? Now one notes that animal metaphors or metonyms (cf. 'I saw that cow coming') are not intertranslatable, but have connotations provided they are unmarked for sex or age. Thus pigs appear to be universally associated with uncleanness and stench (the worst 'physical' taboos), but 'bitches' and 'curs' are too specific to be often transferred. Domestic animals like dogs, cats, sheep, donkeys, goats, cows, while they are liked individually, like slaves, women, kaffirs, foreigners, servants and the working classes, are intrinsically inferior to men and represent inferior qualities: knavery, spite, credulity, stupidity, lechery, ugliness in English, but different qualities in other languages. Horses, the royal animal, are strong in English, healthy and diligent in French, and possibly hard-working in German, though *Ross* the noble steed is a blockhead. Insects are vermin in all languages, but bees and ants (*emsig*) are virtuous exceptions. The farmyard is no more sympathetic, geese being stupid, peacocks proud or vain, hens prostitutes in French, chickens cowardly, ducks darlings in English—but lying rumours in French and German.

Finally, animals more remote from our lives may be more objectively described: tigers, wolves, hyenas, lions, elephants, bears, rhinos—at least none are stupid, but all have special connotations: a lion is brave in French, the centre of attraction in German and English; a tiger fierce in English and German, but more sly and cunning in French; an elephant is clumsy, insensitive and never forgets in any Western European language, all due to his appearance and perhaps length of word, not to fact: in Russian, he has no connotations.

(2) The translator may **replace the image in the SL with a standard TL image** which does not clash with the TL culture, but which, like most stock metaphors, proverbs, etc., are presumably coined by one person and diffused through popular speech, writing and later the media. Obvious examples for one-word metaphors are: 'table', *Tafel, tableau*; 'pillar', *Stütze, soutien*; 'leg', *pied*. Examples of complex metaphors are 'other fish to fry', *d'autres chats à fouetter* (no German equivalent); 'when in Rome, do as the Romans do', or 'if you can't beat them, join them'; *man muß mit den Wölfen heulen, il faut hurler avec les loups*; 'jump into the lion's mouth', *se fourrer dans la gueule du loup*. A good translator is bound to view these and a thousand more such complex metaphors (there is less wrong with one-word metaphors) with scepticism; they are usually so 'mothy' (*mangé aux mites*), so clichified, often so archaic, the idoms and proverbs which foreigners learn by the thousand and use more often than the natives, which apparently only the Russians take a personal pride in. Sometimes they are pithy; more often, the image is as unrealistic (broth, iron, etc.) as the metaphor is archaic—only in German (e.g. *unter Dach und Fach*) are they held together by rhymes more often than in other languages. There is often a case for converting such metaphors to sense in the translation, whether they exist in the TL or not, simply because they are so stereotyped.

Before I leave this translation procedure, I note the special intralingual device which all speech communities have for 'protecting' speakers and listeners from taboos, i.e. euphemism. Taboos commonly relate to anything that is sacred or prohibited, from the deity and the sanctuary, to birth, sex, decay and death, and in particular to smells and tastes relating to uncleanness. Euphemisms are invariably metaphors and the images often have to be replaced by a cultural equivalent, unless the translator is trying to inform the reader rather than affect him in a way similar to the SL reader. Where sex is referred to in Biblical Hebrew as to 'know' or 'touch a woman' or to 'come together', there are innumerable equivalents in modern languages, of which 'making love' or 'love' is perhaps the most obvious euphemism.

(3) **Translation of metaphor by simile,** retaining the image. This is the obvious way of modifying the shock of a metaphor, particularly if the TL text is not emotive in character. *Per se*, a simile is more restrained and 'scientific' than a metaphor. This procedure can be used to modify any type of word, as well as original complex metaphors:

'La fenice è Dorabella' (*Così fan tutte*).
'Dorabella is like the Phoenix of Arabia' (but see below).
'Ces zones cryptuaires où s'élabore la beauté' (Barthes).
'The crypt-like areas where beauty is manufactured.'
'La brosse du peintre tartine le corps humain sur d'énormes surfaces' (Claudel).
'The painter's brush spreads the human body over vast surfaces, like butter over bread.'
'Banquiers irresponsables et orfèvres-escrocs.'
'Irresponsible bankers behaving like swindling gold-manufacturers.'
(N.B. *Orfèvre* is used literally as well as metaphorically.)
'If you are an officer.'
'Si vous avez les qualités d'un officier.'

(4) **Translation of metaphor (or simile) by simile plus sense** (or occasionally a metaphor plus sense). Whilst this is always a compromise procedure, it has the advantage of combining communicative and semantic translation in addressing itself both to the layman and the expert if there is a risk that the simple transfer of the metaphor will not be understood by most readers. (Paradoxically, only the informed reader has a chance of experiencing equivalent-effect through a semantic translation, i.e. transfer of image, whilst the lay reader is simply given the sense of the image.) Thus *tout un vocabulaire moliéresque* (Barthes) can be translated as 'a whole repertoire of medical quackery such as Molière might have used'. Thus the French phrase becomes quite clear without the reference to Molière.

However, the main emphasis here is on the 'gloss' rather than the equivalent-effect. It would be possible to reverse the emphasis, say by translating *Die Klassiker des Marxismus–Leninismus* as 'the classical writers of Marxism–Leninism, Marx, Engels and Lenin, the precursors of socialist society', etc., where more emphasis is given to equivalent-effect, to the equally knowledgable second reader, and the layman is looked after only secondarily.

'La fenice è Dorabella': 'Dorabella is a model of faith, like the Phoenix of Arabia' (though this will not do for the libretto). A simpler example, used for clarification only, might be, *C'est un renard*, 'He is as sharp and cunning as a fox'. Note also that some metaphors are incomplete without the addition of a sense component, *C'est un boeuf pour le travail*, 'He's a glutton for work'; 'dilly dally', *flotter dans l'indécision*. All the above procedures have the advantages of fulfilling Mozart's classical formula for the piano concerto, pleasing both the connoisseur and the less learned.*

(5) **Conversion of metaphor to sense.** Depending on the type of text, this procedure is common, and is to be preferred to any replacement of an SL by a TL image which is too wide of the sense or the register (including here current frequency, as well as the degrees of formality, emotiveness and generality, etc.). In poetry translation, compensation in a nearby part of the text may be attempted (though I am rather doubtful about the artificiality of this frequently recommended procedure); but to state that in poetry, any metaphor must always be replaced by another is an invitation to inaccuracy and can only be valid for original metaphors (of which more later).

* See letter to his father, 28 Dec. 1782.

In principle, when a metaphor is converted to sense, the sense must be analysed componentially, since the essence of an image is that it is pluridimensional—otherwise literal language would have been used. Further, the sense of an image will usually have an emotive as well as a factual component, an element of exaggeration which will be reduced in the translation in inverse ratio to the liveliness of the metaphor. Thus to translate 'She is as good as gold' by 'Sie ist sehr artig' would only be appropriate if the English were a virtually 'throw-away' statement. Otherwise, the components of permanence, value and reliability should be brought out. *Gagner son pain, sein Brot verdienen* are both so 'crummy' that 'earn one's living' is the only sensible translation. On the other hand, 'he's crummy' requires contextual as well as componential analysis. For a *person*, the major components are probably 'unpleasantness', 'decay', 'incapacity', 'small-mindedness', 'being behind the times', and the translator would have to choose from these, as well as some minor components.

(6) **Deletion.** If the metaphor is redundant or otiose, there is a case for its deletion, together with its sense component, provided the SL text is not authoritative or 'expressive' (that is, primarily an expression of the writer's personality). A decision of this nature can be made only after the translator has weighed up what he thinks more important and what less important in the text in relation to its intention. Such criteria can only be set up specifically for each text on an informal basis; to set up a hierarchy of values to be maintained in each translation and to determine a hierarchy of equivalence requirements, all based on a text-analysis scheme, as has been proposed by Coseriu (1978), Harris (1975) and House (1977a) is in my opinion fruitless. (For the same reason most componential-analysis schemes do not serve the translator—but componential analysis does.) A deletion of metaphor can be justified empirically only on the ground that the metaphor's function is being fulfilled elsewhere in the text.

(7) **Same metaphor combined with sense.** Occasionally, the translator who transfers an image may wish to ensure that it will be understood by adding a gloss. Beekman and Callow (1974) quote James iii: 'The tongue is a fire' and suggest that the translator may add 'A fire ruins things; what we say also ruins things'. This suggests a lack of confidence in the metaphor's power and clarity, but it is instructive, and may be useful if the metaphor is repeated, when the fire image can be retained without further explanation. (Compare translation labels in inverted commas, where the inverted commas are later dropped.)

* * *

I now propose to discuss the translation of recent metaphors, usually neologisms, which may be fashionable in the SL community; a few examples: *casser la baraque*, *dans le vent*, 'the name of the game', 'head-hunters', *building disease* (F), *Eintagsfliege*, 'tug-of-love', 'walk on', 'low-rise', 'juggernaut', *Rückstau*, 'bunching', 'flak', 'stick'. These 'metaphorical' neologisms include general technical terms—'juggernauts', *mastodontes, monstres*—where, if there is no accepted equivalent, the translator has either to describe the object or to attempt a translation label in inverted commas—thus the French (*sic*) expression *building disease* could be 'translated' as 'high-rise building mania'. Again, a complex metaphor such as *casser la baraque*, meaning both to 'try to destroy the established order by violence' (or 'destroy the system') *or* to 'score a smashing victory' can be treated like a stock metaphor, either by replacement of image, a reduction to sense, or a combination of sense and metaphor. *Rückstau* and 'bunching' or 'tailback' more or less translate each other. 'A tug-of-love' would almost certainly have to be explained in any language—*lutte acharnée entre les parents pour avoir la garde d'un enfant*—it appears to be coincidence that such a phrase has been found, but since the reference is likely to become more common, it is likely to be imitated in other languages. (I need hardly add that 'flak' in its new English sense cannot be shot back at the Germans.) Lastly, a metaphorical neologism peculiar to the SL culture may be transferred, whilst an international technical term ('snake', *serpent, Schlange*) is always translated, though preferably by an authorized translator connected to an appropriate international organization (cf. *la livre verte*, 'the green pound').

Lastly, and this is perhaps the name of the game—I consider how original metaphors, ancient or modern, are translated into the modern TL for the first time. Here one may say that the more the metaphor deviates from the SL linguistic norm, the stronger the case for a semantic translation, since the TL reader is as likely to be as puzzled, shocked, etc., by the metaphor as was the original reader. Several factors may influence the translator: the importance of the metaphor within the context, the cultural factor in the metaphor, the extent of the reader's commitment, the reader's knowledge. Thus a passage such as 'A coil of cord, a colleen coy, a blush on a bush turned first men's laughter into wailful mother' (Joyce), if it is a metaphor at all, is universal rather than cultural (or relativist) in its imagery, and the translator's problem (which I shy at) is to reconcile the meaning with the alliteration here, rather than to bring out the Irishness of 'colleen'. No cultural adaptation would normally be required, although if 'cords' and/or 'bushes' were not considered to be within the TL reader's experience or intellectual grasp, and the emotional impact of the passage on him were important, the translator might replace them with a more generic word such as 'bond' or 'natural growth'.

If the metaphor were predominantly cultural, I do not think the problem is insoluble as Dagut (1976) suggests in his brilliant article. Because a sentence from a Hebrew novel translates literally as, 'Bound like Isaac for the sacrifice by my love and to make it known', which in the English translation reads as, 'Bound by my love and helplessly to make it known', Dagut assumes that the metaphor is 'virtually untranslatable', and that 'helplessly' is a poor substitute for the metaphor; but in fact both the metaphor and a part of the sense could be introduced as 'Bound like Isaac for the sacrifice, and ready to suffer for my love in the eyes of all', which appears to convey more of the meaning of *'ne 'ekad'*. In this case, both Dagut and his translator, moreover, assume that the English reader has a greater ignorance of Old Testament culture than one might readily expect.

Further, when I examine passages of the French translation of *Ulysses*, I note that there are few original metaphors that are not semantically translated, though there is much under- or over-translation: thus, 'their heads thick-plotting', *leurs crânes bourrés de combines*; 'gaggles of geese', *jabotements de jars*; 'dishonours of their flesh', *stigmates de leur race*; 'give a back-kick', *donner un coup de pied en traître*; 'the sun flung spangles, dancing coins', *le soleil semait des paillettes, monnaies dansantes*. Note that whilst the images are kept, some words are turned to, or toned down to, their symbolical meaning, e.g. 'flesh' as race, 'back-kick' as *coup de pied en traître*. Thus my view is that whilst Kloepfer (1967), criticized by Dagut, exaggerates in suggesting that the bolder and freer the metaphor, the more easily it is translated, because he is ignoring the symbolic content of any original metaphor, in principle he is right, because the image of an original metaphor, unlike that of a stock metaphor, should normally be transferred, and again Dagut may be at fault in overlooking the fact that an original metaphor is likely to have fewer local cultural associations than an idiom, and therefore can be transferred more easily. Whether it is justified to translate 'dishonours of their flesh' as *stigmates de leur race* rather than *déshonneurs de leur chair*, I cannot say, though I doubt it; it is only justified if the translator thinks the English version has an overriding aesthetic value which is missing in the literal version, and I do not think it has.

However, original metaphors present further difficulties in that the best ones often have not only complex but double meanings, e.g. 'Death *stunned* its functions' (O'Casey): here French has *étourdit*, and German *betäubte*, which translate both senses (shock, stop), but in other cases, the translator has the problem of polysemy or word-play and either chooses one of the senses or reproduces both and loses the word-play.

Note that universal metaphors may be based not only on the parts and processes of the human body and the main features of nature and the weather, but also on the facts of sex, so that, however strange, an image like the following has to be reproduced somehow in any language, since it is not cultural:

'Quel dieu, quel moissonneur de l'éternal été
Avait, en s'allant, négligemment jeté
Cette faucille d'or dans le champ des étoiles.'
[V. Hugo, *Booz endormi.*]

'What God, what harvester of the eternal summer
Had, as he left, negligently cast
This golden sickle into the field of stars.'

Here again, however, whilst the main sexual image remains, adjustments may have to be made. Freud himself, writing to André Breton, wrote that the sexual symbols of dreams could not be interpreted until the circumstances of the dream were known.

As well as the universal and the cultural, there is the personal or idiolectal element in original metaphor, the irrational element peculiar to the imagination which the surrealists cherished, which can only be interpreted within a much wider structure of images. Again, this has to be translated by primary meanings since there are no rational points of reference:

'Un brasier déjà donnait prise
En son sein à un ravissant roman de cape
Et d'épée.'
[Breton—see Hugnet, 1934.]
'A charcoal pan had already offered a hold
In its womb to an entrancing
Cloak and dagger story.'

The translator follows the metaphors almost as blindly as though they were deliberately mixed. (Carelessly mixed metaphors, however, he decently normalizes if he has the chance.)

I now consider the translation of original metaphors in newspapers, periodicals and textbooks. Many of these are ephemeral and can be ignored, but some areas, such as jazz and pop, sport, finance, computer technology, advertising, slang (written in novels and autobiography), thieves' cant (here metaphor shades into code), the 'underworld' plus all private languages (e.g. the notorious American Citizens' Band Radio—the CB Bears), the work of some outstanding journalists, since metaphor is the main feature of imaginative writing, are notable for their abundance of recent and original metaphors. From the translator's point of view, the easiest of these fields to handle appears to be pop and jazz: a glance at *The Jazz Scene* (1961) by Francis Newton, alias Eric Hobsbawm (see appendix on Jazz language), suggests that many relatively recent metaphorical terms such as 'groovy', 'swing', 'rock', 'punk', 'funk', 'soul' are likely to be transferred as they are into most foreign languages. Stock and original metaphors are prominent in many West European financial columns, and basically serve the purpose of jiggering up a series of passionless statistics, or ruthless mergers; 'Rey boote den Verwaltungsrat aus und übernahm selbst das Zepter', 'Rey got rid of the Board and took over the reins, the roost, the head, the controls'.

Metaphors creeping into foreign medical texts are usually removed in English or German, but similes should be retained, e.g. 'La pose rationnelle de l'indication, le respect des contre-indications, la surveillance clinique et biologique stricte du traitement, voilà le triptyque de la thérapeutique anticoagulante à laquelle il faut reconnaître tous ses bienfaits', 'Anticoagulant treatment has many benefits, provided (a) it is administered carefully as indicated, (b) contra-indications are observed, (c) it is strictly monitored both clinically and through laboratory tests'. Sporting metaphors strive for the vigour of their objects: 'The pace-bowler found no lift or seam movement' (cricket); 'Bubbly Brighton go up at last, as champagne corks detonate—last-gasp goals'. A glance at English football reports (which I do not normally read) suggests to me that hardly a sentence gets written without a stock ('cliff-hanger') or original metaphor. Whether these metaphors should be reproduced semantically (by equivalent metaphor or sense) depends on whether they are written for accurate description (the true purpose of metaphor) or merely for effect, for ornament, for sensation, its main media-use (KAFKA IN IRAN), in which latter case the translator may prefer compensation to translation, that is, producing his metaphors elsewhere where he thinks they will have maximum effect. For the five senses, visual, descriptive words dominate the vocabulary and are mainly transferred to characterize touch, sound, smell and taste.

However, in serious non-literary texts, original or recent metaphors must be treated with the same respect as those in serious literature.

* * *

As yet, there is no methodology of the translation of slang. Nunberg (1978) has pointed out that 'the vast majority of slang and colloquial words are either metaphorical, or have some marked phonaesthetic or formal peculiarities': he instances 'grass', 'pot', 'tea', 'weed', 'dope', 'herb', 'boo' (sound-effect) and 'Maryzine' (a translation) all for 'marijuana' (in fact all these are metonyms); further, that while these words have roughly the same referent, their use tells the reader or listener quite a lot about the user, the conditions under which he uses them and the period, since slang is evanescent but sometimes recurrent. Further, he suggests that 'slang' itself is a peculiarly British/American English term in relation to which *argot* and *gergo* are pejorative. There is a great variety of age, period and social class in slang, instanced by 'busted', 'tapped out', 'in the red', 'broke', 'strong', 'skint' (also possibly marked for sex). Lastly, slang words have to have their meaning and connotations re-evaluated and revalued every 6 months.

Since slang is so sensitive to time and local culture, the translation problems hardly lend themselves to generalization. In non-literary texts on slang, the words will normally be transcribed and glossed according to the readership. In fiction and journalism which include slang, whenever the TL has no equivalent words, the translator has a choice between transcription, which gives his version a certain local colour, and literal translation, which, if there is cultural overlap, makes the metaphor comprehensible. 'Code-words', such as 'acid', 'freaked out', 'high', 'speed', 'uncool', etc., all metonyms, should I think be translated and put in italics as a warning to the reader that they are recent neologisms in the SL and can only be understood in context (some pointers may have to be given) in the TL.

The italics isolate the slang word from 'normal' speech. The translation has to take account of the morphology of the TL in the case of 'transparent' neologisms. (Thus for 'freaked out', *verkäuzigt, frasqué, fredainé* might give the TL reader a better idea of the imaginative world of hippy slang than a mere transcription.) This 'translate in italics' method can only be used for texts studded with slang where the context of the italicized word points to its sense and where the TL cultural equivalents do not exist. In isolated cases, slang is translated on the same lines as metaphor, bearing in mind that except for common events, slang equivalents are rare, and the translator may have to put in the slang where he can.

* * *

I have shown that one may regard metaphor as an attempt to *cerner*, delimit, define an object or process, physical or mental, more closely; as a decoration to show resemblances (now a rare poetic process) (Empson's 'mutual metaphor'); as an attempt to produce emotive effect, sometimes the vehicle of the salesman and the media, or general interest; and, as Richards (1965, 1968) does, as the constitutive basic element in language, where it later becomes dead or literal language. I have, after listing seven procedures for translating metaphors, tried to show why translation theory is inevitably mainly concerned with the only serious purpose of metaphor or metonym, and that whilst the translator cannot translate neologistic metonyms without coining a neologism himself, which he would have to acknowledge with inverted commas and a footnote, he has to assess the status of the metaphor before he translates. What I have not demonstrated, but hope to have indicated, is that metaphor is at the centre of all problems of translation theory, semantics and linguistics, and, following Dagut, I hope that linguists will treat it less trivially than they have up to now, bearing in mind that it will not lend itself to logical notation and is rather remote from Chomsky's world of linguistic acceptability. Both Wandruszka (1978) and Firth (1968) have stated that a sound translation theory is the basis of a sound theory of language and philosophy. As I see it, a re-evaluation of metaphor must precede a new understanding of translation, linguistics and philosophy . . . 'To see a world in a grain of sand' (*Auguries of Innocence*, William Blake).

8. The translation process and synonymy

In the early days of translation theory, when *Fremdsprachen* began appearing (1956) and Eugene Nida wrote *Towards the Science of Translating* (1964)—this was the first time that linguistics began to concern itself with translation—it was sometimes hoped to evolve a single theory, a semiotic, if not a linguistic theory, that would encompass all translating that would perhaps also produce a single scientific method applicable to all translation human and machine. A few years later, Catford wrote his *A Linguistic Theory of Translation*, and stimulating as it was, it only covered a small part of translation difficulties, and its multiple 'shift' procedures were rather simple and mechanical. Since then Nida and Koller have recommended dynamic equivalence as the only true method of translating; in fact Nida says that translation is entirely communication whilst Neubert and Kade have distinguished the invariant (cognitive) and the variant (pragmatic) element in translating, Jäger (1975) has produced a theoretical book, and almost everyone has produced ingenious and useless diagrams of the translation process.

Remarkably, in the last 2 years we have also had two new closely resembling theories of translation. Harris (1975) has propounded his 'natural translation', meaning 'any translation done in everyday circumstances by bilingual people who have no special training for it. Three-year-olds translate spontaneously in the presence of listeners who they do not think speak both languages, and later develop a criterion of "correct" translation—a translation competence in the Chomsky spirit.' (Personally I regard translation as a complex, artificial and *un*natural process, requiring an exceptional degree of intelligence.)

In a later paper (1977) Harris and Sherwood argue that the 'data for translatology (the scientific study of translating) should come primarily from natural translation rather than from literary, technical and other professional or semiprofessional branches of translation as in the past'. Harris and Sherwood compare 'translatology' with linguistics, but, like Seleskovitch, apparently think the two disciplines unrelated.

Harris and Sherwood's arguments are mainly concerned with proving (unsuccessfully I think) that translation is an innate skill in bilinguals. They take about twenty case histories relating to bilinguals (children and adults) in an interpreting, not a translating situation. Various examples of good and bad translation are produced (interference, undertranslation), and there appears nothing 'innate' about bilingual translating skill: by definition, a bilingual can interpret to some degree of competence, and that is all. More relevantly, the authors produce no evidence that their data are going to be of the slightest assistance to a translator faced with a technological, institutional or literary text—the only valid criterion if natural translating is to be included in translation theory. In fact, 'translatology' gets forgotten in the course of the paper. The paper is of greater interest to the psychologist than to the translation theorist, and has an interesting passage on the 'pleasure that translating may give to a (young) translator', which is an understatement. The mental torture of translation, the long obsession with words and facts, the maze, the continually jostled kaleidoscope, the chess-game, the sudden eureka relief, the 'I've got the translator's smirk' are all facets of a psychological process. Further, the brilliant Seleskovitch (1976, 1977) has explained her interpretative theory of translation which is based on sense, not words or sentences; non-verbal not linguistic meanings; awareness of purpose, not of language; consciousness and language reflexes, not deductions from contrastive linguistics; Seleskovitch admits that written translation goes beyond interpretation, but she does not discuss the distinction between spoken and written language. Further, though she gives some brilliant examples of interpretative translation: e.g.

'Today most people don't have enough self-discipline.'
'Les gens se laissent complètement aller aujourd'hui.'
'I expect my children to have a university education.'
'Il va de soi que mes enfants feront des études.'
'I approve of separate social lives for husbands and wives.'
'Il est normal que mari et femme sortent séparément.'

she fails to point out that all three translations show not only loss but serious distortion of meaning, and if these utterances were artistically or politically or scientifically important, her theory would be a dangerous one to base a method on. Whilst both Harris and Seleskovitch show clearly enough that a linguistic theory of translation is inevitably inadequate unless it takes situational context, addresser and addressee into account, their own almost identical theories rest almost entirely on intuition and reflexes, and allows for perhaps far too wide a choice of translations for each utterance, since only the 'sense', not the words, are important. Moreover, they fail to take account of many bilinguals' notorious incapacity or awkwardness in translating from one to the other of their languages, (or differences in how the languages were learned), probably due to the fact that they take too much of the sense for granted, out of courtesy to their listeners. Seleskovitch's theory has many valuable elements including even the obvious fact that in many cases, particularly for run of the mill utterances where what I have called 'semantic translation' (roughly, where every word is 'sacred') is not required, there is quite a wide choice of usually equally and indistinguishably imperfect but adequate translations, and no perfect translation.

However, the basis of Seleskovitch's theory is unsound. Translation and interpretation have to be based on words, sentences, linguistic meaning, language—because apart from the interpreter's paralanguage and body language (not always clear in both), they have no other material foundations. Meaning does not exist without words. Meaning arises from sights (signs, movements, colours, shapes, etc.), sounds, smells, tastes, surfaces (touch, feel, texture), as well as drives, feelings, ideas, memories, images, etc., that reach consciousness; but all these can only be mediated by words, assisted sporadically by mental images. Certainly, there are periods when both the translator and interpreter have to suppress their memory of the SL words, etc.—the translator at least when he is reading through his version for the last time (and several times before his penultimate close comparison between original and translation), the interpreter, according to Seleskovitch's pupils, when he starts interpreting. Moreover, as a training against 'literalism', i.e. the uncomprehending, slavish one-to-one renderings served up by so many students, which I condemn as much in semantic as in communicative translation (in a semantic translation, 'fatal' is as likely to be 'awkward' in German and 'inevitable' in French as it is to be 'fatal'), the method is sound. Further, if intelligently applied, it will show that whilst it is easy enough to prove that a million translations are bad because they contain plain errors, it is not so easy to make an objective choice between translations that either stress the 'force' or the 'meaning' of the utterance. Lastly, the method stresses the importance of the point, the intention, the tone of any utterance, without which no translation can be effective, but in my opinion it ignores too much subsidiary meaning, too much detail. It oversimplifies. It tends to put an idiomatic, rather glib, slick and conventional version at a premium. Thus, in another of Seleskovitch's examples: 'Capable married mothers should have career opportunities', 'Il faut que les femmes qui ont des enfants puissent, elles aussi, exercer un métier', the important idea conveyed in 'capable' (presumably that women who run their homes capably should have career opportunities—although Seleskovitch appears to ignore this sense—possibly, all married women capable of pursuing a career should have the opportunity of doing so) is missed. Note that although Seleskovitch claims to ignore the words of the original, she cannot ignore any of its key-words. Further, although her lecture is entitled 'Why interpreting is not tantamount to translating languages', and it is stated that 'translators go one step further than interpreters and try to adjust the expression of sense to the linguistic meaning of the original language', Seleskovitch proposes a theory that 'covers both interpretation *and written translation of contemporary texts'*—why only 'contemporary' texts?—and is in fact a take-over bid to include both translation and interpretation. There would be no other reason for her approving reference to Freud's interpretative translation of John Stuart Mill. (Freud read the original passage by passage, closing the book before translating each passage—but Seleskovitch forgets Freud's notorious photographic memory.)

Seleskovitch concedes that the 'aesthetic value of *belles-lettres* raises particular problems of form which have to be taken into account *per se*' and therefore presumably have nothing to do with her theory. (A theory of translation that does not account for the translation of the greatest literature is *Hamlet* without the Prince.) Further, she makes the extraordinary statement that theories of translation based on language claim that languages cannot be translated because of their deeprooted differences (to my knowledge, no modern translation theorist believes in the strong version of the Humboldt–Whorf–Sapir thesis, and in particular the Leipzig School rejects it completely). It is difficult to understand Seleskovitch's final thesis: 'translation of language and rendering of sense are not to be confused; neither are linguistics and the science of translation', nor her peculiar distinction between 'sense' and 'meaning'. I can only maintain that translation is concerned with words, that it is only partially a science (in any event, there is nothing scientific about the Paris School's 'interpretative theory'), and that in as far as it is a science, it can only be based on linguistics.

Seleskovitch's theory is amplified (with abundant stimulating examples) by herself and her collaborators in the valuable December 1976 issue (no. 24) of *Études de Linguistique appliquée* (Didier).

The theorizing has all been too general and too simplified. Translation is a skill and an art as well as a science. Dynamic equivalence is not possible when the original writer is writing to please himself rather than any reader, or when the translation's reader has not the same information as the original's reader. The invariant material element in a text is certainly translatable, but as languages look at objects so differently it may be as difficult to translate as any ideological text. Basically, any general theory will sooner or later be split up in the conflict between the various 'interests' in a translation, where the conflict between the interests of the first writer and the readers of the translation is stronger than that between the norms of the source and target languages, where the translator has to decide whether the culture or the message implicit in the utterance, the (linguistic) meaning of the communicative force is more important. A foolproof translation theory, like a foolproof translation, can only be found in performatives, with standardized instructions, standardized patterns, the 'rehearsed response': *Den Hahn zudrehen*—'turn off the tap!' 'No smoking'—*Défense de fumer, Rauchen verboten*—these, and many more like them, are the only form of perfect translation, measured by their success (their effectiveness) rather than their truth—*im Anfang war die Tat, nicht das Wort*—and admittedly they are a little dull.

If I dismiss any prospect of a general theory of translation, on the ground that no valid theory can be built on so many variables, then I am not suggesting that theory has no place in the study of translation. I am suggesting that we have to remember that 'our purpose is to be useful' (to quote Benjamin Britten), to be useful to translators, and to assist in raising the generally rather low standard of translation, at least in the United Kingdom. So far, Professor Butler has said, translation theory has had little impact on translation, although this argument hardly bears examination. Chapman's and Dryden's translation theory had considerable influence on English literary translation in the seventeenth and eighteenth centuries (Steiner, 1975) and the idea that after 21 years of *Fremdsprachen*, theory has had no influence on translation practice in the GDR must be absurd. Further, Nida has many disciples and missionaries who acknowledge the strength of his ideas in many Bible translations. It is, however, true that theory has had little influence on modern English literary translation, where most works have suffered from lack of a reviser to correct gross errors, not style (usually they are translated by one person or a husband and wife team that appears equally subjective), rather than lack of theory; that Weightman (1967) who has written superbly on translation theory (he is also the translator of Lévi-Strauss) no longer believes in it, and that the majority of English translators, traditionally English, i.e. pragmatic, to a man, are either contemptuous of or hostile to translation theory.

When Seleskovitch points out that translation has nothing to do with the type of sentence used by linguists to exemplify semantic contents such as 'John plays golf' or 'My dog has wings', we would all agree; but when she says that 'Carefully defined semantic equivalents are rarely of any use when conveying information in another language' she is surely mistaken, since this process, which I have called cognitive translation, and Brislin (1976) 'decentring' and is sometimes referred to as the intermediate language (it is 'similar' in any language) is often the basis, the raw material from which one inches towards a decent translation, whether it is communicative or semantic. I am suggesting that Seleskovitch's attempt to solve the problem (and it is a big problem) by ignoring the words, by disregarding contrastive linguistics, by using spontaneous translation as a model in favour of total communication, while it may act as a corrective to some of the neat conversions of say Tesnière, Malblanc, Vinay and Darbelnet, Friedrich, etc., invites inaccuracy.

However, I propose now to take another insufficiently discussed and more modest problem, that of synonymy. It is often said that translation is a form of synonymy, and I will begin by rebutting this, taking as my example the English sentence:

'My friend has gone to the theatre.'

The closest synonymous version I can think of here is:

'My mate has left and is now in the playhouse.'

(Mate is the working-class equivalent of 'friend' and 'playhouse' is clear (Schauspielhaus) but never used now, except as the name of a theatre.) Now, if you look at the German: 'Mein Freund ist ins Theater gegangen', you will see it is an almost perfect (isomorphic) fit, except that it does not cover a girl-friend or a female friend (not the same thing). Thus the German version is far closer to the English original than the synonymous English version. The example illustrates the not always recognized fact that the meaning of any word is explained better and more neatly by translation than by, say, synonym, paraphrase or even by pointing. More pointedly, it illustrates (*Theatre* is *Theater*, not usually *Schauspielhaus*) that translators must use words (as well as all components) of equivalent frequency, and not as they are still told to at school, at least in England, choose a synonym instead of an English word that looks the same as a German or a French or Russian word—there are perhaps as many 'true friends' as there are *faux amis*.

Further, the point illustrates that the translator's first job is to translate or to transcribe; only when this is not possible, for all kinds of reasons of situational and linguistic context, connotation, etc., must he resort to synonyms, then to componential analysis, then to definition, and finally to his last (but not infrequent) recourse to paraphrase.

Let me now return to another aspect of synonymy, synonyms in grammar, which are often closer and more numerous than in lexis. Take the German sentence: 'Es ist unmöglich, das Problem zu lösen.' We have the following potential translations:

1. It is impossible to solve the problem.
2. Solving the problem is impossible.
3. The problem is impossible to solve.
4. One cannot solve the problem.
5. A solution to the problem is impossible.
6. The problem is insoluble.
7. To solve the problem is impossible.
8. There is no solution to the problem.
9. The problem has no solution.
10. Solving the problem is an impossibility.

Since 'impossible' can be replaced by 'not possible', 'insoluble' by 'not soluble' and 'one' by 'we' or 'you', we now have fifteen possible translations. Further, in context, the sentence might become 'inability to solve the problem', 'the insoluble problem', 'being unable', 'owing to our inability' and 'the problem' could be replaced by 'this problem'. Note that the German by back translation can do all that the English can, except use gerunds and participles adroitly, but its use of noun-infinitives is more adroit. With all that, one would normally expect 'Es ist unmöglich, das Problem zu lösen' to be translated by 'It is impossible to solve the problem' since it keeps the same stresses as the German. Note that any replacements by lexical synonyms (e.g. 'resolve', 'settle' for 'solve'; 'question', 'point', 'argument' for 'problem') are further from the sense than the grammatical synonyms. This then becomes a plea for more grammatical dexterity and flexibility, and against lexical licence, in translation practice.

I now discuss an aspect of lexical synonymy. Ullmann (1957) has stated that complete (isomorphic) synonyms exist only in technical nomenclature, that some by no means infrequent technical terms are completely interchangeable. As translators, we know that this is incorrect, *a priori* because of my principle of equivalent frequency, and in fact because all words have different connotations of situation and/or user's origin (education, class, profession, dialect, etc.). Ullmann gives two words for the inflammation of the blind gut, 'caecitis' and 'typhlitis', but caecitis is not even mentioned in the shorter dictionaries, two words for sounds made by friction of breath in narrow opening, 'fricative' or 'spirant', but 'spirant' is hardly used in British English, and has a broader meaning than 'fricative'. And again, I suggest to you that there will always be cases where a German writer or translator will be able to give sound reasons for preferring *Lautlehre* to *Phonetik, Sprachwissenschaft* to *Linguistik, Bedeutungslehre* to *Semantik* or the now pretentious *Semasiologie.* If the translator is aiming at good style (in communicative translation) or is engaged in semantic translation, one should normally be able to find objective reasons for preferring one word to another, but this does not hold good for larger units: where a 'straight' translation is not possible, preference between ten or more equally good translated sentences or paragraphs may be a matter of personal taste.

The richness of English synonymy, drawing as the language does on three main sources (Germanic, Romance and Classical) not to mention Norse, a later injection of Germanic, and having now the same powers of word-formation (notably double, triple, quadruple, etc., noun compounds such as 'output bus driver'—device for amplifying output signals) as German has often been commented on. How does a translator handle a set such as 'quick, fast, speedy, rapid, swift, fleet' or 'dark, murky, sombre, gloomy, dismal, dingy, obscure, dim, dusky'? Stylistically, some words can be used for the interstices of the source language: thus since 'murky' has no German equivalent, it might be justifiably used to take over parts of *dunkel, finster, trüb,* or *düster* just as *dunkel* and *finster* perhaps share the semantic field of 'dark'. In the above cases, I doubt whether componential analysis would serve the translator as well as the type of collocational analysis made many years ago by the great Albrecht Reum or more recently by E. Agricola in *Wörter und Wendungen.* The meaning of a word (or of a set of words) is to be found not in its use on single occasions but in a summary of the accumulation of their various usages, and the form of tabulation favoured by componential analysis—a tree diagram or a plus/minus statement of dimensions for single words, or a matrix table for a set of words—is likely to be of more use to the lexicographer than to the translator reviewing a tangle of words in his own (target) language. Here he may require a thesaurus before making an intuitive choice. When considering a source language word, however—take *büßen*—he may want to set up a componential analysis with *sühnen, wiedergutmachen, Genugtuung geben, abbüßen, Ersatz leisten, tilgen, bereuen,* before selecting the English word which, out of context, will embrace the maximum number of semantic components.

However, his choice will be subject to three later revisions: the word has to be re-examined in its referential, its linguistic and finally its communicative context, where its sense may be redistributed elsewhere in the sentence.

The problems of translating referential synonyms are sufficiently well known. They may be used (a) to avoid repetition, (b) to secure cohesion, (c) because (as above) the author writes badly, (d) in the interest of redundancy, to expand the text, (e) to provide, almost incidentally, additional comment about the topic ('Palestine is a small country—it is the Holy Land'). Referential synonyms are sometimes difficult to detect, and the translator is 'lost', if he fails to do so. Deictics such as 'that', 'the', 'it', 'which', are usually clear enough, but a 'general' or 'empty' verb ('do, operate') or noun ('arrangement') or even adjective ('significant') may function as referential synonyms for more specific corresponding elements in the same or the previous sentence.

Philosophers often point out that a communicative act consists of a modality plus a proposition, and the essence is in the proposition. Thus Strawson (1970b) says of sentences such as

'Unfortunately, Socrates is dead'
'Fortunately, Socrates is dead'

that 'it is far from clear that their truth conditions differ', and thus that they are synonyms of a kind. To a translator, far from being synonyms, they are contradictory statements, and the modality is more important than the proposition. If I change the sentence to 'Fortunately (*or* Unfortunately) Mao-Tse-tung is dead' this becomes clearer, and the attitudes of the two speakers rather than the proposition (which may be true or false) are the two essential facts that contradict each other.

Returning to grammatical synonymy, note that the translator is usually only permitted to move towards greater naturalness: thus 'Then he killed the tiger' cannot be translated by 'Dann wurde der Tiger von ihm getötet'—both sentences are rather artificial in any event—not only because the focus of interest is changed, but because the German sentence is stiffer than the English and is less probable.

Other pseudosynonymous sentences appear to be (a) 'This is not a Picasso!', (b) 'This is not a work of mine!' said by Picasso discovering a forgery. Cognitively, there is a thin distinction. In (a), Picasso does not say whether he painted the work; in (b), he does not say whether Picasso painted it. The implied difference is that in (a), Picasso painted the original, whilst in (b) he probably did not. Connotationally, the first sentence is arrogant and affected, whilst the second is a straight denial. The translator whose object is to help the reader would want to bring out any such distinction implicit in the original.

From a translator's point of view, synonyms in collocation are of five kinds: (1) traditional formulas, (2) emphasis, (3) bad writing, (4) intended to make delicate distinctions and (5) lists that do not often correspond with a TL text.

For standardized terms, such as 'last will and testament', 'without let or hindrance', 'in good repair, order and condition', or 'goods and chattels', only *letztwillige Verfügung, ohne Hinderung, in gutem Zustande, Hab und Gut* will do, being standardized in both languages, and again *Objekte und Gegenstände* (there must be many more German ones) can only be translated as 'objects'.

Synonyms are often collocated to emphasize a point, whether it is a colloquial expression such as 'frightfully, terribly fond', or even in an encyclopaedia: 'I legnami risultano cosi cariati, marciti, fradici'. In the last example, the three qualifiers could be artificially separated out as 'decayed, rotted, crumbling', showing a process, or more likely the strongest qualifier could be chosen and suitably reinforced: 'The timber is found to be completely rotted.'

Synonyms are in fact sometimes collocated in such a way that it is not clear whether the purpose is emphasis or distinction, or it is merely a badly written phrase. Thus Norman St. John Stevas recently spoke of 'an education in the arts or the humanities'. An arts degree (i.e. literature/history, geography) is a degree in the humanities, but humanities does not normally include the arts. If the two are to be distinguished, then 'arts' is *schöne Künste* and 'humanities' is perhaps *humanistische Bildung*. Did the speaker mean 'both', or 'either'? Fortunately the German translator does not need to know, as *oder*, like 'or', has both meanings. Again, a sentence such as 'he appreciates and values books' may simply mean 'er schätzt Bücher besonders hoch', but if the synonyms are to be differentiated, it may mean 'er schätzt und legt Wert auf Bücher' or, as a job, 'er schätzt und bewertet Bücher'.

Note also that a translator may be faced with a series of closely related lexical items, semi-synonyms that represent entities, events or qualities (these are the lexical stock) for which there is no one-to-one equivalent in the TL. The translator may have to replace them with a smaller number of items including, say, a generic term to account for two or three of the missing items. Thus, Italian can use suffixes to show varieties of size: 'Tronchi e rami vengono segati in cantieri e ridotti in travi, panche, panconi o tavolini, tavole, travicelli, correnti o morali, correntini o listelli, scorzoni.' Here the translator has two choices: he can either ignore the list and write down all the (English) technical terms for the varieties of shapes which tree trunks and branches are sawed into in timber yards; or, he can summarize the list as 'beams, boards and battens of various sizes' (to cover the *-ini, -elli, -oni*, etc.), possibly adding, depending on the interest of the reader, the Italian technical terms, including the alternative terms which are likely to be missing in English.

9. Translation and the metalingual function of language

For the purpose of this chapter, the metalingual* function of language is defined as the capacity of a language to describe or to illustrate one or more of its own peculiarities. This capacity could be instanced, say, in an article on phrasal verbs in English; in a passage stating that a particular word is used in a special sense, e.g. literally, or that it has recently developed a special sense; and finally in a passage, literary or non-literary, deliberately including word-play and any linguistic ambiguity.

When a passage concerning a grammatical peculiarity of the source language has to be translated, one must assume that the second reader requires more information than the first, and therefore that 'equivalent-effect' is not a realistic aim; the translator also has to decide whether the reader is a specialist with some knowledge of the SL or whether he is coming 'cold' to the passage. Thus terms such as *Umlaut* are normally transcribed in German grammars for learners, unfortunately without a literal translation ('change of [vowel] sound' with diaeresis) which would help the learner. In a clause such as *Die Bezeichnung Ablaut, die von J. Grimm geprägt wurde*, a normal translation would read: 'The term *Ablaut* (or vowel gradation) which was coined by J. Grimm' if the text related to the German language specifically, but both the German term and its inventor might be relegated to footnotes or even omitted if the text were concerned with vowel gradation generally. On the other hand, an English text discussing such old phenomena but fairly recent terms as 'phrasal verbs' or 'subject participle clauses' would not normally translate adequately without (a) a transcription of the term, (b) a loan translation in inverted commas, to show its literal meaning, and possibly as a proposal for neologism, (c) a definition (if not already in SL text), (d) a SL example, (e) an interlinear translation of the example to demonstrate the term's syntax, (f) a functional translation (I distinguish 'functional translation' as the most effective translation of a term in a particular context from 'communicative translation' as a general method). Thus in an English grammar for German linguists, the German translation of the sentence: '"*Killing my friend* gives me no pleasure" is an example of a subject participle clause' might be: '"*Killing my friend* gives me no pleasure" (wörtliche Übersetzung: "*Tötend meinen Freund* bereitet mir kein Vergnügen"; funktionale Übersetzung: "Wenn ich meinen Freund umbringe, empfinde ich kein Vergnügen") ist ein Beispiel eines Subjekt-Partizipsatzes (Subject Participle Clause), d.h. einer Gerund- oder Partizipgruppe, die die Stelle eines Subjekt-Gliedsatzes eingenommen hat.' Thus the reader can inspect all the relevant facts.

* The concept is a wide one. The metalingual function is usually described as language's capacity to describe or define itself or its features.

Secondly, if a word in the SL is used in a particular sense, the translator has several choices: 'Au 16e siècle des centaines de Français étaient coupables de libertinage, pris dans le sens vieilli de "licence de l'esprit en matière de foi".' The sentence could be translated as: 'In the sixteenth century, hundreds of Frenchmen were guilty of *libertinage*, in the obsolete sense of the French word, meaning freethinking in religious matters.' Alternatively, the above sentence from 'guilty of' could be replaced by 'libertinism', 'libertinage', or 'freethinking in religious matters'. The translator must be guided by his assessment of the reader's knowledge and interest.

Again, a translator is entitled to delete a special sense of a term, if it is of no interest to the reader, or to reproduce it as a linguistic curiosity. Thus: *le marché noir ou le cours parallèle, comme on le qualifie de façon euphémique* could be translated as either 'the black market' or 'the black market; the French also refers to it euphemistically as *cours parallèle* (parallel rate) *or* parallel rate (*cours parallèle*)'—the bracketed translations could be omitted, depending again on the interest and knowledge of the reader (cf. *médecine parallèle ou héterodoxe ou empirique:* tr.: alternative medicine).

The translator also has a choice when a text gives alternative terms for the same referent. Thus: *'La mobilisation active est une des bases fondamentales du traitement des maladies ostéo-articulaires. On parle aussi de kinésithérapie active ou de cinésithérapie, ou de gymnastique thérapeutique: ce sont des synonymes.'*

This could be translated as: 'Active mobilization is a fundamental element in the treatment of diseases of the bones and joints. It is sometimes referred to as active kinesitherapy or remedial exercises.' (There is no reason why the translator should not add other current synonyms.) If the text specifically refers to French practice, the reader may also be interested in having the three synonyms transcribed. Again, if the synonyms in the TL are not as frequently used as those in the SL, the translator is justified in excluding them.

Translating word-play in literary and non-literary texts embraces (exceptionally) two different problems. In non-literary texts, the reader usually requires all possible information. For example: 'Das Ehepaar X lebt auf ziemlich großem Fuße. Nach der Ansicht der einen soll der Mann *viel verdient* und sich dabei *etwas zurückgelegt* haben, nach anderen wieder soll sich die Frau *etwas zurückgelegt* und dabei *viel verdient* haben' (Freud, *Der Witz*, p. 26, Fischer Bücherei). This is translated by James Strachey as: 'Mr. and Mrs. X live in fairly grand style. Some people think that the husband has earned a lot and so has been able to lay by a bit (*sich etwas zurückgelegt*); others again think that the wife has lain back a bit (*sich etwas zurückgelegt*) and so has been able to earn a lot' (Freud, *Jokes and their relation to the unconscious*, p. 66, Penguin Books, 1975).

Thus the punning element is retained, but the German is reproduced as the joke illustrates the rearrangement of precisely the same verbal material—in the English version there is a slight change. (In other instances, Strachey cannot do this so neatly; on p. 54 he has to translate a dozen words in a footnote, warning that 'If all this is borne in mind, what follows will be intelligible'.)

James Strachey explains in his preface why he has rejected previous methods of dealing with examples of word-play which consisted of either dropping them altogether or replacing them with the translator's examples. The second method, adopted by A. A. Brill, the book's first translator, substitutes the translator's insights for the author's. (Incidentally, some of Brill's examples were gratefully quoted by Freud in later German editions.) Brill replaces the above joke as follows: Two witty statesmen, X and Y, met at a dinner. X, acting as toast master, introduced Y as follows: 'My friend Y is a wonderful man. All you have to do is to open his mouth, put in a dinner, and a speech appears, etc.' Responding to the speaker, Y said: 'My friend the toast master told you what a wonderful man I am, that all you have to do is to open my mouth, put in a dinner, and a speech appears. Now let me tell you what a wonderful man he is. All you have to do is open anybody's mouth, put in his speech, and the dinner appears' (*Wit and its relation to the unconscious*, tr. A. A. Brill, p. 36, T. Fischer Unwin, 1916). Brill adds a few comments similar to Freud's (note that the sexual background of Freud's *geradezu diabolisch guter Witz* is missing) and then quotes a joke by Oliver Wendell Holmes, which Freud adds to a later edition without translating it into German, giving it as an example of the untranslatability of jokes with this technique. (In fact, *all* jokes are translatable, but they do not always have the same impact.)

James Strachey's principles of translation are in the circumstances the only correct ones, and must be followed in all cases where the words are as important as the thought, and 'dramatic illusion' (i.e. the translation should read like the original) less important. Strachey's translation is a model (see also his discussion of *Witz, Scherz, Komik, Humor,* etc.); it is, however, significant that his neologism 'parapraxis' for *Fehlleistung* has been generally replaced by 'Freudian slip'. Whilst in-groups and word-droppers readily acquire neologisms, an opaque expression like 'parapraxis' is unlikely to find general acceptance, particularly among linguistic puritans.

The translation of proverbs in non-literary texts is straightforward if the TL has a recognized equivalent. Otherwise, the translator has the option either of translating the foreign proverb and showing its reference to the text, or of absorbing the proverb in the text. Thus in an article on pollution in Italy, where the proverb has no English equivalent: '"Tutti i fiumi portano al mare" dice il proverbio e, in un certo senso, ciò è vero. Ma che cosa portano oggi al mare i fiumi? Tutta la sporiciza e i veleni che gli uomini gettano entro di essi, sopraffacendo il provvido potere autodepurante del quale la natura li aveva dotati,' it seems to me the most satisfactory version follows the first solution, although it is less direct than the original: 'The Italians have a saying that all rivers lead to the sea, by which they also mean that money attracts money. Now, in the first sense, this is true. But what kind of wealth are rivers carrying to the sea today? Nothing but the filth and the poisons that people throw into rivers, destroying their natural and beneficial self-purifying power.' (Alternative: 'There is no doubt that all rivers eventually lead to the sea but all they carry with them is the filth and the poisons. . . .')

I now have to consider word-play or polysemy in texts where 'dramatic illusion' is essential, that is, in translating plays and poems, and desirably other literary works.

Here, most frequently, the translator can only capture one of the two senses, e.g. for 'season'.

> 'Or as sweet-seasoned showers are to the ground'
> (SHAKESPEARE, Sonnet 75.)
> 'Wie süß gewürzter regen ist fürs feld'
> (tr. STEFAN GEORGE.)

In the repartee between Polonius and Hamlet (*Hamlet* Act III. ii: *Polonius:* I did enact Julius Caesar: I was killed on the Capitol; Brutus killed me. *Hamlet:* It was a brute part of him to kill so capital a calf there), there are three puns (brute, part, capital), two sets of alliterations (killed, Capitol, kill, capital, calf) and a connotation of 'stupid' for 'calf'.

The Schlegel translation is as follows: '*Polonius:* Ich stellte den Julius Cäsar vor: ich ward auf dem Kapitol umgebracht; Brutus brachte mich um. *Hamlet:* Es war brutal von ihm, ein so kapitales Kalb umzubringen.'

Schlegel has preserved only two puns and one set of alliterations, and the dialogue loses a little in force.

When a literary passage includes a double meaning within a lexical unit, the translator first attempts to reproduce it with a word containing the same double meaning: 'To be or not to be—that is the question (Sein oder nicht sein—das ist hier die Frage)' but the word-play cannot be preserved in Spanish. If this is not possible, he may try to substitute a synonym with a comparable double meaning: 'The *fractions* of her faith' (*Troilus and Cressida*, V. ii), *Die Trümmer ihrer Lieb' und* (Tieck) *Treu*.

Again, if this is not possible, he has to choose between distributing the two senses of the lexical unit over two or more lexical units:

> And yet the spacious breadth of this division
> Admits no orifice for a point as *subtle* . . .
> (*Troilus and Cressida*, V. ii)

> Und doch gewährt die weitgespaltene Kluft
> Um einzudringen nicht den *kleinsten* Zugang
> Für einen Punkt, *fein*, wie Arachnes Faden
> (Ludwig Tieck)

or sacrificing one of the two meanings (e.g. by replacing the two meanings of 'infernal' by the word 'verdammt', as GDR translator did to Sean O'Casey's annoyance).

In translating imaginative literature—where it has been often said that the translatable element is the poetry, a stimulating, flatly untrue and typically 'literary' comment—the biggest loss in meaning (i.e. the total effect on the reader) is due to the peculiar metaphorical properties rather than the sound-effects of the foreign language. Metaphor is the core of poetry and metaphors based on nature and its fruits are usually rooted in a particular environment. Normally, a translator finds he can at least follow some of the original's assonance and alliteration (if he is translating poetry, he often follows metre and rhyme), but given that metaphor, both stock and original, is in itself a kind of implicit accompanying translation of a word or idiom (metaphor therefore translates or metaphorizes meaning) often rooted in the source language or its culture, it is not surprising that it is not possible to transfer the 'two' versions to another language.

I note that in a, say, twenty-line *Hamlet* passage, about a dozen metaphors are missing in Schlegel's version. Since stock metaphors are a kind of cultural deposit on a language and reflect a speech community's cultural focus (just as original metaphors usually reflect a writer's personal interests), the difficulty in translating them is again a reflection of cultural distance, which is usually considerable even in two contiguous language areas. However, this paper has been concerned only with metaphor as an aspect of word-play.

In imaginative literature, events and people have a more or less symbolical character, which is invested in the more general words that denote them. In a passage from Valéry's *Variété* (*Stendhal*) describing the period 1810–1830: 'Quelques-uns se sentaient confusément sur la tête tout un échafaud de coiffures, une perruque, une calotte, un bonnet rouge, un chapeau à plume tricolore, un chapeau à cornes, un chapeau bourgeois'—connotation, metonymy, metaphor, word-play merge into each other. What begins in a language as a connotation (*sens virtuel*) is developed till it attains its own separate sense, a pun on what was once its primary sense. The translator then may have to decide, as in many cases of metalanguage, whether to follow the more general concrete or the more culturally influenced sense, or, as in the above passage, he may combine them both: 'Some had the confused sensation of wearing a whole pile of headgear hanging over them like a scaffold—the nobleman's wig, the priest's scull-cap, the red cap of revolution, the patriot's hat with tricolour plume, the cocked hat, the bourgeois hat.' Note here that all objects are culturally bound except possibly *coiffure*, and that *chapeau* is at least more generalized than *perruque* (virtually obsolete). With their connotations, they are even more localized but not confined to French culture.

However, in the following too-well-known poem by Heine, the 'two cultures' almost neutralize each other, and the tropical translator would have problems with *Fichtenbaum*, which appears much more specific than *Palme*, and the gender of the two trees.

> Ein Fichtenbaum steht einsam
> Im Norden auf kahler Höh!
> Ihn schläfert; mit weißer Decke
> Umhüllen ihn Eis und Schnee.
>
> Er träumt von einer Palme,
> Die fern im Morgenland
> Einsam und schweigend trauert
> Auf brennender Felsenwand.

In translating any specimen of metalanguage, there are usually problems and alternative solutions, and whilst, *pace* Catford, nothing is untranslatable, a supplementary gloss (in the TL and the SL) is often required. Metalanguage is often signalled by expressions such as 'so-called', 'by definition', 'so to speak', 'literally', 'sometimes known as' (for example: 'sometimes collectively known in England as "fancy cheeses"' should be translated as: *qui, en Grande-Bretagne, sont parfois désignées sous le nom de 'fancy cheeses'* [*fromages de luxe*]; it would be incorrect to write: *sous le nom de fromages de luxe* [*fancy cheeses*]), 'often referred to as', 'figurative', 'in the full sense of the word', 'with a similar meaning', 'in a restricted sense', 'synonymously', 'in this sense', 'as another generation put it' or by italics or inverted commas—I list them as some writers are apt to translate them literally or ignore them with nonsensical results. However, metalanguage, except in imaginative literature where either the force or the meaning of figurative language may have to be sacrificed, can often be neatly handled.

PART TWO

Some Propositions on Translation

Introduction

There is no such thing as a law of translation, since laws admit of no exceptions. There can be and are various theories of translation, but these apply only to certain types of text, and all are at various points between the continuum of transmitter and receiver emphasis. There can be no valid single comprehensive theory of translation, and no general agreement on the element of invariance, the ideal translation unit, the degree of translatability, and the concepts of equivalent-effect and congruence in translation, although all these questions are worth pursuing, particularly if interesting examples are produced in support of an argument. (Excellent books have been written producing true and pertinent instances in favour of misguided theses: purely theoretical treatises on translation are even less profitable than most purely theoretical treatises.) In spite of the claims of Nida and the Leipzig translation school, who start writing on translation where others leave off, there is no such thing as a science of translation, and never will be.

If I now set up some rules of translation, I am aware that they are somewhere between Aunt Sallies and reference frames. I am merely suggesting that translators should test some of their problems against them. A word can be legitimately stipulated to mean anything ('let us assume for the purposes of this essay that "egg" means "love"'); context is the overriding factor in all translation, and has primacy over any rule, theory or primary meaning.

Linguistics of translation

1. Range and acceptability of collocations

Where there is an accepted collocation[1] in the source language, the translator must find and use its equivalent in the target language, if it exists. A collocation consists basically of two or three lexical (sometimes called full, descriptive, substantial) words, usually linked by grammatical (empty, functional, relational) words, e.g. 'a mental illness'. The collocates within a collocation define and delimit each other by eliminating at least some of their other possible meanings; the defining may be mutual and equally balanced, but more often it is closer for one collocate than for the other. Thus 'to pay attention' is a collocation, since it reduces the number of senses in which 'pay' can be used to one. The word 'attention' is not so radically affected, but it excludes 'attention' in the sense of 'care, solicitude'. 'To buy a hat' is not a collocation, since it does not appreciably delimit the sense of 'buy' or 'hat'. However, collocations shade off into other grammatically linked word-groups without a sharp division.

A collocation is the element of system in the lexis of a language. It may be syntagmatic or horizontal, therefore consisting of a common structure; or paradigmatic or vertical, consisting of words belonging to the same semantic field which may substitute for each other or be semantic opposites. These become collocations only when they are arranged syntagmatically.

Syntagmatic collocations can be divided into seven main groups:

(a) *Verb plus verbal noun.* Examples: pay attention, suffer a defeat, run a meeting, make a speech. The verb is the collocate for which the translator must find the appropriate equivalent. The verbs in these collocations merely have an operative function (they mean 'do') and no particularized meaning since the action is expressed in the noun. Some verbal nouns have a small range of collocates; others, like *discours, Lob, Dienst*, have one obvious collocate (*prononcer, spenden, leisten*).

(b) *Determiner plus adjective plus noun.* The appropriate adjective has to be found for the noun. There is a much wider range of choices than in (a), and the force of this category of collocation is usually only established by contrast with another language. Thus 'a large apple' but *une grosse pomme*; 'a tall man' but *un homme grand*; *un grand homme* but 'a great man'; *un beau garçon* but 'a good looking man'; 'a pretty girl' but not (usually) 'a pretty boy'. Some nouns have one particularly suitable adjective in an extensive variety of areas, particularly for physical qualities (e.g. woman: dark, slim, middle-aged, short, young) which, for other objects, would require different adjectives, whilst other nouns (e.g. 'criticism') have a narrow sheaf of adjectives for each segment of a variety of areas (*approfondi/gründlich; anodine/nichtssagend*).

(c) *Adverb plus adjective.* The most suitable adverb must be looked for. These collocations tend to cliché (e.g. 'immensely important'). The collocation is much rarer in Romance languages, where its equivalent transposition is 'adjective plus adjectival noun', e.g. *d'une immense importance.* Note however *vachement dur*, 'damn hard' or 'bloody hard'. This collocation, which is more restricted and less frequent (therefore far less important) than (a) and (b), is much at the mercy of fashion.

(d) *Verb plus adverb or adjective.* This is a much smaller category: the adverb or adjective must be looked for. Examples: 'work hard', *fleissig arbeiten*, 'feel well', 'shine brightly', 'smell sweet', *hart arbeiten.*

(e) *Subject plus verb.* There are two groups: first, the noun and verb may mutually attract each other: 'the dog barks', 'the cat purrs', *das Tier frisst*, 'the bell rings', 'teeth chatter'. In some cases, particularly when referring to animals, the verb usually has no other subject. In the second group, there is merely a fairly high expectation that a particular verb will follow the subject: 'the door creaks', *le clocher pointe, les champs se déroulent*, etc., and here the right verb must be looked for. In French, some of these verbs are often found as past participles or in adjectival clauses qualifying their subjects (used as *étoffement* with low semantic content), and then they require no translation in English: *la maison qui se dresse sur la colline*, 'the house on the hill'.

(f) *Count noun plus 'of' plus mass noun.* This restricted collocation consists of a term denoting a unit of quantity and the word for the substance it quantifies. The appropriate unit must be looked for in the target language, e.g. 'a loaf of bread', 'a cake of soap', 'a pinch of salt', 'a particle (or a cloud) of dust', etc., if it exists.

(g) *Collective noun plus count noun.* The collective noun has to be discovered: e.g. 'a bunch of keys', 'a flock of geese or sheep', 'a pack of cards or hounds'.

Wider and less easily categorized collocations include nominalizations (in particular, nouns premodified by one or more nouns), introducing the name of an object (or unit of quantity) by a term for its size, composition, purpose, origin, destination, etc., which is now rapidly superseding the 'noun plus "of" plus noun' collocation; the whole range of phrasal verbs, and various items of a sequence including activity/agent/instrument/object/attribute/source/place, etc.: e.g. 'bake/baker/oven/bread/fresh, new, stale, musty/flour, yeast/bakery'.

Stylistically and semantically, clichés are a subgroup of collocations in that one of their collocates has diminished in value or is almost redundant, as often in 'grinding to a halt', 'filthy lucre', etc., and the translator may be entitled to replace a cliché with a less common collocation, if it clarifies the content without distorting it.

Paradigmatic collocations may be based on well-established hierarchies such as kinship ('fathers and sons'), colours ('emerald is a bright green'), scientific taxonomies and institutional hierarchies where the elements of the culture for each language often have their own distinct linguistic likeness (*Abbild*), although the extralinguistic object may be the same. Alternatively they may consist of the various synonyms and antonyms that permeate all languages.

Antonyms may be classified under three heads:

(a) Objects which complement each other to form a set ('land, sea, air'), or a graded series ('ratings, petty officers, officers).

(b) Qualities (adjectives or adjectival nouns) which are contrary, which may have a middle term (e.g. 'interested/disinterested/uninterested'), or are contradictory. Contradictory polar terms are shown formally, i.e. through affixes: 'perfect/imperfect, loyal/disloyal'. (Suffixes have much stronger force than prefixes: cf. 'faithless/unfaithful'.) Contrary polar terms are usually shown lexically: 'hot/cold, young/old, faithful/treacherous'. In a text, such collocations usually appear as alternatives: e.g. 'hard or soft; clear, obscure or vague'.

(c) Actions (verbs or verbal nouns). In two-term collocations, the second term is converse or reciprocal: 'attack/defend; give/receive; action/reaction'. In three-term collocations, the second and third terms represent positive and negative responses respectively: 'offer/accept/refuse, besiege/hold out/surrender'.

Actions may also complement each other as in (a): 'walk/run, sleep/wake'.

There are two types of synonym collocation. The main type is the 'inclusive' collocation which includes (a) the hierarchies of genus/species/subspecies, etc., and may indicate the degree of generality (or particularity) of any lexical item, and with it the appropriate category (*Oberbegriffe* or superordinates): e.g. 'the brass in the orchestra'; 'pump or grease-gun'; 'an equity on the market'. *Flèche* is a generic term for 'spire', and a specific term for *flèche* (slender spire perforated with windows); (b) synecdoche, where part and whole are sometimes used indiscriminately with the same reference (e.g. *chariot/porte-outil*, 'strings/violins'); (c) metonymy, where 'Bonn' and 'the West German government', 'the City' and 'British bankers' may again be interchanged. The second type of synonym collocation is usually an old idiom such as 'with might and main' and 'by hook or by crook' (see Proposition no. 14 where it forms an exception)—which is likely to have a Germanic (*auf Biegen oder Brechen*) but not a Romance (*coûte que coûte*) one-to-one equivalent.

Collocations are the lexical (not grammatical) tramlines of language. Where a translator finds current and equally common corresponding collocations in source and target language texts, it is mandatory to use them; they are among the invariant components of translation. They may be factual or extra-linguistic, denoting institutional terms (e.g. *le Président de la République*) as well as linguistic. A translator must be conversant with them not only to follow them but also to know when to 'break' them (going off the tramlines) when they are broken in the source language text.

2. The core of a thought: logical structure

In any fussy or obscured syntactical (surface) structure, the translator's job is to find the underlying (deep) structure. In my opinion, the most useful procedure is to discover the logical subject first, then its specific verb, and let the rest fall into place. The basic structure, from which all others flow, is: animate (human) subject plus operator (transitive verb) plus inanimate direct object, and this should be looked for first. For example: (a) . . . *dans lesquels l'initiative parlementaire pourrait encore s'exercer pleinement*, 'where Parliament could still take a full initiative', (b) *Il est rare qu'une solution pleinement satisfaisante d'un problème soit proposée par les orateurs au ministre*, 'it's not often that speakers in Parliament propose a fully satisfactory solution of a problem to a minister'.

3. Three series of semantic categories

Lexical items have perhaps three series of semantic categories; the translator may have to test an item against each series, in order to establish the sense of the word in the context. (I use 'sense' for one type of meaning of a word.)

The first (ordinal) series consists of six categories of application:

(a) *The primary or nuclear sense (sememe)*: i.e. the first and immediate sense suggested by the word alone, without or completely out of context. Most words probably have primary senses broadly accepted by educated people, e.g. lexicographers. 'Time' is a concept before it is an occasion; 'green' is a colour, not a feeling; one 'pays' money before one pays one's respects, regards, attention, etc. The primary sense, which is determined by usage, is sometimes absurdly confused with its illusory 'true' or 'literal' sense when the word has been taken from another language ('virtue' means 'courage') or its etymological meaning ('nice' means 'ignorant', or later, 'delicate'). The primary sense is always the most frequently and/or widely diffused sense of the word at a particular period of time. The earliest etymological sense of a word is sometimes superseded as primary sense by two or more secondary senses. This occurs particularly in the case of compounds such as *concours, aufheben, einstellen* and some English phrasal verbs ('put up', 'take in', 'get on'). A frequency count would establish a theoretical primary sense, but these words cannot be translated in isolation, and they usually have two senses. When a word has a concrete and figurative sense the concrete is usually primary (*ponctuel* is an exception); many words with conceptual senses have lost the concrete senses with which they originated. Note that in spite of purists and archaicizers, the primary sense of 'nice' remains 'pleasant'.

(b) *The secondary senses*: these are established in series of related collocations. Thus 'time' premodified by an adjective or a numeral may be an 'occasion'; in a historical context, it may be a 'period'; premodified by 'long', 'short', etc., it is 'an amount of time'; in music, it is the term used to classify basic, rhythmical patterns. Similarly *assurer*, whose primary sense is, I think, to 'provide' (e.g. electricity) has secondary senses 'to assure', 'to make stable' (collocated with a concrete noun as direct objective), 'to insure' and 'to assure' as technical insurance terms. (In conversation, 'to assure' is the primary sense.) It is often an empty verb and therefore omitted in translation (e.g. *la mairie assure une permanence le dimanche*: 'the office at the town hall is open on Sundays'.

(c) *Derived secondary senses*. These are the variations or nuances on each secondary sense. Whilst secondary senses do not overlap each other, their sets of derived senses are more or less mutually synonymous (e.g. assure, guarantee, certify, maintain).

(d) *Nonce senses*: these are the senses that occur only in one collocation: e.g. time-saver, time-ball, time-bargain, *assurer le pavillon.*

(e) *New senses*, i.e. new senses of a word. These may be called *semantic* (as opposed to *formal*) neologisms.

(f) *Hapax senses.* These are meanings that are only found in a single example or citation.

Unless the text is basically expressive (as in James Joyce), the translator must not create semantic neologisms or hapax senses without explaining them.

The second (qualitative) series basically comprises four categories of meaning: physical, figurative, technical and colloquial. More delicately, we can distinguish seven categories:

(a) *Physical or concrete.* Existing in material form, and perceptible to the senses (e.g. apple, high, throw, position (of a place)).

(b) *Conceptual or abstract.* Perceptible to the mind (e.g. height, brave, dread).

(c) *Figurative or metaphorical.* Basically, this is the transfer of a material to a conceptual sense, and therefore the transfer of (a) to (b), e.g. *sunny* smile, etc. Figurative language ranges all the way from fossilized, i.e. virtually imperceptible ('I weighed him up') and cliché to recherché, original and idiosyncratic, which it may be difficult for the translator to spot, let alone to translate. In length, it ranges from the single word, where it may also be a simile, a metonymy, a synecdoche, a personification, an eponym,* a hyperbole, etc., through the phrase or idiom (*ein Strich durch seine Rechnung, sauter aux yeux*, 'by hook or by crook'), the proverb, the parable, the fable to the allegory. Since none of these linguistic (not necessarily literary) devices immediately reflects extralinguistic reality, the translator may be compelled to change the vehicle or the scenario in order to preserve the tenor.

(d) *Technical or specialized.* Here a particular sense of a term is officially or traditionally standardized within a trade or profession. This category is distinguished because it is isolated from the webs of meanings and synonyms that often make up the physical and figurative categories of a word.

(e) *Cultural.* The special sense depends on a group reference, e.g. gay, trip, revisionist. The particular prejudicial and prejudiced cultural senses of some words have to be noted by translators.

(f) *Familiar, conversational, slang*, e.g. 'old' in 'old boy'; often only in collocations, e.g. 'son of a gun'.

(g) *Zero:* words in collocation whose meaning is virtually swallowed up, e.g. 'pay' a visit.

Single items may have their senses in (a) and (b), or (a) and (c), but not in (b) and (c). Items in (d) may also be in (a), (b) or (c). Thus *massiv* (G) is (a) 'solid', (b) 'heavy' or 'massive' (*massiver Angriff*), (d) as noun, a 'massif'. *Accident* (F) is (a) 'unevenness of ground', (b) 'chance event, often misfortune', (d) medical disorder, as in 'cardiovascular accidents'. These are a few examples from the categories.

* Formerly called 'antonomasia': e.g. *pasteurize, limoger.*

The translator sometimes makes his worst mistakes by selecting from the wrong category. It is then difficult to know whether a word is applied in its material, conceptual, figurative or technical sense, the latter not known to the translator. A *chapeau chinois* may be a 'Chinese pavilion' or a 'jingling johnnie' (d), but as a simile it is more likely to be (a) a 'coolie's hat'. Restricted meanings in (d) are clear and monosemous in one field of technology, but they often have a different meaning in another, and, of course, there may be two or three terms for it within the technology, depending on the register, that is, who is using the term. In both (b) (*ignorer,* ignore, *réaliser*, realise, *contrôler*, control) and (d) (*couple, vernier, tolérance, sujet, accident, objet trouvé, résistance*) the influence of English has to be accounted for. In the microcontext (i.e. narrow context) of: *Ce n'était pas seulement une règle à calcul, c'était aussi un nombre d'or qu'il avait à la place du coeur, nombre d'or* appears to offer a choice from (a) 'golden number', (b) 'wealth', (c) 'a magic formula', (d) 'a golden section' (a formula in fine arts (A : B B : A + B) for a perfect ratio), (c) 'an efficient tool'; only the macrocontext can decide.

Finally, concrete and figurative applications must not be confused with primary and secondary senses respectively. In numerous cases, the figurative or conceptual application of a word becomes its primary meaning (e.g. *étonner*, charm, etc.).

The third (logical) series consists of four categories of semantic application, whose normal definitions I propose to adapt slightly:

(a) *Denotation* (contextual). The direct specific meaning of a word, optimally shown ostensively (i.e. in photo or diagram or by printing) and described as far as possible in summary observable terms; the cognitive meaning. The denotation of 'Auschwitz' is 'Oswiecim'.

(b) *Intension* (extra-contextual). Property or group of properties connoted by a term which are essential to the thing named; the set of attributes belonging to anything to which a term is applied. Therefore the intension of 'Auschwitz' may be any 'small Polish provincial town', but for the translator, it depends on the function of the word in the passage. Again, the intension of 'knife' includes '(sharp) (metal) (thin) blade, handle, cutting' depending on the passage. Semic or componential analysis may be subsumed under intension, and is required when one-to-one word translation is out of the question, and the translator does not want to transliterate, since the term will mean nothing to the TL reader.

(c) *Extension* (extra-contextual). The total range over which something can be extended or extends; the class of things to which a term is applicable; the group of things denoted by a term.

'Auschwitz' has no denotative extension, but its connotative extension is 'Buchenwald, Dachau, Oranienburg, Ravensbruck, Belsen, Mauthausen, Treblinka, Belzek, Wolzek, Sachsenhausen', etc. The denotative extension of 'knife' is 'pocket, table, bread, carving, etc., knife, sword, dagger'.

(d) *Connotation* (contextual). That aspect of meaning of a particular word or word-group which is based on the feelings and moral ideas it rouses in the transmitter or receptor. It is colloquial; the meaning conveyed or suggested apart from the thing it explicitly names or describes. It is a more or less powerful implication. It may be precise, e.g. the 'filth' of 'mud', or imprecise, e.g. the 'cosiness' of 'home'. It may, in normal usage, greatly exceed or even exclude the denotation of the word, e.g. in 'Auschwitz'. The connotation of 'Auschwitz' is its primary meaning: 'mass-murder, genocide, unprecedented crime'.

A fourth possible special series of categories applies to adjectives or verbs relating to (a) objects, (b) persons, (c) concepts derived from actions, qualities and substances. Thus (a) a green vase, (b) he's green, (c) green envy; (a) *des mots truculents*, (b) *un homme truculent*; (b) *un homme détestable*; (c) *un pronostic détestable*; (b) *il tient à la liberté*; (c) *la force des peuples tient à leur jeunesse*; (a) *un vin frais*; (b) *une fille fraîche*; (c) *un accueil frais*. Thus all words can be related to people, things, or the properties derived from them.

4. Evaluative language

The translator has to detect and assess evaluative language, which expresses the SLT author's or reader's or his peer group's explicit or implicit value-judgments, not to mention the value-judgments of the prevailing SL or TL culture. Some words, such as 'good', 'fair', 'terrible', 'passable', 'excellent', 'superb', have a vague meaning until they are placed on a scale which can be derived from the writer's values or those of the group where the words' currency originates; the words may then have to be 'converted' to correspond to the value-scales of an analogous person or group in the TL culture. Other words are partly evaluative and partly informative (perceptive, stupid, pigs (police), star, judicious, etc.). German has an apparently unique series of ameliorative informative pejorative verbs: *überraschen, verblüffen (erstaunen), befremden*, but most languages have series for die, kill, man, woman, love, smell, eat, drink. A third set of words are at face value informative and obtain their evaluative aspect from the culture they derive from: e.g. democracy, bourgeois, conservative, revolutionary, communist, monarchist, revisionist, formalist, etc. If the evaluative aspect of these words is not carried over into the target language, the translator must assist his reader, possibly with a footnote, better by characterizing the translated word (proletarian ideal, revisionist subversion, narrowly conservative, etc.) to preserve the thought-content of the original. Moreover the translator may have himself to evaluate the degree of subjectivity in the evaluations made by the SL writer.

5. The scale of linguistic intensity

Language is written on a scale of intensity as well as evaluation; all words expressing actions or qualities to some extent are ranged on a cline between strength and weakness, energy and inertness. Evaluating the degree of intensity is apt to be subjective. It is difficult to translate a noun phrase such as 'mild hostility', as 'mild' is perhaps somewhere between *léger* and *modéré* and *leicht* and *mäßig*.

6. Register or socially conditioned language

The SLT author uses self-expressive language deliberately when he expresses his own views, and unconsciously, either through psycholinguistic markers or through 'register' which has become an imprecise blanket term to cover all the socially conditioned features of language. Sociolinguists such as Gumperz (1975) and Goffman (1975) have noted that in certain roles and/or situations, people speak (or phone or write—notes or texts or letters or diaries), as employers, engineers, dustmen, sons, lovers, strangers, graduates, illiterates, beggars, presidents, marxists, etc., and will have a specific verbal repertoire, expressed phonologically, syntactically and lexically, although this repertoire may often be a marginal and even insignificant part of their discourse. The main social determinants of speech or writing behaviour are, according to Goffman, age, sex, class, occupation, caste, religion, country of origin, generation, region, schooling, cultural cognitive assumptions, bilingualism, etc. ('Each year, more are reported'). They are also influenced by the mode and the occasion, both equally socially conditioned, of the speech or writing event. Their main interest to a translator is that they provide him with a certain lexical field, which at best he should assimilate by appropriate reading in the SL and TL (particularly TL) and some characteristic word 'deformations' (noted particularly in French medical literature), as well as syntactic markers (e.g. passives and noun phrases premodified by two or three nouns in electronics literature) running through the texts. If the 'register' is extremely remote from standard educated language, the translator may have to abandon his endeavour to maintain functional equivalence and produce an information translation, a kind of reported speech. The socially conditioned nature of language is particularly important in dramatic literature and in advertising. Normally, the translator should no more imitate class or regional dialect (unless they are his own) than he should antiquate his writing to translate a classic—it sounds too artificial; one false note will find him out. In advertising, the pictorial illustration may give the translator a better clue to style than the SL text.

7. Language and reference

All non-literary passages, most sentences, are partly language, partly external reality; partly sense, partly reference; partly pragmatics, partly semantics (following Peirce and Morris); partly stylistics, partly cognition. A linguistically difficult sentence may be defined as a sentence where one-to-one translation is impossible and the unit of translation is likely to be at least sentence to sentence. Assuming the informative dominates the expressive and the vocative function, and he is confident that he understands the reference perfectly, the translator can 'go to town' on the sentence: he usually jettisons the SL syntax and clarifies the lexis, frequently strengthening and simplifying its oppositional or dialectical elements: 'En matière d'arthrite les différentes thérapeutiques, loin de s'exclure l'une l'autre, ne peuvent que bénéficier de l'addition et il faut répéter à tous les échos que Royat n'exclut pas la chirurgie de bonne indication, qui, elle-même, n'exclut pas l'usage de la pharmacopée. En fait, la crénothérapie et les médications diverses sont de bonne indication. Le seul problème, pour nous chirurgiens est de savoir dans quelles conditions l'action est opportune.' In these sentences, *Royat* tallies with *crénothérapie, chirurgie* with *action, pharmacopée* with *médications*, and all three treatments are either opposed or combined under *thérapeutiques*. Once this structure is perceived, the translation of the sentence presents no problems: 'The various treatments for arthritis are not mutually exclusive: in fact the three main kinds of treatment are all the more effective when they are combined. No opportunity should be lost of emphasizing that mineral water treatment (e.g. at Royat) can be applied in conjunction with surgery, when it is strongly recommended and surgery need not preclude the use of drugs. In fact, both mineral water and various drugs have shown good results and the only problem for the surgeon is deciding under what conditions to operate.'

On the other hand, in a referentially difficult or ambiguous passage, the translator, particularly if he has no access to the author of the SL text, must play for safety, erring on the side of word for word literalness if he must, and retaining any ambiguity, which, however, he must point out in a footnote. Since he cannot guide the TL reader, he can only transfer the facts of the SL texts as neatly and wholly as possible.

8. On ambiguity

Most sentences carry a deal of lexical and grammatical ambiguity, which may be linguistic or referential; hopefully all this ambiguity will be cleared up by the micro- and the macrocontext. Where the ambiguity remains in spite of the macrocontext, the translator has to determine whether it is referential or linguistic, or between the two extremes. Thus in the sentence: 'Brusquement un malade présente une efflorescence de production pathologique', *efflorescence* is referential if it means 'rash, eruption', but linguistic if it means 'outburst' (more likely in the context of delirium, in an affected and idiosyncratic style of writing). A referential ambiguity must always be retained and pointed out, if it cannot be cleared up by an expert. A linguistic ambiguity may enrich a text as both meanings may be intended, and the translator should attempt to reproduce the ambiguity, but if he is unable to do so, he normally translates one of the meanings and lets the other go. Whilst lexical ambiguities are more common, grammatical ambiguities arise when the point of stress in a clause or when relationships between word-groups or clauses in a larger unit are not clear, i.e. one does not know 'what goes with what'.

9. Language as code and system

The translator is continuously made aware of the functional and structural nature of language, which appears to him in the common dynamic-functional simile of a game of chess and the static-structural simile of a crossword puzzle. Thus one mistranslated word may still make half-convincing nonsense of a passage since it forces valid senses (sememes) on to other words and phrases in the passage. When the word is corrected, the whole passage is switched along different lines. Here is an example, adapted from Giraudoux's *Suzanne et le Pacifique*: 'Il balançait des écorces d'oranges creuses sans les couler, il se retirait de deux mètres quand du côte de la Chine on le tirait, il semblait de toutes ses vagues ne regarder que vous seule.' 'He threw away some orange peel without putting it furtively aside, he drew quietly back two yards when he was pulled in the Chinese direction, he appeared with every fresh wave of emotion to look at you alone.'

When *il* is corrected to refer to *le Pacifique*, which is the last word in the previous sentence, this becomes: 'The ocean rocked some bits or orange peel about without letting them sink, it softly withdrew a few feet when it was pulled towards China, it appeared to look at you alone with its every wave.'

For the translator, language is a code which he is well aware he will never break, a system he cannot wholly grasp, because it is lexically infinite. All he can do is make assumptions about it, in accordance with the benefits he derives from it, depending on the yield that suits the users at the time; the assumptions, like the sense of the words, will change continuously. He is frequently faced with too little extralinguistic reality and too much linguistic ambiguity—words either too far out of their usual collocations or so frequently in them that they become meaningless cliché, fitting as loosely as yale keys in the huge locks of their context. Never was the inadequacy of language to designate extralinguistic reality shown up more clearly than in Lord Birkett's remark at the Nuremberg trials: 'All this evidence! But one picture would be worth a thousand words.'[2]

10. Varieties of interference

One touchstone of a good translator is his sensitivity to interference, which affects terminology and language, the encyclopaedia as much as it does the dictionary. There are perhaps nine aspects of interference:

(a) Collocations or lexemes with similar form in SL and TL, but different meanings.

(b) As above, but with the same meaning, and therefore to be translated 'straight' (therefore, strictly, non-interference!).

(c) SL syntactic structures inappropriately superimposed on TL.

(d) SL word order, or word phrase order, inappropriately reproduced.

(e) Interference from third language known to the translator.

(f) Primary meaning of word interfering with appropriate contextual meaning.

(g) Stylistic predilections of translator.

(h) The primary meaning of a word, interfering with an important secondary meaning, which is also not quite so close to the related word in the TL: '*Le chalutier bénéficiera de douze jours et demi de repos par mois de mer, comme son camarade du commerce*'—'his counterpart in merchant ships'. (*From Advanced Non-literary Texts*, Lécuyer and Virey.)

(i) The translator's idiolect, including his regional and social dialect.

When one is continuously aware of all these pitfalls, one is perhaps on the way to becoming a good translator. On the other hand, a good translation shows neither deliberate opposition nor subservience to interference; its language is uncontaminated by it.

11. Connotation and denotation

Continuum, scale, balance, cline, pendulum, see-saw—the translator's job finally consists of weighing one factor against another. Occasionally, he has to choose between the connotative and denotative semantic features of a lexical unit. In a recent article in *Figaro*, Bertrand de Jouvenel, the veteran diplomat, referred to *l'orme du mail* as one of the glories of France (together with the rose-window in Chartres Cathedral). The connotation for an educated middle-aged reader might be the eponymous title of Anatole France's novel; further, a kind of Hyde Park Corner, where fierce political opponents can discuss their differences. But the connotations of *mail:* peaceful, old, traditional, secluded, beautiful are more powerful. The denotation, however, is 'the elms in the public walks in certain towns'. But the rendering must be simple and uncluttered; the towns have to be abandoned; I suggest 'the elms in the old avenues'.

12. Metaphor again

When the translator is faced with a common problem, that of rendering the image of a stock SL metaphor by its sense (usually because there is no stock equivalent), he has to bear in mind that the sense normally has several semantic elements. Thus *une route riante* (cf. *des campagnes riantes*) has elements of picturesqueness, gaiety, giving pleasure, 'sunniness', and of course laughter, with the general implication that the road is set in beautiful scenery. If necessary, one could make a componential analysis, contrasting the plus or minus features of *riant* with *souriant, rayonnant, épanoui*, and any other item in this semantic field—setting (town or country), intensity, momentariness, formality and animation might be some of the dimensions—and then selecting, say, *two* features for translation: 'beautiful country road'. More likely, one would attempt a translation label such as 'scenic route' in the hope that it will stick, since *route riante* is an official term in Belgium.

We have to bear in mind that language when seen diachronically consists entirely of metaphors. Dead metaphors have lost all metaphorical sense, and are the 'normal', literal, sane, rational, logical, clear, precise, 'scientific' stock of language. As 'metaphors' they present no translation problems, and are translated literally (*penser* = think) where possible. The essence of the sense of both stock and original metaphors is that they encompass a wider range of meanings than literal language, but that they are less precise. Normally, original metaphors have a wider range of meanings than stock metaphors; they are more suggestive and, at least initially, even less precise. Thus a reporter, wanting to summarize the situation in Iran in one heading, wrote KAFKA IN IRAN. What is a translator to make of this? If Kafka is well known in the TL culture, he sighs gratefully and translates literally; otherwise, as a heading: Bureaucracy, Police State, Chaos or Misery in Iran could be considered; a third, less committed alternative would be to try another equally large and indefinite metaphor, such as Fog or Nightmare or Dostoyevsky or Darkness in Iran, or even 'Alice in a Persian Looking-glass'.*

Metaphor is the concrete expression of the ability to see resemblances or contrasted differences (which is one definition of intelligence as well as imagination), the normal sign of innovation in language as is invention in life. The translator, except when working on imaginative writing of any kind (football or financial reports as well as poetry) or attempting to enliven a dull, as well as poorly written, text where the informative function of language is prominent, is more likely to be reducing metaphors to sense than to be creating them.

13. Simile, metonymy, synecdoche

Similes are more precise, more restricted and usually less radical, less committed than metaphors, since they limit the resemblance of the 'object' and its 'image' (vehicle) to a single property ('cool as a cucumber'). Thus they are generally easier to translate than metaphor (simile is a 'weaker' method of translating a metaphor), and the main problem is cultural, i.e. does one transfer or adapt the simile—is *d'un blanc de neige* to be 'snow-white', or, in a Middle East country, 'white as egret feathers'?

Metonymy, where the name of an object is transferred to take the place of something else with which it is associated, normally requires knowledge of the TL culture. Stock English metonymies such as 'the Crown' for the Monarch, 'Shakespeare' for Shakespeare's works, 'the bed' for marriage or 'sex', 'the kettle' for water, *la cave* or 'the cellar' for wine (*on buvait la cave du comte*, but 'he keeps a good cellar') often cannot be translated word for word; institutional metonymies such as Rue de Rivoli, the Kremlin, the White House, Bonn, may or may not require explanatory expansion in the TL, depending on the knowledge of the putative typical reader; original metonymies, which are rare, since metonymies normally imply a recognized and known contiguity, adjacency or causal relationship between one object and another, are translated communicatively unless they are important. Thus an aphasiac who substitutes 'fork' for 'knife' (Jakobson, 1971) would be corrected if interpreted to a third party, but the 'similarity disorder' must be retained if reported to a doctor. Synecdoche (i.e. part for whole, species for genus, or vice versa) is treated similarly, and though its metaphorical element is often fossilized it cannot usually be translated literally. Thus 'hands' is *l'équipage, les hommes,* 'sail ho!' is *navire en vue*, 'cut-throat' is *coupe-jarret* and 'willow' becomes *batte de cricket.*

14. Idioms

If one defines idioms as phrases or word-groups whose meaning cannot be elicited from the separate meanings of each word of which they are formed (e.g. 'hard up', *être dans la dèche*, 'have on', *faire marcher*), then one first notes that these are never translated word for word; that since idioms are either colloquial or slang, it is often

* I am grateful to my colleague John Smith for this suggestion.

difficult to find a TL equivalent with the same degree of informality; and that idioms pass out of fashion rapidly, so that bilingual dictionaries are their ready victims: *tu me cours sur l'haricot*, 'You give me the willies', 'You get on my tits' (*Harrap's New Standard French and English Dictionary*). Since translators are meant to work into their 'language of habitual use' (Anthony Crane), they are not usually 'caught out' by idioms, unless they are mesmerized by their dictionaries. But many expatriate translators and teachers have a pathetic penchant for idioms, forgetting that they are often affected, pretentious, literary, archaic, confined to one social class, modish, clichified or prolix (e.g. 'by hook or by crook', 'on a shoe-string', 'grind one's axe', 'Simon-pure', 'in a pucker', 'between Scylla and Charybdis', 'between the Devil and the deep blue sea', etc.)—in fact as tiresome and unnecessary as most proverbs—and many people prefer to use literal language combined with some original metaphors. Further, 'last (but) not least' (not an idiom) is now a German, not an English phrase.

Theory of translation

15. Well written and badly written texts

The translator has to assess the quality and value of the writing in the source language text. The common translator's distinction between literary and non-literary texts, assuming that the importance of the first lies in its formal elements and of the second in its factual content, and therefore that the first must be translated closely and the second freely, is mistaken. An opposite, and equally misguided view is that a non-literary text, being scientific, must be accurately translated, whilst a literary text, being artistic, allows infinite licence in translation. It might be more profitable to regard the non-literary text as denotative, and therefore to be translated slavishly in all its surface detail, and the literary text as connotative,[3] and therefore to be translated to reveal its latent meaning, to point the allegory in the story, the moral in the action, etc., as well as its sensuous qualities (sound effects, such as metre and onomatopoeia, and visual images) if one accepts Molière's dictum that the two main functions of art are to please (the senses sensuously) and to correct (morally).

However, the basic distinction is not between literary and non-literary texts, but between good (or effective) and bad (or ineffective) writing. If a text is well written, whether it is literary or scientific, historical or technological, its formal components are of prime importance, and the translator must respect them and fully account for them in his version, not by any kind of imitation but by transposing them through deep structure ('what does this really mean?') to congruent formal components. It is as misguided to talk about the 'art' of literary translation and the 'skill' of non-literary translation as to imply that science is inferior to art. The translation of poetry is often more difficult than any other kind of translation only because poetry is the only literary form that uses all the resources of languages, and therefore there are more levels of language to be accounted for.

The translator is, however, entitled to treat the formal components of a badly written text, whether popular or technical, with considerable freedom, since by replacing clumsy with elegant syntactic structures, by removing redundant or repetitive items, by reducing the cliché and the vogue-word to a plainer statement, by clarifying the emphasis and tightening up the sentence, he is attempting to give the text's semantic content its full value. (Thus he is performing a double translation, first intra-, then interlingual.) Nevertheless, the translator is often at risk in declaring a text to be badly written. A text that is ponderous, contorted and ornate, that sins against the fraudulent canons of simplicity, clarity and brevity may indeed be well written if it expresses the author's personality without distorting his message; it is only badly written if the message is lost in the conventional received jargon which appears designed to make its own irrelevant but 'with it' impression.

16. Translation is for the reader

A translation is normally written and intended for a target language reader—even if the source language text was written for no reader at all, for nothing but its author's pleasure. The translator has to assist his reader. In plain terms, it is usually more important for him to make or indicate the sense of a passage than to funk the issue by rendering it 'correctly'. He may have to explain or transpose allusions, supply reasons, emphasize contrasts. Even if the SL text is generalized and abstracted on the analogy of non-figurative art or has what seems like surrealistic or stochastic interventions, it is his duty to make his version a little more accessible to the reader, to find at least some pattern in non-sense. Styles which are dense and intellectualized may also require assistance from the translator. A passage such as:

> 'La IVe République donnait déjà le spectacle de ces grands directeurs qui assuraient la continuité du service public tandis que passaient les ministres mais ce devait être avec le régime suivant que les experts jouiraient du lustre et de l'éclat d'un semblant de règne. Technicité accrue de problèmes déclarés plus complexes, dessaisissements et démissions du parlement, gouvernements dotés d'une espérance de vie plus longue, on distinguait de moins en moins entre ministres techniciens et hauts fonctionnaires à vocation politicienne, on jugeait qu'une bonne gestion administrative autorisait l'impasse sur la participation politique des citoyens',[4]

cannot be left as it is, and has to be helped along or tricked out, particularly when the writer's function is presumably informative rather than self-expressive, and when the translator notes that a certain construction (in this case the post-modified noun-phrase used absolutely) is a favourite quirk in the author's idiolect and, being elliptical, tends to hamper comprehension.

The more difficult the language, the more versions are feasible, and the more evidently the act of translation consists of an 'active' interpretation after a 'receptive' comprehension. The above passage might translate as follows:

'The Fourth Republic had already offered the spectacle of powerful heads of departments maintaining the continuity of the public service while ministers came and went, but it was in the regime that followed that the experts were to enjoy the show and splendour of seemingly absolute power. The increasingly technical nature of admittedly more complex problems, the enforced or voluntary surrender of power by parliament, the governments' expectation of a longer tenure—these circumstances made it more difficult to distinguish between ministers with specialist knowledge and higher civil servants acting as politicians, and it was generally held that emphasis on good management was responsible for blocking the electorate's advance to participation in politics.'

17. The naturalness of a translation

Normally, the translator should write within his own idiolect or his conception of the SL text author's, always provided the text appears to be written naturally. The translator must not use a word or phrase that sounds intuitively unnatural or artificial to him. For this reason, it is right that one person should translate *on a beau dire* as 'whatever one may say' and another should reject it and use 'say what one may'. From the point of view of the third reader, i.e. the translation critic or teacher, ten different versions of the same text may be equally acceptable. *Quot homines, tot scripta.* Unanimity over the translation of most sentences would be artificial. If a translator accepts a suggested rendering because of the authority behind it, rather than because he feels it intuitively (idiolectally) right for him, this rendering is likely to clash with the rest of his version—it will not cohere.

For me, a sentence such as 'Les coefficients respiratoires sont médiocres et ne portent guère à l'audace' translates as 'The respiratory quotients are poor and scarcely encourage radical treatment' and a sentence such as 'Tendenze ancora più estreme permettono oggi di escludere l'operatore umano anche in certe fasi di produzione complete' as 'Due to even more radical trends, the human operator is nowadays eliminated even from certain complete production stages'. Obviously, I prefer to be 'radical'.

The primary meaning (sememe) of *audace* is too emotive and of *estremo* is exaggerated to me, and I translate both words as 'radical' naturally in these situations. The word 'radical' in the above sense is a basic active constituent of my idiolect, and might be out of place in this sense in the work of nine out of ten other translators.

18. The frequency rule again

The equal frequency rule has precedence over the rule[5] that normally a translator should not translate an SL item into a TL item which would normally and naturally have another equivalent in the SL. Thus it may be legitimate to translate *perturbation* (Fr.) as 'violent disorder'; for the translator, the theoretical reason why the SL writer did not put *désordre violent* is that he, unlike the translator, had a more effective word available.

19. The importance of the truth

When extralinguistic reality is wrong in the SL text, the translator must say so. Misstatements must either be corrected or glossed. This responsibility is more important than monitoring the quality of the writing in the SL text. However, the above rule applies only where the informative function is dominant. Where the SL text is propaganda or art, the translator may have no such responsibilities.

20. The limits of synonymy

Translation is in a sense an exercise in synonymy, but that is no justification for the virtually indiscriminate and unreasonable habit of replacing accurate and obvious equivalents with synonyms, often practised by the translator to show, whether he knows it or not, that he has guarded against interference. Thus in a text with a mainly informative function, *informazioni* is 'information', not 'data', *sforzo apprezzabile* is 'appreciable effort', not 'much effort', etc., whatever they may be in a text with a persuasive function.

21. The three linguistic scales or hierarchies

Even the translator who keeps insisting that it is the thoughts not the words that count can sometimes be forced into the admission that whatever the unit of translation in a text or any part of it, it should be as small as possible. The only 'perfect' translation, after all, are of the 'dog bites man' variety. The unit of translation is likely to be smallest when the writing is creative or legal–administrative.

In persuasive writing, the unit of translation might be the paragraph for emotively written advertising, the sentence or the holophrase for public notices, the word or phrase for a legal text.

Translation is complicated by its own use of two kinds of units. The grammatical scale of morpheme, word, word phrase, clause, sentence, paragraph, is generally known. The lexical scale, which is perhaps more important in translation, has not to my knowledge been worked out. Possibly it consists of: seme (minimal element of meaning)/sememe (one meaning of a word)/lexeme (uninflected words)/collocation (transposable construction), e.g. adjectival clause, participal phrase, verb–noun phrase, reducible to deep structure autonomous (*selbständig*) theme–rheme unit contrasted theme–rheme units/complete section of text (or paragraph or topic unit). The last three units are sometimes replaced by: extended metaphor/proverb/allegory. The fact that there are two different scales, and in particular the divergence of the collocation and the word-phrase, explains why machine translation has often come to grief. (The third linguistic scale, the phonological—phoneme/syllable or tone/foot/-breath or tone group—counts only in poetry translation.)

22. Paraphrase

All rules of translation are basically negative; they attempt to reduce the error factor, they all register an inability to produce an exact translation. All translation rules are an attempt to circumvent the translator's last resort, paraphrase, which too easily becomes periphrase. Paraphrase is an extended synonym and inevitably an expansion and a diffusion of the original text. It is only justified when an item of terminology (technical institutional cultural, ecological, scientific) cannot be handled in any other way, e.g. by TL equivalent, transcription, neologism, by reproducing the 'encyclopaedic' tenor for the linguistic vehicle. A paraphrase can only draw on encyclopaedic knowledge, if it is justified at all; a linguistic paraphrase is never justified. A paraphrase runs counter to the thesis, which I broadly support, of W. Agtby, the Prorektor of Handelshojskolen at Aarhus, that the best translation is likely to be the briefest, i.e. the one nearest to the number of lexical items used in the SL text. The smallest unit of paraphrase is the synonym, and this too must only be used when the primary meaning is inappropriate. In ordinary language, I see no reason for translating *eindrucksvoll* or *impressionnant* as anything but 'impressive'.

23. Jargon

Jargon is variously defined as an idiom peculiar to a trade or profession, an occupational register of language, or an esoteric slang unintelligible to the layman. One would expect it to be rich in terms of art, neologisms, acronyms, eponyms, etc. Whilst this is often the case, another characteristic is its converse: the frequent use of general or abstract terms, viz. deverbals, deadjectivals and denominals.[6] When jargon is well used, these terms are preferred to concrete and specific terms in order purposely to cover a wider field; hence the use of 'accommodation unit' rather than 'house' or 'dwelling' which once enraged Churchill, or the use of 'mentally handicapped' rather than 'mad, lunatic', etc., which Evelyn Waugh preferred. Such jargon is not only accurate, but also, as in the latter example, useful in combating stupid prejudices by eliminating a traditionally emotive semantic feature in a term.

Where jargon is misused, these terms are unnecessary and sometimes ambiguous; they are often used for their effect and prestige value, as in advertisements (e.g. 'a new generation of Dulux', 'New Dimension furniture', 'three concepts from John Player'), being longer, more sophisticated than concrete terms, and derived from Latin or Greek.

In a mainly informative passage, the translator should get rid of unnecessary or ambiguous jargon. In the following passage: *le caractère inflammatoire de la douleur, exagérée par la moindre mobilisation et entraînant la mise au repos antalgique de l'articulation, le plus souvent en position vicieuse*, the underlined words are jargon, and the sentence could be clarified as 'As the inflammation causes pain which is aggravated by the slightest movement, the joint, which is usually in an incorrect position, has to be rested as a pain-killing measure'. Further examples of jargon in the same article are:

possibilités articulaires: 'ability to move their joints'.
possibilités fonctionnelles: 'freedom of action'.
réveil inflammatoire: 'recurrence of the inflammation'.
si l'enraidissement paraît inévitable, qu'il se fasse en position de fonction: 'if the stiffening appears inevitable, the patient should see that it happens when the joint is in use'.

The common characteristic of this and much other jargon is that it is generic. It is only its firm position in the linguistic and situational context that disambiguates it.

However, the translator is always at risk in narrowing the semantic area of jargon. If he suspects that the source text writer intended to use a large, easily adaptable and disposable phrase, he must retain it in English, even though English does not embrace such abstractions so easily. On no account must the foreign equivalent of 'accommodation unit' be translated as 'house'. In doubt, the translator must play for safety by preferring the more literal version. In fact, in as far as he practises a science that reflects etralinguistic reality he never ceases to play for safety.

Conversely, technical jargon can be removed if it is heavy and used for effect: *Dans cette conception, la bouffée délirante, entité nosgraphique, n'existe plus*, 'According to them, a delirious onset is not a distinct illness at all'.

24. Emotiveness in Romance languages

Utterance in Romance is more emotive than in Germanic languages. Thus a sentence such as '*Le lieutenant-général Bayerlein ne fut pas plus heureux que son camarade Witt*' (referring, rather hypocritically, to the casualties of their respective divisions) could be translated as 'Bayerlein had as many casualties as his colleague Witt'. Romance languages tend to personalize inanimate subjects, charge *formules de politesse* (e.g. the close of a letter) with sentiment, and exaggerate apologies such as '*je suis désolé*' as well as greetings such as '*enchanté*'.

25. The paramountcy of the equivalent-effect principle

Werner Koller[7] has rightly pointed out that the principle that the translator should produce the same effect on his own readers as the SL author produced on the original readers (first stated, I believe, by P. Cauer in 1896 and usually referred to as the principle of similar or equivalent response or effect, or, by E. A. Nida, as the principle of dynamic equivalence) is becoming generally superordinate, both in translation theory and practice, to the principles of primacy of form and primacy of content. The principle of equivalent-effect is the one basic guide-line in translation, and it is ironical that it is so little recognized by school and university teachers who either favour a 'stylistic' bias, which produces a high-flown travesty dedicated to the 'spirit of the original', or a 'content bias' ('ideas, not words') which reproduces information, shedding emphasis, expressiveness or persuasiveness, and reduces all meaning to cognitive meaning. Moreover Nida, by contrasting dynamic only with formal equivalence, thereby omitting cognitive equivalence, fails to show the range of dynamic equivalence's various foci (i.e. *Schwerpunkte*). At the same time many students, searching an illusory 'truth', favour a formal bias (i.e. dogged adherence to the SL syntax), or are content with primary meanings, usually obtained from dictionaries, and their versions are evidence of frequent interference.

However, the equivalent response principle is mentalistic and needs further definition. According to Koller, the reader referred to is 'the normal reader who has average encyclopaedic knowledge'! The definition is vague, and even if author and translator have similar readers in mind, the 'pragmatic' factors of register will affect the style of the translation. If the readership is different, the TL text will be further from the SL text, and similarity of effect correspondingly harder to achieve. (The problems are simplified when a text is written to be translated, as in some advertising and propaganda material, and the SL reader does not exist.) Koller asks many questions about the intended effect on the second reader, without supplying any answers. One assumes that if the emphasis of the text is on information, both sets of readers will be primarily interested in its content. Presumably, clarity, simplicity and orderly arrangement are the qualities required for conveying the information, and are therefore the essential elements in achieving the similar response. If, however, the text attempts in some measure to persuade or direct the reader, this affective function is likely to dominate the informative function. Where there is a nuance of suasion, encouragement, scandal, optimism, pessimism, determent, etc., the reader is likely to react more strongly to it than to the information it relates to, whether the latter is previously known or not. The essential element that must be transferred is the affective/persuasive, which takes precedence over the informative, which often basically makes the translation worth doing, which persuades the publisher to commission. Even if it can only be read between the lines (like the yes/no tendency of an important statement) it is the crucial element. It is the peculiar flavour, the *sapor*, which in speech is in the tone, not the words, which has to be conveyed.

It is, therefore, mistaken to maintain that the cognitive is the primary and the affective is the secondary element in language. Witness how in French, the indicative gives way to the subjunctive in statements of unquestioned fact that are coloured by feeling. Similarly, the connotative tends to override the denotative meaning, and metaphor is more important than the physical fact. When one has to make a choice between 'call the police'[8] or 'call the constable', the former version is likely to be more emotive, where emotiveness is required, even though the latter is a more 'accurate' (cognitively) translation.

This excitatory function, whether it appears in commands, rules, instructions, propaganda, notices, etc., has, unlike the other two functions, widely different syntactical realizations in European languages. The success of the translation with a strong excitatory function can be crudely assessed by its practical effect on the reader (e.g. did he buy the product? did he keep off the grass?) but this may not be possible. When a statement has a performative function, it is often written in formulaic language, and the effect on the first and second readers is not taken into account.

Similar response where the function is expressive is difficult to analyse, since it depends on a unique personal relationship between one originator (with the exception of folk ballads etc.) and one reader. One does not know if the reader is going to be most affected by the content (say, insight into social conditions), the ethical truth of the text, or a quality of the language, or the rhymes and rhythms. The same text may be effectively translated variously accordingly. Usually, a translation that concentrates only on the content can hardly achieve similar response, but it is useful as a stepping stone to the SL text. A translator who aims at something other than producing a similar response cannot claim to be attempting a full translation, but this does not mean that all translations should never sound like translations. Thus if the SL author deviates widely from the collocational, lexical, syntactic, metrical, prosodic, semantic norms of his own language, one would expect the TL text to do likewise, and to have the flavour of a translation. An English translation of Thomas Mann's *Dr. Faustus* (or *Krull*) should be convoluted and pedantic so that the reader should feel that Serenus Zeitblom could never have been English: nevertheless, it should still have a similar effect on him as on the German reader. Thus the main stream of translation theory, which advocates equivalent response, can be paradoxically reconciled with Walter Benjamin's[9] brilliant way-out view that translation fills in a gap in the second language, but perhaps only where masterpieces are being translated. *Nomina numina.* The more important the text, the more literal the translation.

26. The persuasive function

There is a parallel in the relationship between the text's persuasive and informative function and the translator's subjective and textual levels. The stronger the persuasive element in the text (unless it is formulaic) the more the translator is likely to stretch his imagination, to exercise his choices, unconsciously to let internal images, memories of sense-impression, records of activities imbued with feelings suffuse his language. The translator is at his most creative when he is handling the persuasive function.

27. The limits of context

Context determines meaning, but, at least in 'ordinary language', it does not determine all meaning. In the use of single words, many proper nouns can be translated out of context, in particular the names of countries, rivers and towns, though some of the latter two are duplicated in other parts of the world. The names of the months and the days of the week are usually used in their single concrete sense. Many technical and scientific terms, particularly if they are compounds in origin (e.g. telephone), can be translated 'straight': nylon, oxygen, aluminium. But no other category of single word apart from the above is translatable without reference to context. However, a vast number of compounds (railway station, *Arbeitnehmer, classe témoin*) are monosemous, and the ratio increases the larger the lexical unit. A translator is not *always* justified in demanding to inspect the micro- or macrocontext before he translates.

28. The degree of choice

How much choice has a translator? The question may be approached through a number of generalizations:

The greater the difference in grammar and lexis between the SL and TL languages, the greater the degree of choice.

The stronger the cognitive or representational function, and therefore the weaker the pragmatic function in the SL text, the lesser the degree of choice.

The better one understands the linguistic meaning of a text, the less choice the translator has in formulating his words; but, the more difficult the linguistic meaning, the more variations are likely to be available.

The better the translator understands the referential meaning, the more easily he can 'transfer' it to language and the larger number of linguistic variations he can use. Correspondingly, the more obscure the referential meaning, the more the translator has to 'cling' to the SL words.

In theory, there should be less choice in the translation of objects, qualities and processes or actions than of mental concepts. However, the notorious gaps in language failing to name or distinguish between generic and specific terms and cutting up colours in various ways have been frequently noted. Theoretically, all physical phenomena should be translatable accurately, as they are concrete and in the sensible world, whilst mental concepts should be untranslatable, as they are ideal and peculiar to one individual. In fact, as the physical is only grasped through the mental, this theory is only applicable in the most general terms.

I now reverse the perspective and consider the question practically. A translator should have no choice in translating technical and institutional terms where the correspondence has been standardized either officially or by usage. As soon as a term of art has been recorded by an association such as the British Standards Institution (BSI), the *Association française de Normalisation* (AFNOR), the *Deutscher Normenausschuss* (DNA) and the American Standards Association (ASA), or in any glossary of repute, a translator merely causes harm and confusion by using any term but the one generally accepted. Further, one has no options when one translates the great majority of common objects and the majority, but not so large a one, of actions, processes and qualities, grammatical words and common collocations.

29. When to translate words and not ideas

Normally, one translates ideas, on which the words act as constraints. If ever one is permitted to translate words, not ideas, it is when the reference in non-literary translation or the sense (*Sinn*) in literary translation is still obscure after all aids have been consulted in vain. Anthony Crane[10] has pointed out the exceptional verbal correspondence in Samuel Beckett's own translation into English of his novel *Comme c'était*, where obscure language is precisely translated, as though it were denotative. In normal literary translation, however, the emphasis is on connotation, not denotation.

It is commonly stated that one should translate ideas not words. The concept is mentalistic, and relates two different orders of things, but it is useful as a warning against taking the SL words as their face value, against translating from and/or into the primary meanings of words. To be accurate, one translates words that are used in context, that is, words that are lexically conditioned and constrained by collocation and connotation, grammatically by syntax, intonationally by word-order, sometimes phonetically by assonance, alliteration, onomatopoeia, and moreover they are normally referentially bound; one does not normally translate words in isolation, or assume they are being used in their primary sense, unless they appear randomly. In imaginative writing, words are usually referentially bound, even though the reference may have symbolical value only (e.g. 'red' symbolizing 'blood', or 'death' in Wilfred Owen's poems); non-literary writing is always referentially bound, and in a grammatically and collocationally acceptable sentence such as 'The King of France is wise' (the ordinary language philosopher's delight) the translator makes no difference between such a fancy and the equivalent fact, but may have to add a footnote to explain that the king does not exist. Again, when a translator finds a misprint or a neologism that is referentially clear and indisputable ('La sueur est sécrétée par les glandes écaines,' eccrine glands), he has to note that *écaine* is not usually found.

30. Reference

For the translator, *Bedeutung* (reference) has two interlocked faces: (1) the mental, which imaginatively and intellectually apprehends the extralinguistic reality, or, in the case of concepts where there is no such reality, some kind of symbolical equivalent, (2) the linguistic, which is the simplest and clearest possible reduction (paraphrase or précis) of the *Sinn* (sense) of the text. Thus in a newspaper report, the reference of 'the girl in the red dress' might be 'Mary Reddaway', whilst in a story it might be a symbol of beauty, or mystery, and so on. The sense denotes or defines the reference, it is the linguistic structure built over it. Reference is as close to the basic extralinguistic reality as the translator can get; it sticks to the bare fact, where sense is allusive or descriptive. Reference has 'meaning in isolation' (Russell). What we say or write is sense, what we point to or name is reference. The translator frequently transfers from sense to reference (the neutral element), from the domain of the dictionary to that of the encyclopaedia, before returning to the sense in the target language. He must know who 'the girl in the red dress' is before translating.

31. Art or science

In the most general theory, the translation of language relating to animate and inanimate objects, appearances and processes in the visible world should be a science, since the referents are more or less measurable, whilst the translation of language relating to concepts or colouring physical phenomena affectively, not being measurable, should be an art. This broad theory, like the behaviourism on which it is based, has a restricted truth, but breaks down repeatedly. It fails to take into account that most words, whether they name physical phenomena or not, have an affective colouring, whilst many concepts, such as life and death, are more concrete than objects; the reality is only experienced through the mind.

Looking at the question more realistically, one could distinguish art and science in translation with more assurance by positing that translation is a science where there is one correct or one objectively superior rendering of a word, phrase, clause, etc., and an art where there are more than one equally (or less than) adequate rendering. Translation is therefore demonstrably a science when one is handling terms of art that have an accepted equivalent and terms where one has to find the nearest possible equivalent; thus a term such as *Mottenfrassnekrose* cannot to my knowledge be found in a reference book, but the search for an equivalent (mottled or focal or piecemeal necrosis?) is scientific, since one is dealing with a demonstrable fact, although the German author uses an imaginative and unusual metaphor. In general, accepted equivalents are sacred, and everything else is free (within a narrow cone of choice) to the translator. Stylistics, cultural and pragmatic colouring, all equivalents that are not standardized or generally accepted—all this comes within the scope of the art of translation, provided that scientific methods are used to eliminate all other possibilities before the moment of choice arrives. It may, however, not be possible to weigh scientifically the merits of connotation against denotation, emphasis against lexical accuracy, over- against undertranslation. Diagrammatically, the science of translation (viz. the translation of terms of art) may be as shown as follows:

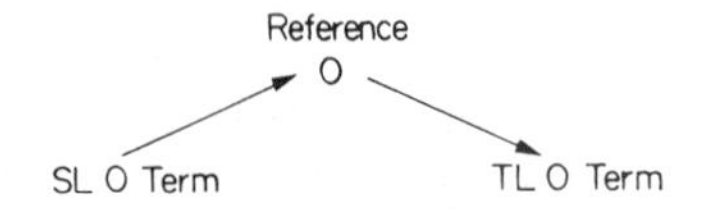

There is one obligatory transfer from SL term through common reference to TL term, and not necessarily any direct connection between SL and TL sense (e.g. loom—*métier—Webstuhl—telaio*).

The art of translation (viz. the translation of 'language'), all non-standardized lexical units and (structures) is shown as follows:

The basic artistic process is the selection between almost equally good variants; this is an exercise in stylistics requiring the translator's taste, wit and elegance; his *Vorstellung* and idiolect are powerfully at work. Reference is no longer required as a guide-line.

Needless to say, this artistic process is only the final stage in translating non-standardized lexical units and grammatical structures. The basic process is again scientific, the translator by a continuous process of hypothesis and verification through reference eliminates all inaccurate variants and reduces valid variants to the lowest possible number:

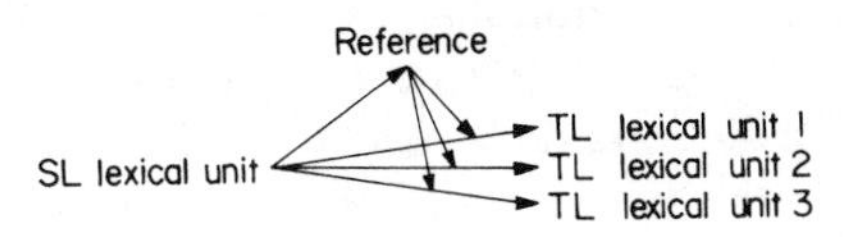

32. Literal translation

If a word for word, primary for primary meaning translation has functional equivalence, any other translation is wrong. No translation is ever too literal or too close to the original—the criteria are irrelevant. 'Er liebt seine Mutter' can only be translated as, 'He loves his mother'. (Such correspondences are rare and usually only found in *langue*-type sentences in more or less old-fashioned modern language course textbooks rather than in the *parole* of ordinary language. Thus sentences such as 'The cat lies on the mat' or 'Das Mädchen liebt seine Mutter' are unacceptable as *parole*, where 'lies' is replaced by 'is lying' and *Das Mädchen* by a proper name or pronoun.)

Provided functional equivalence is preserved, any syntactic structure both smaller and larger than the sentence should be transferred in order, together with the order of its word components. The better written the sentence, the more important the rule becomes. 'The proper words in the proper places' (Swift) must correspond in the SL and TL texts. I see no reason for translating Paul Claudel's, *De là, l'attrait curieux qu'ont pour nous les petits tableaux hollandais*,[11] otherwise than by: 'Hence the curious attraction that small Dutch pictures have for us.' Anything else is 'wrong', unless perhaps the word 'hence' does not come naturally to the translator, and he is forced to use 'This shows' or 'This is' instead. Any attempt to translate *attrait curieux* as 'peculiar charm', 'strange fascination' etc. (both English collocations would turn out differently in retranslation), arising from the bad old school and university instruction 'Always use a "different", i.e. non-cognate word', is not acceptable.

In the wider sense, all translations must be as 'literal', i.e. as close to the original as possible. In the narrower 'word for word' sense, literal translation is only useful as a preliminary technique for discovering an acceptable translation.

33. The translator's idiolect

From his idiolect, the language of his habitual use, with its personal peculiarities of grammar, lexis and word-order, the translator creates his linguistic reproduction (*Abbild*) of a situation he sees through the SL text. His idiolect at once incidentally expresses his own style and character and regulates the naturalness of his translation, ensuring that it is modern and full. The effectiveness of the version is finally dependent on the elegance and sensitivity of the translator's command of a rich language.

34. Variance

When a passage in the SL text goes beyond the stage of abstraction that is normally acceptable in the TL, and is not expressive (or 'espressionistic' in Herbert Read's sense of 'expressing subjective emotional experiences')[12] the translator inevitably changes the syntax and minimally the lexical content of the original 'La continuità della viabilità ordinaria è assicurata da 94 sottovia e 21 cavalcavia' ('Traffic normally runs uninterruptedly over the whole motorway, which has 94 underpasses and 21 flyovers').

In the above translation, the link between 'uninterruptedly' and 'underpasses' has been weakened. If the sentence were given to twenty competent translators, it is unlikely that the same version would come up twice.

The more difficult a sentence is linguistically, in its 'sense' rather than its 'reference', and the further it is removed from its deep structures, the greater the number of translations will be acceptable. The difficulty may lie in the obscurity, the complexity or the degree of abstraction of the thought in the sentence. The greatest spectrum of variance in translation lies in the communicative, which is also the stylistic element.

Since language systems differ phonologically, grammatically and lexically (although the degree of difference varies from language to language), translation is an unnatural, artificial and artistic activity, always in varying degrees. Even the declared invariance of terms of art is usually artificially standardized, and represents a referential not a linguistic equivalence.

From a mentalist-idealistic point of view which takes universals as a basis of thought and language, variance in translation will be more conspicuous in the grammar than in the lexis, and in the vocative and to a lesser degree, the expressive (in the clash between the SL writer's self-expression and the translator's) aspect of the text rather than the informative. The more remote a surface structure in a SL text is from its deep structure, the more differently it is likely to reappear in the TL text. In fact, even the basic structure, animate subject–animate verb–inanimate direct object, may have to change in a translation, although it is the construction least likely to change.

Lexically, the words most subject to variance are those expressing nuances of feeling and quality (basically adjectives and their derivatives in other parts of speech) that are mentally perceived. Sociocultural differences apart, the greatest divergences are often in texts describing subjective states, where a language has some of its rarer and most esoteric words. (Within each register of a language, the least frequently used words are likely to be the hardest to translate.) Thus Roget's category on Dejection has an enormous stock of words (many admittedly obsolescent) very few of which have obvious French or German equivalents.

35. The 'socio-cultural' parole

Neubert has referred to the linguistic, situational and sociocultural aspect of translation. Presumably he excludes the subject element *Vorstellung*, since he regards translation as a science. In my opinion, when the sociocultural aspect is thus introduced it becomes the substantive element in the translator's work, the *parole* (Frege's *Sinn*, J. R. Firth's '*text*') with which he is primarily concerned, and which may be 'reduced' on the one hand to *langue* (and then to 'deep structure') and on the other to 'situation' (reference).

Thus as I interpret Neubert, most portions of a text can be reduced to two basic parallel interpretations which may be of assistance to the translator, although he does not adopt them: the Morning Star is 'the star (that) shines in the morning' as well as 'Venus'. Thus a subsidiary extension could be made to my translation schema:

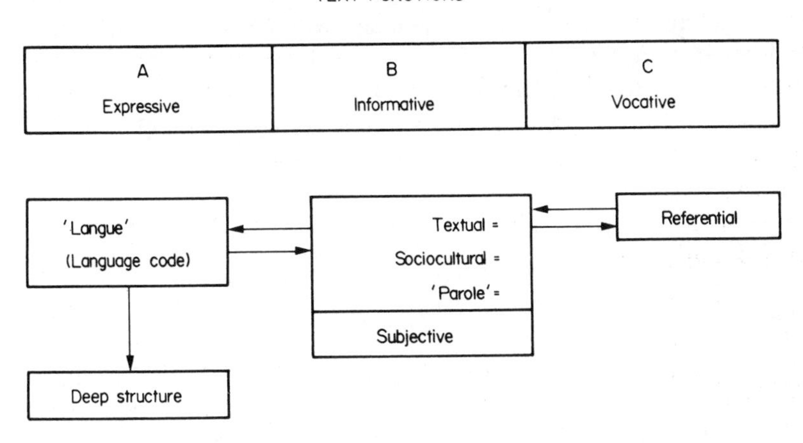

36. Terms of art again

My definition of 'terms of art' is slightly widened to include all lexical items that have a specialized use in a situation connected with a scientific, artistic or technological process or with a professional activity of any kind; it includes all jargon. Terms of art must be translated by the appropriate term in the TL provided they are used as terms of art. If however they are used figuratively, or in a more general way (many terms of art, e.g. 'input', 'know-how', etc., pass quickly into ordinary language) they become non-standardized language, and may be variously translated, e.g. 'La psychiatrie a *secreté* une antipsychiatrie, la gynécologie une antigynécologie dont les sources sociopolitiques ont *la même nappe phréatique*' ('produced . . . the same underlying causes'); 'Les aides publiques n'ont pas un caractère *exorbitant du droit commun*' ('are not at variance with the law').

37. The occasion for a translation

Neubert (1968) has slightly confused occasions with methods of translation. One and the same text, whatever its original purpose, may be translated (a) with its original purpose retained, i.e. as self-expression or to inform, persuade or direct the target-language reader; (b) to explain itself to the target reader; (c) for a new group of readers, laymen, children, opponents, special audiences for a particular occasion, etc.; (d) a generation or more later; (e) to illustrate the mechanics of the SL. For each of these occasions, the text will be translated differently and the intention of the original must still be elucidated.

38. Unit of translation

The concept 'unit of translation' (UT) normally refers to the source-language unit which can be recreated in the target language without addition of other meaning elements from the source language. Ideally, the UT is one word, hence 'literal' is often equated with the truth. However, as a concept the UT hardly assists the translator, since as soon as he meets any difficulty he is expanding it, or, if he begins by translating ideas rather than words, he continuously contracts it.

39. Ideal translation

'Translating a poem, if its creator is a craftsman, is like rescoring a piece of music for a different set of instruments or a different kind of musical ensemble' (Smith, 1978). Does this underrate the difficulties? A translation can no more be definitive than the interpretation of a piece of music, or a solo performance in an orchestral work. The concept of the 'ideal translation' (Jäger, 1975) is unreal. Translation is an 'endless' procedure, except in the case of 'performative' statements. Other translations can never be finished, only laid aside. They can always be improved. And, for any linguistically difficult passage, there are often several equally good (if in some respect inadequate) solutions. Moreover, since it is assumed that the TL reader is alive, a translation is written in the modern language, and therefore there is a case for revising it every 30 years. Whilst the canons of Classical (therefore 'ideal') art may govern some translations, others are as close to Romantic or Surrealist intuitions as their originals.

40. Aesthetic function

The poetic or aesthetic function is centred in the sound effect of language, including metre, repetition and euphony. Where it is the dominant function the sense becomes irrelevant; the translator will therefore ignore the sense, as in examples and catch-phrases for phonetics ('the rain in Spain') or in translating some of Christian Morgenstern's poems.

At other times, the function is combined with the expressive and informational functions, as in Jakobson's (1960) example *l'affreux Alfred*, where 'frightful Alfred' would be superior to 'odious Alfred' as a translation purely for reasons of equivalent sound effect.

The aesthetic function is essential in poetry whether it is combined with the expressive function (lyrical poetry of the first person), the informative (narrative poetry of the third person), or the vocative or transactional (dramatic poetry of the second person). In cases where the poetic function plays a minor part, the translator may have to ignore it. As it is centred in the SL, loss of meaning is usually considerable! Any translation of a phrase such as 'I like Ike' will require ingenuity, but it would normally be transferred.

41. The central concern of translation theory

The central concern of translation theory is to determine an appropriate method of translation.

42. Own language mastery comes first

A translator has to know his own language, his subject and the target language—in that order. Excellence in the first requirement often saves him from hideous mistakes in the second and the third.

43. Pendulum swing in translation style

Fifty years ago, translations were mainly too stiff and bogus-literary (see Knox, 1957). Now, translations are mainly too colloquial and too emotive.

44. The expanding process

As with translation problems so with the translation. A translator may start with the standard 'micro'-procedures: transcriptions, literal translations, translation labels, loan-translations, transpositions, modulations (see Vinay and Darbelnet, 1976), componential analyses (to fill in lexical gaps), etc., processes subject first to syntactical constraints and lexical systems. But then as he reviews the sentences, the paragraph and the text, and becomes less word-bound, clause-bound, sentence-bound, even thought-bound, he closes always more narrowly on his intention, which is either to realize the meaning of the author or to produce precisely the required effect on the reader. Note that here communicative and semantic translation coincide. Even in Gouadec's (1974) illustration: 'The calm supreme assurance of her eyes finally repelled his fear', 'La profonde sérénité de son regard finit par chasser ses craintes'—a clichified translation of a clichified sentence by H. E. Bates—some evidence of this eccentric, centrifugal movement away from *finit par* (syntactic constraint—*servitude*) towards *sérénité* (calm assurance) and *craintes*, both optional, both contextually indicated, can be seen. Thus finally, with a few 'strokes', the translator may go beyond all the findings of contrastive linguistics, the *Sprachenpaar*. Starting with the word, he may move through the 'ranks' (Halliday, 1961) of the grammatical units to the final level of discourse or rhetoric, the 'personal use made by the writer of the opportunities offered him by a language-system' (Gouadec, 1974).

45. The right true end of translation

The most exciting kind of translation is where it is consciously interpretation, hermeneutics, exegesis. Where the text is obscure, and so remote in time and space and learning that the language goes beyond metaphor to symbolism, the translator has to interpret substantially, unless he is to leave the task to his readers. In a case such as Confucius' 'Within the four seas, all men are brothers' (Wright, 1976), the text requires both historical and intuitive interpretation. One does not know what the 'four seas' are, the social status of 'men' (gentlemen?) nor the precise metaphorical value of 'brothers'. The same criticism has been made of Pericles, whose democracy probably consisted of 'pure' Athenians only and excluded slaves and Spartans.

Further, the comments of some sinologists lead one to think that Chinese communists' literal and physical interpretation of Marxism on a personal as well as political level ('self-cultivation') may have contributed to the reorientation that has become so opposed to Soviet bureaucratism (the idea, not the bureaucracy).

The responsibility of translators for interpretations of the books that have influenced world history, and have often constituted the foundation of intellectual hegemony in various cultures, has been great and usually neither acknowledged nor examined. Translation theory may now help to make them conscious of his responsibility.

Lévi-Strauss (1974) maintains that poetry and myth are at opposite ends of translation; poetry can only be translated with many kinds of distortions, whereas the value of the myth persists even in the worst translation. The substance of myth is neither in the style nor the manner of narration nor the syntax, but in the story (*l'histoire*); myth is language (*langage*) but language working at a very high level, above the linguistic basis it started from (like a plane taking off from its runway). There is a rough truth here. Poetry is subject to distortions, not always as many as Lévi-Strauss suggests. If myth can be seen only as action, or behaviour (*histoire*), then it is less at the translator's mercy than a descriptive text. If myths are universal, partly independent of period and place, they should be less liable to misinterpretation after their initial translation. However, Lévi-Strauss appears to put myths beyond language (while denying it), and even the degree of literalness or figurativeness of elements of myth may have to be at least partly assessed by linguistic analysis, viz. translation.

46. The indeterminacy of translation

In principle, translation can convey facts (starting from proper names, figures, cyphers and physical objects), orders, instructions, questions and 'messages' perfectly. Its rendering of descriptions, feelings, mental attitudes is usually imperfect. But even this is assuming that we are dealing with explicit, non-ambiguous even if polysemous SL texts.

In the sentence 'The cat sat on the mat', the word 'mat' is semantically underdetermined for translation purposes into several foreign languages, although in English it may be perfectly adequate, depending on its intention and its context. Similarly in the title of an article *La folie des médicaments, la folie* as 'craze' or 'folly' would make equally good sense, and the word is again insufficiently determined. In general, the farther a word is from the centre of the SL situational or linguistic context (perhaps in parenthesis, as an item in an uncoordinated list, as part of a title), the less semantically determined it is and the more the translator then has to 'interpret', on the basis either of the probability of the situation described or of his understanding of the SL author's intention or outlook.

The preceding paragraph represents my attempt to make sense out of at any rate part of Quine's notorious contributions to translation theory (1959, 1960). Quine makes several points in favour of the 'indeterminacy' of translation; he suggests that at least 'radical' translation into an unscripted language is impossible, while translation between culturally-close languages such as Frisian or Hungarian into English is mere 'intracultural verbalism' rather than translation.

But on the main issue, the gap between inadequate analytical hypotheses on which the translation of sentences depends, he is pathetically short of examples—'gavagai' and 'neutrinos lack mass' have become famous through their singularity.

Quine conceals his scepticism about translation with a certain wit and urbanity.

When he states that 'For translation theory, banal messages are the breath of life', he is warning the translator to be suspicious of the absurd and the exotic. In a few contexts, this is salutary; it is the security that rests in the translator's cliché. Again, Quine's reference to 'free-floating, linguistically neutral meaning' (a hint of decentred or logical or deep structure) suggests that inside the (world-famous) philosopher, there is some kind of a translation-theorist. But again, when he states that 'we' can, but 'the native' cannot, capture this meaning, it is not surprising that this behaviourist and slave to the Whorfian hypothesis despairs of translation.

I must stress that the reason why it is not possible to translate 'the cat sat on the mat' adequately into, say, French or German (apart from the formal aspect of the sentence, the rhymes and the monosyllables) is not because of the 'indeterminacy' of translation as such, but because of the lack of specific information in the English sentence, or generic terms in the foreign language. If the missing information is supplied, the translation in Quine's sense at least will be adequate, and there should be the correspondence in truth-values between the SL and TL text, which, he claims, is so often missing.

However, where the SL text is ambiguous or vague (see Kempson, 1977) in four respects:

(1) *reference*, e.g. for 'hall'—is it a *salle* or a *vestibule*?;
(2) *sense*, e.g. 'his book'—the text fails to specify the relation between 'his' and 'book' (*qu'il a écrit, qu'il a acheté*?);
(3) *lack of lexical specification*, e.g. 'neighbour'—male or female?; 'go'—on foot, by train, by plane?; etc., or
(4) *disjunction*—with two equally possible interpretative possibilities (e.g. 'the applicants had either a degree or teaching experience'),

the translator has to guess or interpret, and assess his degree of accuracy in an appended statement.

Quine on the other hand is questioning not so much the determinacy as the possibility of translation on all occasions except where the SL text is 'physically' stimulated, a thesis which has been refuted by Dummett (1978) in a more convincing argument than any I could put forward.

47. The translation processes

There are three basic translation processes:

(a) the interpretation and analysis of the SL text;
(b) the translation procedures, which may be direct, or on the basis of SL and TL corresponding syntactic structures, or through an underlying logical 'interlanguage' (the *tertium comparationis*);
(c) the reformulation of the text in relation to the writer's intention, the readers' expectation, the appropriate norms of the TL, etc.

The processes are to a small degree paralleled by translation as a science, a skill and an art.

Techniques

48. Equivalent frequency of usage

The principle of equivalent frequency of usage in source and target language applied to grammatical structures and lexis is particularly useful as an additional method of verifying a translation. Thus to translate 'he baked' as *er buk* would be out of time and out of place (only a pedant would use the German phrase), and to translate 'Ich habe keine Ahnung' as 'I have no premonition' would give *Ahnung* too much particularity. Both translations violate the general principles of equal generality, formality and affectivity, as well as equivalent frequency of usage. Whilst semantic equivalence is the only basic principle of translation, it can only exist if there is the maximum equivalence of form and frequency in usage.

49. Words outside their normal contexts

A word that is divorced from all its usual collocations and appears to be being used entirely out of context should be presumed to be applied in its most common or primary sense; in particular, if it is used as an item in a list of objects, or as an illustration. Thus in Aragon's *Les lilas et les roses, délirants* must be 'delirious' in *Aux vélos délirants aux canons ironiques*. Again, in the sentence 'Médecin-alibi, médecin-ôtage, médecin-fétiche, c'est ce que recherchent parfois nombre de parents aux prises avec un enfant difficile', *ôtage*, being out of context, must be applied in its primary sense of 'hostage'. ('Many parents struggling with a difficult child want to use their doctors as an alibi, a hostage or a fetish.')

When a word has one main physical and one main figurative meaning, the physical or emotional nature of its collocate, however unusual, will give a clue to the sense intended. 'Green ideas' are not likely to have any colour, but to be unformed, if I may interpret Chomsky's notorious 'Colourless green ideas sleep furiously' in a way that was not intended.

50. The back-translation test

A source language word should not be translated into a target language word which has another obvious one-to-one equivalent in the source language. Usually, *geschmeidig* should not be translated as 'soft' because 'soft' is *weich*. Well established collocations (*weich sitzen* = 'sit comfortably') are the exception to this rule.

To translate *avec mesure* in 'Il dit avec mesure les choses les plus fortes', it may be advisable to split *mesure* into its semantic components as 'with measured restraint', as 'moderation' would be *modération,* 'restraint' *retenne*, 'reserve' *réserve*, etc. The third reader, i.e. the translation critic, is always entitled to reject any part of a translation that he considers to be too free, however elegant, if he himself can turn it back closely and elegantly into the source language, and show a substantial discrepancy with the original text.

There may be reasons for not splitting a word into its semantic components when translating. In 'Il n'a pas le sens de la mesure', any collocation to translate *mesure* would be clumsy, and the rhythm of the sentence requires a one-to-one equivalence such as 'he has no sense of restraint'. However, the back-translation test, though useful, is never decisive.

51. Translating as interlanguage

Where the target language has a number of synonyms to express the sense of a source language word, the translator should choose the word he considers stylistically most fitting (congruent, *adéquat*) rather than the word that most obviously translates the source language word. Thus in the sentence, 'Le cueillette était achevée,' *achevée* may be translated as 'over' since French has no particular other word to render 'over', although *achevée* might more obviously be translated as 'ended', 'concluded', 'finished', 'completed', etc. It is the hallmark of a good translation to use resources of lexis and grammar (e.g. English verb-nouns, German *Formwörter* like *auch, halt, eben, mal*) which are not available in the source language, and it is the mark of a specious, inaccurate translation to use them where they are unnecessary. A bad translator will do anything to avoid translating word for word; a good translator abandons a literal version only when it is plainly inexact. The unit of translation cannot be generally determined, but it is always the smallest segment of the original which provides an acceptable equivalent to a segment of the target language text. Nevertheless, a translation frequently operates in the lexical and grammatical interstices of the source language.

52. National characteristics?

Certain conceptual terms in each language notoriously remain untranslated: 'standing', 'fairness', 'humour', *sympathique, Gemütlichkeit, mañana, esprit, démarche*, etc. When they are likely to be understood by the receptor and are generally accepted, they can remain, but it is no business of the translator to add to their number: probably, certainly if one accepts the universality of the human spirit, they are all evidence of some translator's incompetence.

53. Stress and meaning

Where the translator has a problem involving a clash between stress (indicated in the word order) and lexical accuracy, he normally prefers lexical accuracy. But the stress can always be preserved if a non-animate subject governs an animate verb (which is deleted), e.g. 'Sa santé ne lui permet aucun excès', 'Owing to his health he must not overstrain himself', or if an active verb can be converted into a passive, with the same lexical meaning: e.g. '*A l'optimisme d'O'Connor correspondait le pessimisme de Rommel*',[13] 'O'Connor's optimism was matched by Rommel's pessimism'.

54. When and when not to repeat a word

A lexical item repeated in the same or the following sentence of the source language text must be correspondingly repeated in the target language text, unless the original is poorly or loosely written. It should not be rendered the second time by a synonym or a 'kenning' (periphrastic expression used to replace a simple name). Thus in the sentence, 'Die tragende Grundlage der kommunalen Selbstverwaltung ist die intensive Mitwirkung der Bürgerschaft und der von den Bürgern gewählten Gemeindevertreter an den Geschicken der Gemeinde', *Gemeinde* must be referred to twice, perhaps as, 'The essential basis of local self-government is intimate co-operation in the life of the *Gemeinde*, the unit of local government, between the citizens and its representatives, who are elected by the citizens.'

Conversely the translator is entitled to replace referential synonyms ('the Iron Duke', 'the Iron Chancellor', *le vainqueur de Sidi-Barrani, le galant commandant de l'Afrika-korps*, etc.) by proper names, if the information given is superfluous and the writing is undistinguished; much other writing is filled with less obtrusive redundancies and synonyms, not to mention passages where species and genera stand in haphazardly for each other in a pseudo-elegant attempt to avoid repetition (or, at best, undue emphasis), and it is up to the translator to detect these.

55. Cultural allusions in non-'expressive' texts

A translator should not reproduce allusions, in particular if they are peculiar to the source language culture, which his readers are unlikely to understand. If the allusions are peripheral to the text, they should be omitted. For example, in a popular history of the Second World War, describing Rommel, 'Il n'avait rien de ces manches à sabre que raillait Stendhal, et tel ce héros de Plutarque, avait appris à coudre la peau du renard à la toison du lion',[14] might be translated as 'He was no trigger-happy brute, and had learned to combine cunning with strength'.

56. Alternative terms

When a source language text has alternative terms for an object, and the target language only one term, the translator normally uses the one term only. If, however, one of the two source language terms has a special interest, being technical, archaic or particularly 'transparent' in its descriptiveness, the translator should take some account of it, usually by reproducing it, in brackets in the text, or in the notes with an explanation. For example: 'Dürers Festigungskunde umfasst "Meinungen", d.h. technische Methoden, eine Bastei (Schütte) zu bauen und den Plan eines Sperrforts (Klause) zu entwerfen.'[15] The text makes further references to *Schütten* and *Klausen*, alternating them with *Basteien* and *Sperrforte* respectively.

The translator may disregard *Meinungen*, which is quoted from Dürer's 'Treatise on fortifications', but to be helpful to his reader, supposedly an informed student of Dürer, he should perhaps put *Schütte* in brackets after 'bastion' and *Klause* in brackets after 'blockhouse' to translate *Bastei* and *Sperrfort* respectively, also explaining the archaisms in a note.

57. Titles

A title is best left untranslated until the rest of the assignment is completed. Informative or figurative titles can then be checked against the sum of the content. Even a plain title such as *La prévention: de l'école au lieu de travail* may then be better adjusted as 'Preventive medicine at school and work'. English titles tend to be shorter than others.

58. Almost empty words

Most languages have some lexical and grammatical features of low semantic content which may have no equivalents in the target language; there is often no need for the translator to take account of them. Thus French has *expressions charnières* such as *toutefois, or, quoi qu'il en soit, néanmoins*; *incises* such as *concluait-il*, and the *étoffement* of the verb (e.g. *dresser un plan*). German has its *Füllwörter* or *Flickwörter* (*doch, eben, ja, wohl*, etc.) and *konnte*. English has 'can' plus the verbs of the senses, and its unique 'operating' verbs (do, have, put, go, get, come, keep, let, make, take, be, etc.), the brilliant discovery in C. K. Ogden's *Basic English*.

59. Quotations

When a quotation from another source (speech, book, etc.) is included in the source language text, it should normally be rendered more literally than the rest of the text. The translator is not responsible for its 'functional equivalence', since it is not addressed to the reader of the target language text. It is its own 'authority', and the translator must take no liberties with its formal elements. The translation should be easily identified when compared with the original quotation; possibly the greater the authority, the closer the translation.

60. The text and the notes

If one is translating important information which is likely to puzzle the proposed reader, it is better to write the background into the text to make it meaningful rather than as a note. The translator assumes that the first reader is better informed than the second and the information succinct enough to be inserted unobtrusively.

Thus in a popular history of the Second World War, the name 'Mihailovich' is likely to mean nothing to the reader in 1979. It could perhaps be expanded to 'General Milhailovich, the Yugoslav royalist partisan leader'. Another translator might substitute 'fascist' for 'royalist partisan', but this would be emotive and confusing except in some marxist groups. Again 'resistance' might be better understood than 'partisan'. The text should be self-sufficient. Notes should contain only variants and corrections. Fröland (1975) has pointed out that this recommendation can be abused by the translator, as can any by anyone. I am here mainly referring to non-specialized literature. Notes and glossaries are essential (preferably at the end of the book rather than at the end of the chapter or at the bottom of the page), if they are in the original.

61. The possible redundancy of SL metalanguage

It is easy enough, when one is working mainly on the level of reference, of the material world, of terminology and its standard collocations, to forget that language and its ambiguities are involved at all, to translate almost one-to-one straightforward sentences such as, 'Insuline, électrochoc, neuroleptiques ont successivement guéri les bouffées délirantes, et cela d'autant plus facilement qu'elles sont spontanément curables par définition,' without noticing that if *bouffée* is (correctly) translated as 'outburst' or 'attack', the phrase *par définition* becomes redundant in English, as the metaphor is not transferred.

62. Third language proper nouns

When the SL text mentions a non-SL surname, the translator should always check it. *Le réaction exogène de Bonhoefer* (*sic*) reads suspiciously. The reference is to Bonhoeffer, the eminent psychiatrist, the father of the hero Dietrich.

63. Deletion

Theoretically, the translator has to account for every portion and aspect of cognitive and pragmatic sense in the SL text. In fact, he is justified in pruning or eliminating redundancy in poorly written informational texts, in particular jargon, provided it is not used for emphasis. He may sometimes reduce a 'filler' verb (e.g. do, take, pay, effect, etc.) plus its deverbal noun to its basic verb, where the difference in meaning is inappreciable; 'La décomposition de ces matières organiques se fait sous l'action des bactéries saprophytes'; 'Such organic matter may be decomposed by saprophytic bacteria'. Obviously this is subeditor's work which is often done within one language. Moreover there are other stock constructions (adjectival clauses and past participles where the verb is semantically weak) where the verb can again be deleted in translation (*La maison située sur la colline, la maison qui se dresse sur la colline, la plaine s'étendant devant nous, un crayon destiné à son usage*, etc.). Lastly, it is sometimes necessary to delete the enclitics (*Flickwörter*) used as connecting words to mark continuation or slight contrast at the beginning of a sentence in some languages, notably German (*doch, überhaupt, eben, allerdings, pure* (It.)).

64. The text writer's idiolect

In a mainly informational text, it is legitimate to ignore the writer's repeated idiolectal peculiarities: 'La contagion interhumaine n'existe pas davantage' ('Furthermore, the disease does not spread from person to person'). 'La contagion n'a pas été davantage signalée à l'école que l'enfant a continué de fréquenter pendant les trois semaines qui précèderent sa consultation' ('Moreover, the disease was not reported at the school which the child still attended during the three weeks before he saw a doctor'). The writer uses *davantage* merely to emphasize his points or make slight contrasts.

65. Terms of art variants

Terms of art are usually the invariant element in translation, but within a language they may have several variants. Illnesses, for instance, occasionally have three: the layman's, the doctor's, and the specialist's classical term (e.g. ringworm, tinea, *tinea circinata*; butterfly-sore, localized rash, *lupus erythematosus*). The terms should normally be matched in each language, assuming say that an article in a British medical journal is to be translated for a corresponding foreign journal. However, the general English preference for less formal terms and simpler syntax and the English professional man's relative ignorance of philosophical terms must be respected: thus *pieds malodorants* are 'smelly feet'; *makroskopische Diagnose*, 'clinical diagnosis'.

66. Similes and images

Any simile, image or comparison should usually be as familiar to the TL as to the SL reader. Sometimes this requires adjustment: 'La chlorure d'Al n'agit que pendant le temps d'un bal ou d'un concours.' 'Aluminium chloride is only effective (as a deodorant) for a short period, say that of a public dance or examination.' I am assuming that the two local referents are more common in France than in England.

67. Tone

The tone of a passage is the key to its communicative effectiveness, and has to be determined by the translator. Tentativeness, urgency, menace, flattery, persuasiveness all have certain markers which are more apparent in the syntax than the lexis, and may be reflected in the tense, mood and voice of a few significant verbs. 'Dica' says a Roman shopkeeper, meaning 'Can I serve you?'. Other markers may be emotive words, or absurdly unreal references: e.g. 'If you don't get this right, I'll push your head into the radiator!' Tone is not necessarily mysterious; for R. Hasan[16] it appears to consist of 'high level semantic components'. For the translator it requires a considerable acquaintance with modern stylistic analysis. Otherwise he will not be competent to translate, say, the self-doubt of Kafka's subjunctives. Syntax, which is a more generalized and abstract measure of language than lexis, gives the feeling-tone of a text.

68. Referring

One assumes that a translator looks up any word about whose meaning, in the context, he may have the slightest doubt; that any reference to a bilingual dictionary is only preliminary to a check in two or three monolingual dictionaries, which indicate (a) modern usage, (b) appropriate register, (c) a range of collocations, (d) degree of frequency, formality, emotiveness, generality, intensity and approval in all appropriate words. He has to be careful with any type of cognate, false or true, which he has not previously met, particularly if its apparent/transparent meaning makes good sense in the context—it may even have the same meaning as its TL 'equivalent', but a different rate of frequency (e.g. *présence, contestataire, réalité, hommage, phénomène, clairvoyant, lucide*). In choosing from a colloquial, a professional, and an academic term for the same phenomenon (e.g. measles, rubeola/morbilli), he has to consider mainly the standard register in the equivalent TL context, occasionally weighing a wayward use in the SL text and even the advantages of 'elegant variation' in his own version. If there is no 'professional' equivalent he may have to use the 'academic term', which is likely to be an internationalism. Thus if a 'painted lady' (a butterfly) does not exist in the TL, he has to use the learned term *Vanessa cardui* (which is in Webster).

Further, in investigating proper nouns and terms of art, he will look particularly at the type of reference book between the dictionary and the encyclopaedia, which defines concepts and procedures, and which pays as much attention to the connotations as the denotation of all proper nouns (e.g. Antaeus, Parthian, Warsaw, 8th Army). Lexicographers are at last realizing that all well-known proper nouns should be in the dictionary and are part of the language because of their connotations, which are linguistic.

Finally, there are cases even in translating 'standardized' language where one term is only marginally-minimally preferable to another (*détecteur/indicateur/senseur,* sensor/ indicator/detector/sensing device!); these translations are far from interchangeable in every context but in some contexts, after all the criteria of frequency, formality and transparency have been applied, the choice of the one or the other makes as near as no difference, and becomes a matter of 'elegant variation'. Even in medical translation, the reader may occasionally like a rest from such terms as 'tracheobronchial bifurcation', 'where the trachea divides to form the bronchi').

69. Proper names in communicative translation

Where proper names are treated purely connotatively, e.g. 'He is a Croesus', 'She is Niobe', the proper name is normally translated by its connotation, unless it also has the same sense in the TL. The proper name should be componentially analysed, in its context, and may require two or three 'senses' in the translation. (*Midas:* (a) wealthy, (b) increasing his wealth, (c) unable to enjoy his wealth, etc.). In semantic translation, the transferred proper name is mandatory.

70. Lengthy titles

These can sometimes be nicely translated by making them into double titles and reversing the order of words, e.g. for *Contributo anatomo–chirurgico sulle possibilità e sui limiti della vagotomía sottodiaframmatica nella terapia dell'ulcera duodenale* put 'Advantages and limitations of subdiaphragmatic vagotomy in the treatment of duodenal ulcers; an anatomical and surgical approach'.

71. Synonymous adjectives in collocation

Synonymous adjectives in collocation often become clichés which are better translated by adverb plus adjective. Thus: fit and proper, *besonders angebracht*; neat and tidy, *ordentlich angezogen*; dreadful and awful, *äusserst schrecklich.* When they do not become clichés, they should be distinguished.

72. Unfamiliar acronyms

A translator can approach an unfamiliar acronym, as in 'Trattata con ESK, la paziente avrebbe avuto un transitorio miglioramento', in two ways: (1) by searching in dictionaries of abbreviations, pharmacopoeias (in Merck six drugs beginning with ESK were found, but these were all types of penicillin); (2) by considering context and probability. This being a mental case-history, ECT appeared the most likely solution. The usual Italian term was then found to be '*e*lettro*s*hoc*k*'.

A translator normally is not entitled to create TL acronyms, and should convert any *ad hoc* SL acronyms into TL words.

73. The shift of scale

'A genuine translator would have to grope for a set of words no more unexpected in his English context than Sterling's is in its French tradition.' Thus Gombrich (1978), whose essays in art interpretation, together with the works of Panofsky (1970), Wind, Wittkower, Saxl, Ehrenzweig, Male and, for music, Cooke (1959) are, apart from being superb, a frequent stimulus to reflection on translation. Gombrich is criticizing 'the sonorous pathos of Delacroix's lobsters and the crepuscular ostentation of Courbet's apples' as a translation of '*le pathos sonore ou crépusculaire des homards de Delacroix et des pommes de Courbet*'. He points out that the style of French art criticism itself has a *pathos sonore ou crépusculaire* which requires a 'shift of scale' towards the English love of understatement, and suggests that some words like 'theatrical gloom' or 'sombre rhetoric' (he does not decide which) 'would lie sufficiently near the extreme beyond which the sublime tumbles over into the ridiculous'; all this is contrasted with the absence of such melodramatic effects in Goya's still life.

My first comment here is that Gombrich rightly characterizes the above-quoted English translation as inept: 'ostentation' is invented, *pathos* in French is usually pejorative, and *crépusculaire* has a far more pronounced figurative sense both of darkness and decline than in English. Secondly, whilst 'rhetoric' gets somewhere near *pathos*, and 'gloom' is acceptable for *crépusculaire, sonore* is hardly covered by Gombrich. In my opinion, if the passage, which is after all critical and satirical, had been written by Claudel or Valéry instead of Charles Sterling, a French critic, and had therefore reflected the individuality of an important writer rather than the traditional style of French art criticism, semantic translation would have been mandatory, and the 'shift of scale' demanded by Gombrich less radical. I suggest 'the sonorous or murky theatricality'. (Gombrich's paragraph here should be regarded as a *locus classicus* of translation theory.)

74. Not found

If a non-literary translator fails to find a SL word in any literature, he usually (a) translates in line with the context, and (b) states what he has done and in his estimation the degree of likelihood that his translation is correct. But (b) is not always necessary for an unfamiliarly or newly compounded word. If in a dictionary or encyclopaedia one finds a word where one is referred to a second word for its definition, one normally assumes that the second word is more common, and therefore uses it rather than the first word in a translation. Thus 'tubercular analysis, tuberculous patient' not 'tuberculous analysis, tubercular patient', although the two words are occasionally interchangeable. Similarly, 'lymphocytic leukaemia', not 'lymphatic leukaemia'.

75. Extension of expression

Romance language past participles and near-past participles such as *incomplet, imparfait* sometimes have to carry more meaning than they appear to, and translate as 'not yet completed', 'which does not give satisfactory results,' respectively.

76. Key-words in literature

In imaginative writing all key-words acquire symbolical value, and become potential metaphors grounded in the culture. Like key-words in a technology, they are suddenly forced to bear figurative meaning. When such words are translated they may have to be supported with an attribute unless there is a strong cultural overlap between source and target language countries.

77. Translation shifts

An important word (key-word) in a text which is used in a peculiar sense by the writer can first be translated 'literally' with an explanation or definition, and then by a word relating it more closely to the target language translation, used first as a translation label. The latter may be adopted for subsequent recurrence, leading the reader 'gently' into a more accepted use of a word. Thus, Lévi-Strauss in *La Pensée Sauvage* (1962) refers to Clouet (i.e. Clouet's) paintings as *voitures en réduction et les bateaux dans les bouteilles, ce qu'en langage de bricoleur on appelle des 'modèles réduits'*. The latter is translated as 'small-scale models' or 'miniatures', bearing Clouet the miniaturist in mind, so that subsequent mentions of '*modèle réduit*' can, in the context of painting rather than *bricolage*, be translated as 'miniatures'.

Note that *bricoleur* is not translated or explained here. At its first mention it is glossed as 'a man who undertakes odd jobs, Jack-of-all-trades, a kind of professional DIY man' and then left as *bricol/age/eur*, since no one-word translation is possible, and the extended meaning of the word is, in English, associated with Lévi-Strauss.

78. Paraphrase

Paraphrase is the last (but sometimes necessary) resort of the translator.

79. Transcription

This concerns loan words, transferred words, adopted words.

Transcription is mandatory in all the following cases, unless there is already a generally accepted translation likely to be accessible and acceptable to the reader:

(a) proper nouns—particularly names of people (except the Pope) and of geographical features;
(b) addresses;
(c) names of private firms;
(d) names of national public and private institutions, unless they are transparent;
(e) terms peculiar to the institutions, ecology and general culture of the SL countries, where there are no equivalents in the TL countries; and
(f) titles of newspapers, periodicals, books, plays, films, articles, papers, works of art, musical compositions.

In all the above cases, the translator may add a translation or gloss, if he thinks this will assist the reader. He probably will not add a translation of the names of national newspapers or periodicals; he will do so for learned journals, unless the titles are transparent in the SL. When the translator is himself translating the body of a work—see (f)—he may translate or select his own title, but append the original one (translation couplet).

The temptation to translate for the first time names of institutions which are 'transparent' in the SL should I think be resisted, since some such names, e.g. *S. Thomas Klinik*, may or may not be misleading cognates.

80. The wave process of translation

Translation difficulties that begin with one word may be elucidated as the word is seen against its collocation, group, clause, sentence, paragraph and whole text. The only appeal in a dilemma is to a larger unit of discourse (Shattuck, 1971). Hence translation as a process of ever-widening ripples. However the referential meaning has priority over the attempt to elucidate through wider linguistic meanings.

81. Typical phenomena

A 'pub' is as typically English as a *Gaststätte* is German and *bistro* French. As world communication increases, fewer attempts may be made to translate them.

82. Idiolect

One out of 500 words in any text is likely to be used in a faulty or idiosyncratic sense. Unless the text is an important document or is written by an important writer, the translator should normalize the error or idiosyncrasy.

83. Translation balancing act

On the one hand, the translator should not use a synonym where a translation will do, in particular, where the translation is a 'transparently' faithful cognate or the standard dictionary equivalent and has no special connotations.

On the other hand, he should not translate one-to-one where one to two or three would do better, nor reproduce a SL syntactic structure where he can recast the sentence more neatly. The above is the translator's basic tightrope, balancing pole, etc.

84. Acceptability, metaphor and translation

The translator has to translate everything; more precisely, he has to account for every item of his text by some form of translation procedure which may include transcription or 'deletion' (i.e. deliberate omission, say of German 'illocutionary' particles such as *aber, also, bloss, denn, da, doch, bitte, bestimmt, eben, eigentlich, einfach, etwa, gerade, halt, ja, mal, nanu, nun, nur, noch, ruhig, schon, überhaupt, wohl*—see Helbig (1977)—or of redundant subheadings more characteristic of the SL than the TL culture). He usually cannot reject any item as grammatically or lexically unacceptable or corrigible, but he still has to assess the degree of its acceptability/corrigibility before deciding whether or not to normalize it. As a translator he cannot hive off 'stylistics' as extraneous to semantics (Lyons (1977) does this, but still gives stylistics far more space than metaphor), and the last thing he can do is to be as dismissive of metaphor as, for instance, Chomsky, who regards his notorious 'colourless green ideas sleep furiously' as 'nonsensical' (1957)—see Newmark (1973) for a 'translation'—or Lyons, who (since he often looks for logical rather than psychological explanations) will have nothing to do with metaphor, though he naively admits that 'it is by no means restricted to what is often thought of as the more poetic use of language' (*sic*). Lyons finds both tautologies and contradictions to be linguistically unacceptable, and is careful to avoid the obvious metaphorical explanation of 'He is his father's son' (i.e. he has all his father's characteristic qualities) or of the 'anomalous' deviant contradiction 'My mother is younger (i.e. less mature) than I am'. A translator cannot afford this type of logic. He has to find everything 'acceptable', either as serious, as ironical, or as spoof: a sentence like 'I'm me', meaning anything from 'I have the (pertinent) quality which the third party (or the second) lacks' to 'I'm reliable, unlike you', should give him no trouble.

Again for the translator, 'Business is business' has within the context the same 'social' force as 'A rose is a rose is a rose', while 'Abiogenesis is spontaneous generation' being a metalingual statement may require transcription as well as translation and a careful check of the status (frequency, newness, connotation) of the word used to translate 'abiogenesis' in the TL. Any translation theorist must protest as Weinreich (1972) did against 'KF' (Katz and Fodor, 1964), about the frivolous and unhelpful attitude of many linguists towards metaphor, which is the basic device and driving force in language and thought and in the formation of concepts.

A translator has to bear in mind that at a pinch *any* sentence and even any lexical word—additionally, all propositions are potentially figurative as well as spatial and temporal—can (out of context) bear several metaphorical interpretations; that any 'physical' statement can also be interpreted as a mental or imaginative statement; and that the process of metaphor is as intimately connected with translation (of which, as Sir Ernst Gombrich has pointed out, the Latin, French, German etc., forms are a literal translation of the Greek) as with the evolution of language.

85. 'Standardized' into 'non-standardized' language

In the *BASF* magazine, *die Dritte und die Vierte Welt* becomes 'the Third and Fourth World'. The expression is puzzling, because the Third World is a political concept, denoting the non-aligned countries which are outside the two main world power blocs. The Fourth World, as the distinguished translator Ewald Osers has pointed out to me, is a standardized term, social rather than political, increasingly used in development-aid literature for the group of least developed countries (LDCs). The Third and Fourth Worlds therefore overlap, and the explanatory 'overlapping' might have been added by the translator, unless the SL text implied a social distinction between developing and least developed countries, thereby turning standardized to less standardized terms.

According to Gilbert's *Dictionnaire des mots nouveaux, le Quart-Monde* is *le sous-prolétariat, population misérable des pays riches*, which puts the 'Fourth World' in the usually unnamed first and second worlds; but this sense appears to have died an early death.

Since the Fourth World, with its emphasis on bad social conditions, is included within the Third World, which is more of a political term, it may be advisable to translate *die Dritte und die Vierte Welt* as 'the Third and (in particular) the Fourth World'. Normally, a translator finding a generic term collocated with its specific term can only assume either that the text is carelessly written (and that the specific term can therefore be deleted in translation), or, as here, that both terms are deliberately mentioned, but that the SL writer wishes to draw greater attention to the specific term.

Again, the recognized German standard term, *der Klub der fünf Weisen*, cannot yet be translated as it is; a version such as 'West Germany's committee of top economic experts, known as "the club of the Five Wise Men"' may lead to a later literal translation.

86. Phonological translation

It is usually accepted that the phoneme cluster 'fl-' has a certain common meaning in, at least, flame, flicker, flare, flitter, flash, flee, flit—but not in 'flat' or 'flank'. Whether such sounds can be translated, in poetry, in alliterative writing or in proper names, is an open question. German has *prallen, prall, prellen, Prunk, prusten, prahlen, prangen, prasseln, prassen.* If there is an affinity, should 'Flashman' become 'Prallman' in a new translation of *Tom Brown's schooldays* (not that such a translation is called for)?

87. Unfamiliar abbreviations

If he meets an unfamiliar abbreviation, a translator should examine his own text before consulting every possible dictionary. Thus 'n.S.' in an article on 'Nephrotic Syndromes associated with malignant leucomas'.

88. Reference books

Translators are still searching vainly for a large up-to-date Italian or a British-English dictionary (Burchfield's *Oxford Dictionary* supplements will not do); for a large complete German–English dictionary with English as the 'home' language (the A of the *Oxford–Harrap* will be out of date long before the Z is done); for a large German dictionary (Duden has only reached K). Meantime, here are some invaluable reference books: *Keesing's* (Bristol) for prominent proper names in public life since 1937, superbly indexed; *Fontana Dictionary of Modern Thought*, ed. by A. Bullock and O. Stallybrass (Fontana/Collins for key-words in the sciences (beautiful, non-technical, definitions) and the humanities, with relevant personalities indexed); Raymond Williams's *Keywords* (Fontana, 1976); *Payton's proper names* (E. Warne); E. Partridge's books on slang and common phrases; Gilbert's *Dictionnaire des Mots Nouveaux* (no English or German equivalent); Longman's *Dictionary of contemporary English*; the Larousse *Dictionnaire du Français Contemporain* (Dubois) (no German equivalent); *Lexis* (Larousse); *Word power* by E. de Bono; J. C. Cooper's *Illustrated dictionary of traditional symbols*; the *Penguin companions to literature* (for details of translations—new editions overdue); J. Fuller's *Handbook for translators*; *The illuminated language of flowers*, ed. Jean Marsh (Macdonald and Jane's).

89. German titles

Sooner or later, translators will have to standardize the translation of German titles beginning with articles or articles plus adjectives. I suggest that the article in book titles be retained, 'He read *Der Unbestechliche*' (cf. 'He read *The Castle*'), and that of institutions be translated, 'He visited the Bauhaus'. An adjective in the second place should be retained (a) in the nominative case, (b) with a strong inflexion, in *all* contexts, 'He worked in the *Staatliches Bauhaus*.' It seems to me that in translation, titles are not subject to German grammar and should be invariable.

90. Translation and collaboration

Just as no literary masterpiece has ever been written by more than one author, a first-rate translation must be written by one person can only bear the stamp of one idiolect. On the other hand, when I look at most literary translations with their 'incredible' howlers, I am amazed that so many have either not been seen by a second person or have been incompetently checked. The notorious TL husband plus SL wife couples (there are several, but 'obviously' I have the Muirs in mind) are far from foolproof, because the reviser's knowledge of the TL must also be instinctive—thus an SL-speaking partner is disqualified as a reviser. Anyone who submits a translation (or an article on translation theory) without having it checked is courting calamity.

91. From sense to metaphor?

Forty years ago, Ritchie translated *sots ennemis* as 'addle-pated enemies'. Is such a translation ever justified? Where an adjective has an obvious one-to-one equivalent which is also communicatively effective, there is no reason to replace it with a metaphor. However, in 'informative' or 'vocative' texts such a replacement may be valid if it is used as 'compensation' to balance the more common 'metaphor to sense' transition in another part of the text or as a means of enlivening a translation.

92. Peripheral cultural terms

A cultural term on the periphery of the text should normally be given an approximate translation or cultural equivalent (e.g. *Fasnacht* as 'carnival', *Kermesse* as 'fête', *Mustermesse* 'trade fair') rather than be transcribed. One does not want to bother the reader of any type of text with opaque transcriptions of little importance. Again, if *dans une vallée écartée de la Cordillère des Andes* is going to play no further part in the text, it is appropriate to at least delete the *cordillera* and translate 'in a remote valley of the Andes'.

93. Flexibility

The translation theorist in many respects has to follow the translator in being flexible and adaptable. I take a quotation from De Gaulle, 'La France glissera du silence de la mer à l'asthénie définitive', and suggest, as a semantic translation, 'France will slip from a death-like silence to a state of permanent weakness' with, if required, a brief gloss. *Le silence de la mer* is the title of Vercors' book, but only the connotations and the reference (occupied France) are relevant, not the language, and therefore a translation or a transcription of the title within the text would be meaningless.

94. Misprints and lateral thinking

'Elle avait un uvéakolobrom congénital'. Thus a case history in yet another French medical journal. The 'uvea' is clear, but how does one handle the still improbable *kolobrom*? 'If *k* doesn't work, try *c*' is a possible translator's hint, which takes one straight to 'a congenital coloboma of the uvea' (i.e. a fissure of the iris). A translator can sometimes waste hours on contexts, reference books, etymologies, etc., when he should merely be thinking of misprints, misspellings, missing words, etc. Translating is excellent training in lateral thinking, or vice versa.

Sense has to be pursued in the most unlikely circumstances, but somehow reconciled with common sense.

Searle (1979) in a tiresome article has demonstrated that no sentence is independent of context, that 'Le chat est sur le paillasson' may mean anything but what it appears to mean; Wittgenstein shows that if A = 3 and B = 4, A + B is *not* 7 if A is already a part of B. All translation theory can do is to point to and warn of the remotest possibilities.

95. 'Not found' again or neologistic abbreviations

In a medical text, a neologism unpunctuated by inverted commas is likely to be a blend, an abbreviation or a misprint, i.e. not a neologism. In the sentence: 'L'antibiothérapie s'impose en évitant, bien entendu, les cyclines susceptibles de donner une couleur jaune intense et définitive aux dents permanentes de l'enfant' *antibiothérapie* is a transparent blend for 'antibiotic treatment'; cycline as such is not given in any reference book, but any list of antibiotics includes the tetracycline group, and therefore the lay translator is 'forced' to this translation which he has to check with an informant. In the above passage, the proximity of two synonyms *définitives* and *permanentes* forces the translator to use an alternative 'standardized' term for *dents permanentes*: therefore, 'Antibiotic treatment is required, but (clearly) tetracycline preparations which may produce a permanent intense yellow colouring on the child's second teeth must not be administered'. Note that the translation of *bien entendu*, an instance of phatic language, is optional.

96. Dialect words

Dialect words fluctuate in usage and can sometimes enter common currency. Here, even old-fashioned, 'out of date' dictionaries can come into their own: *Un homme errené qui manquait de souffle. Errené* could be located as a synonym for *éreinté* only in the large *Littré*.

97. Headings and titles

These should normally be translated last. A non-literary text or book should normally be factually and accurately described by its title. A literary text may have its title changed to an appropriate connotation. Usually, the translator has control over the title of any text.

A heading or title is static, and describes a finished narration: it should normally be centred on one or two nouns, and have SL verbs converted to present or part participles qualifying them. Thus, '*Vance sucht in Westeuropa Unterstützung für neue Schritte gegen Iran*' might become 'Vance's attempt to get renewed Western European support against Iran'.

98. Double translation

In an article on *Selbstverwaltung der Wirtschaft auf dem Gebiet der Technischen Überwachung* (*BASF* no. 05, 1979, printed in five languages)—'Autonomy in industry: the supervision and inspection of plants and appliances'—the word *Selbstverwaltung*, being a theme-word, is frequently repeated, and, therefore, must be repeated in the various translations. In the context, 'autonomy' is the best choice, but is not sufficiently explicit; and the English translator of the first sentence, 'Dem Begriff der Selbstverwaltung haftet an, dass er sich weithin mit mittlebarer Staatsverwaltung deckt', rightly adds the more explicit meaning: 'The term "autonomy" implies that the activities of a self-administered body tie in closely with indirect administration by the state.' (The French translator's *autogestion* suggests this word may soon lose its political connotation and socialist denotation.) 'Double translation' ('two bites at the cherry') is a procedure where one makes two separate attempts to cover the meaning of a word, in this case 'autonomy' and 'the activities of a self-administered body'.

Aspects of meaning

99. The primacy of feeling

The persuasive element or passage in a text must be treated vigorously and with some imagination by the translator, since it is intended to rouse feeling, if not action, in his reader. Usually it is more colloquial in style than the informative and the expressive element. Syntactically, languages appear to differ far more widely when used to express feelings and give orders and instructions than to make statements. Compare the statement, 'The paint is wet', *la peinture est fraîche/die Farbe ist nass* with the warning: 'Wet paint'/*prenez garde à la peinture/frisch gestrichen.*

Some critics believe that the cognitive function of a text is more important than its persuasive (or expressive) function; that whilst in translation cognitive (i.e. extra-linguistic) accuracy can and must always be achieved, the other factor, the connotative, stylistic or 'pragmatic' (the relation of the receiver and the transmitter to the text in the sense of Peirce and C. W. Morris), defies accuracy, and is therefore secondary. K. Baldinger has referred to it as a 'halo' round the conceptual content; A. Neubert states that only the 'pragmatic' is untranslatable. This widespread idea appears mistaken to me; a glance at the entries for, say, 'Munich' or 'Hitler' in, say, the *Petit Larousse* or the *Quillet–Flammarion* suggests that lexicographers tend to leave out the most important facts for fear of their *Appell* effect on their readers. Thus Solzhenitsyn's remark in his (undelivered) Nobel Prize speech: 'The spirit of Munich[17] is a sickness of the will of successful people; it is the daily condition of those who have given themselves up to thirst after prosperity', could not be understood without an explanation of the significance (i.e. connotation) of the Munich agreement, which is semantically vastly more important than its cognitive definition, i.e. a summary of the agreement.

100. Distinguishing linked synonyms

Synonyms in collocation or close proximity in the source language text must be clearly distinguished semantically in the target language text. This rule applies to pseudo-synonyms such as *vins et alcools*, explication and explanation, *scabreux et hasardeux* as to the great pantechnicon words like *promotion*, development, *matériel, équipement* etc. which must be distinguished, partly through wider context, in any collocation like *construction et aménagement* (which may be 'design and lay-out').

There are, however, provisos. The source language text must be well written, as synonyms are sometimes used carelessly and ponderously, as in *Objekte und Gegenstände*; sometimes mainly for emphasis, as in 'deeply and profoundly', tender and loving', 'direct and straightforward', and because pairs of adjectives sometimes improve the rhythm of a sentence; and in old legal phrases, to cover the Germanic and Romance alternatives, as in 'without let or hindrance', 'goods and chattels', etc. The rule is therefore a tricky one. Sometimes, when, say, *matériel, équipement* are juxtaposed in a long list, it is difficult for the translator to know whether they are different, synonymous, overlapping, or whether the one (possibly *matériel*) includes the other, and whether the writer himself knows.

101. Negatives and contraries

If it is difficult to find a congruent equivalent of an item in the target language, it is often possible to 'decompose' it into a negative and its contrary or contradictory term. An obvious example is 'shallow', *peu profond.* Normally, the force of the positive is weakened in this procedure: *peu profond* is not as shallow as 'shallow'. The best equivalence is obtained if the lexical item has little affective force: e.g. *Les infections en dehors des périodes d'épidémie*, 'infections which do not occur during epidemic periods'. Strictly, *en dehors de* is stronger than 'not . . . during', but as this is an informative communication without expressive or emotive overtones, the equivalent effect is achieved. Conversely, it is often advisable to convert a negative premodifying a lexical item into a positive contrary or contradictory term. For example: 'Non è azzardato pensare che l'utilità delle leghe si sia manifestata all'uomo la prima volta che una spada di rame cozzò contro una spada di bronzo', 'It is quite likely that man first became aware of the use of alloys when a copper sword clashed with a bronze sword'.

102. American neologisms

Some American words pass into other languages before they reach English, and a translator faced with a technical or colloquial neologism in any language should make an early attempt to 'place' it in the great Webster's Dictionary. This, for instance, is where he will find *sociatrie* (sociatry), which is not even in L. Gilbert's excellent *Dictionnaire des nouveaux mots.*[18]

103. Interference

Interference is the translator's worst problem, as it is the language learner's. Failure to recognize interference makes him look most foolish. So many thousand English words—scabrous, scurrilous, fatal, masks, colossal, assure, copious, brutal, reduced, adequate, dislocation, trivial, banal, useful, arrests, efforts, alterations, perforating, solicitations, moment, fraction, massive, promotion, contingent, concern, studio, central, rate, permanence, instance and so on—have other meanings when pronounced in French or German with French or German suffixes. And so many foreign words have one primary etymological sense, but another in the context in which they are now more frequently used, e.g. *si* (conjunction), *prévoir, vorsehen, Anlage, Leistung, Spielart.* Often their motivated transparency makes them more opaque than strictly opaque words. Every year now, more English goes into West German and Russian goes into East German, and when adopted, starts a life of its own, whilst the special language of technology, which is also often the language of the media, spans the world. Borrowed words take up one sense, sometimes the less common one, and leave others behind. A motivated word in one language becomes opaque and non-motivated in another, and conversely. Interference is the chaotic as well as the dynamic element in a language, continually breaking up the system *où tout se tient* (Meillet) creating too many senses for one word or too many words for one thing. There is no even restricted rule for this problem, but only the translator's one unrestricted rule: mind the sentence, mind the word, and finally mind the sentence. 'Translated words always lie, but translated texts only lie when they are badly translated.' (Translated from Harald Weinrich's *Linguistike der Lüge*.)[19]

Working as he does on and in *parole*, never on or in *langue*,[20] the translator can only regard dictionaries, grammars and works on linguistics with caution, and will favour those with the maximum number of citations and a context-sensitive arrangement like a thesaurus. Finally, only a massive common sense, more like a good general's or a statesman's than an intellectual's, will protect him against his own ingenuity, his recherché and exotic brainwaves, which are so often idiotic; so easy to think of the *bois du monastère* as the 'wooden objects (perhaps the furniture) in a monastery', the *cartes traditionnelles du désert occidental remplacées par des cartes de Grèce* as 'the fortunes of Greece now taking precedence over the usual one of the Western desert', until he makes a deliberate pause to review the whole position; so easy to select anything but the obvious sensible interpretation.

104. Bühler and Frege contrasted

The connection between Frege's and Bühler's theories of language and its application in translation can be illustrated by an example. The phrase, *Arbeitnehmer organisatorisch oder räumlich abgegrenzter Betriebsteile (Bundesgesetzblatt 1972, Teil 1, 4. Abschnitt, Paragraph 42, Absatz 2, Satz 1)* is condensed in thought and not easy to render. Being a legal text, it is designed to impress the reader (*Appell*), but this particular phrase is purely informative. Essentially, the translator is concerned with thought (Frege's *Sinn*) or text, but whenever the thought is difficult, he attempts temporarily to put aside the text and make up his mind what is really happening—what truth does the text really refer to? He, therefore, transfers to the level of Frege's *Bedeutung* and considers Bühler's *Darstellung* function. In the above case, we assume that the reference is to a firm's employees who are either organized in separate departments, or who work in separate plants or buildings. The translator now attempts to turn *Bedeutung* back to *Sinn* (a common procedure; converting 'information translation' to 'publication translation'), but it is difficult to do so, since he has to retain the generality of *organisatorisch* and the slight ambiguity of *räumlich*. Therefore, paradoxically, in making his own interpretation of *Sinn*, the translator introduces a subjective element, the level of *Vorstellung*, and takes the *Ausdruck* function of the original into account. A possible translation is, 'Employees in a company's various divisions or in its separate buildings'.

Bühler's *Darstellung* and Frege's *Bedeutung* are precisely equivalent. If a text had purely this function (but it never has), it could in theory be translated literally. Frege's *Sinn* is thought or language, the essential medium of translation. Bühler's *Appell* is often no more than a part of an utterance; it is the directive element in a legal text, the persuasive element in a recommendation, the emotive element in a literary text, or it is an instruction or an order. Its only highest common factor appears to be 'vocative'. Bühler's *Ausdruck* and Frege's *Vorstellung* are both subjective, and the translator should respectively attempt to contain, if not eliminate (which is of course impossible), these elements. However, in a literary work, the elements of *Ausdruck* and *Vorstellung* are likely to be more significant than in other texts. Moreover, here *Bedeutung* is no longer extralinguistic reality; even in a naturalistic work, it makes little difference whether the hero earns 1000 or 999 marks a month. The nature of *Bedeutung* depends on the translator's or the third reader's (the translation critic's) interpretation of the source language (SL) author's artistic theory: in a naturalistic work, it should admittedly be as close as possible to extralinguistic reality; in a symbolist work, it is the reference of the symbols; in 'art for art's sake', it is identical with *Sinn*, or non-existent; for me, it is the *Dichter's* (creative writer's) critique of human behaviour, which is constructed out of basically figurative, allegorical semantic units. It is the translator's job to transpose these figurative units into the target language (TL). 'My love is like a red red rose' will look different in a culture where roses are uncommon and not notably beautiful and play no melody.

105. Trouvailles

Marking examination papers, I take off marks for indisputable mistakes (in extralinguistic reality)—truth-mistakes—and usually half-marks for stylistic barbarisms and infelicities—usage-mistakes. I give valuable and rather subjective 'plus' marks for *trouvailles* or verbal flashes of perception. *Trouvailles* are usually one to at least two words or at least two to one word translations; if they are one to one, the rendering approved of will probably not be found in a dictionary. They may be grammatical or lexical: a grammatically reformed sentence that retains or clarifies an emphasis may be a *trouvaille*, as may the rendering of an unusual collocation. The essence of a *trouvaille* is that it intuits a meaning behind a few words; it exists in between the words in the sense that Mozart wrote that the best music is in the silence between the notes. A good translator may create a *trouvaille* in any kind of text; it is mistaken to think that literary translation is concerned with *trouvailles*, and say legal translation with terminology. On any topic, a *trouvaille* may transmit information on a particular level of evaluative, affective or intensive language. It may show a delicate balance between connotation and designation. It represents a minimal amount of entropy,[21] in Vinay's (1976) sense, and aspires at once to a Racinian elegance and complex simplicity. Although it links the text to extralinguistic reality, a *trouvaille* also has the subjective non-communicable element which Walter Benjamin saw as the essence of translation.[22]

106. The limits of word meaning for accuracy's sake

A word can mean anything at all under the following conditions:

(a) that it has a stipulative licence to do so;
(b) that it forms part of a special code;
(c) that it is spoken or written in error, or is a misprint;
(d) that the author is writing under stress (fear, illness).

In all the above cases, the translator still has to discover the word's meaning. However, under normal circumstances, the meaning of a word can never be wholly dictated or conditioned by its linguistic or situational context. A kitten may be a *chaton*, a *petit chat* or a *petite chatte*, but it is never a *chien*. The semantic contours of conceptual terms are often vaguer and wider, but *système* must not be translated as 'arrangement', unless as part of a recognized collocation (unknown to me)!

Theoretically, at any rate, all words have a minimum semantic content, that is one or two primary semantic components which form part of each of their meanings, and which must therefore be 'transferred' in any translation; these are the boundaries of translation, beyond which translation becomes paraphrase. Certainly, an item is often translated by another item which is not given as its equivalent in most dictionaries, but most frequently it will be 'pragmatically' rather than 'semantically' different (or be in another 'register' and will be found in the thesaurus, as a synonym; a hyponym (approximately, a specific or subordinate term) may also be translated by, as it is often referred to by, its hyperonym (generic or superordinate term), in particular if the one or the other is missing in the TL or SL, but sometimes also as an alternative to the precise equivalent. Frequently, a new meaning of a word is a logical extension of its previous shifts of meaning, and can be accounted for by the translator; thus, *marée* = tide→wave→fish (carried by tide)→fishing expedition.

But what a translator has no right to do is to substitute a secondary or nonce meaning of an item for a primary meaning which fits perfectly in the context; nor may he replace a linguistic allusion to a referent with its ordinary name or technical term, or a paraphrase. For the sake of clarity, he is entitled to bring the linguistic allusion closer to the referent, but he is not entitled simply to name the referent. Thus in the sentence, 'Le grand défaut des mécanismes naturels est d'être insuffisamment prospectifs. Il est sensible dans un domaine comme l'aménagement du territoire, où la durée se compte par décennies', it is illegitimate to translate *mécanismes naturels* simply as 'Nature', which is the referent; 'natural mechanisms' is unhelpful; I suggest, 'The one great deficiency of the processes of nature is that they cannot think ahead sufficiently'.

107. Primacy as commonest meaning

Translators (in particular) are apt to confuse a previous with the present primary meaning of a word. Thus, in my opinion, the primary (most frequent) meaning of the conjunction *si* (Fr.) or *se* (It.) in written language is 'whereas (whilst, although)' (eight times out of ten?), whilst the English 'if' only has this meaning once out of ten. Similarly, *prévoir* usually means 'specify', *assurer* 'provide', *intérêt* 'advantage' more often than 'interest'. Thus the most frequently applied meaning tends to be 'hidden' by the former primary meaning, and the latter tends to be influenced if not motivated by etymology, interference and tradition as preserved in dictionaries and grammars, both of which are so often 'updated' ('new edition', i.e. a few additions!) instead of being completely rewritten. (Again *peut* or *peuvent* means 'may' much more often than 'can', but *ne peut* or *ne peuvent* usually means 'cannot'.)

108. Lexical universals

A translator is always looking for linguistic and/or semantic universals, that is lexical items that have more or less the same application in two or more relevant languages, sometimes called isomorphous units. The most likely instances are words denoting objects common to the ecologies, e.g. sun, moon, earth, sea (German has two words), star, plus sand, plant, flower, rain (Russian has no verb), cloud, etc. if these exist. Even here, past or present linguistic interference causes bifurcation and specialization of terms. Sun and moon appear to be lexical constants, but English and German distinguish between 'sky' and 'heaven', French has two words for 'river' and Russian one for 'wood' and 'tree'. Dutch has the same word for 'sky' and 'air', German normally the same for 'hill' and 'mountain'. Moreover, the connotations of all these words are likely to be different in each language.

Parts of the body, common human activities and kinship terms would appear to have claims to universality, but in fact there are great differences, as languages distinguish between animals and human beings differently, and kinship has gaps, is frequently male-dominated or related to castes and hierarchies. Moreover, Russian does not distinguish between hand and arm, nor, like French, between finger and toe; only English appears to recognize a knuckle, and tongue and language are often the same word. Italian does not distinguish 'hearing' from 'feeling' (as Mozart with his incomparable wit and humanity pointed out in *Figaro*), nor French feeling from smelling, and German tasting is homophonous with costing—the situation appears absurd.

The only semantic invariables appear to be the numbers, and a few terms in that lexical field (minutes, seconds, days of week, months) when applied in their physical sense. Recent inventions are also temporarily isomorphous, and not surprisingly translators are interested in their standardization. Words denoting universal natural objects are likely to be more isomorphous than others, but the theme only confirms the partial correctness of the Whorf–Sapir thesis anticipated by Humboldt. However, in context such words are much easier to translate than those more obviously coloured by the users' feelings and thoughts.

109. Conceptual terms

Ralf Dahrendorf[23] has noted that 'by the very fact of misleading, translations can create terms that can acquire a life of their own'. The comment is correct, but it often has unfortunate linguistic consequences. (The phrase 'acquire a life of its own' often has a sinister connotation in other fields, particularly psychiatry.) Dahrendorf is referring to the common translation of Max Weber's concept of *Stand* as 'status', though it in fact means both 'status' and 'estate'. (An 'estate' is a closed straum of society, based on property rather than money, with a common mode of life and values.) 'This is an example of the exigencies of translations—and of their creativity.' Certainly, concepts when translated (or transliterated) often narrow or deflect their meaning or develop a secondary meaning. Weber's *Stand*, however, appears to have been either variously translated (by Talcott Parsons) or pinned to a single inadequate word such as 'status' or 'stratum' without inducing any creativity at all. A better procedure would be to analyse the semantic features of the concept and include its main ones in a TL collocation, which may be shortened to its head noun where the reference is unmistakable. The intensive meaning of *Stand* appears to be a closed, organic status or stratum, and this appears to be the best clue for a version.

110. Referential synonymy

If the translator is concerned with *parole* and the lexicologist with *langue*, they look at questions of meaning and synonymy differently. The translator recognizes that theoretically and cognitively, no two words out of context have the same meaning. Within a context they frequently do so, either for the purpose of denoting the same object (almost haphazardly, e.g. Barbara Castle, the ex-minister, the red-haired non-driver)[24] or because they are used carelessly, or because the whole weight of the sentence, its truth value, is in the rheme, the new information, in which their separate semantic features are not involved. Thus the following sentences may have the meaning for the translator:

	Theme	*Rheme*
1.	He/Mr. Smith/The man I met yesterday/The dark gentleman in the black suit	ran fast.
	Rheme	*Theme*
2.	I considered	this matter/my problem/ the plants in the garden.

The translator accepts the following propositions: (a) each of the above sets of sentences may have the same truth value; (b) in any translation, the new information should have priority over the old; (c) nevertheless the full linguistic value of the theme should normally be reproduced, even though its semantic features (e.g. the man's name, what he was wearing, when I met him etc.) are of no interest as they are already known. For the translator, the theme has a theoretically infinite number of synonyms, to be used at convenience, whilst the rheme has none at all. (d) If the translator is asked to make cuts, he should cut parts of the theme, never the rheme.

Similarly, the precise meaning of a word may be unimportant, so that any of its appropriate meanings can be selected, provided the truth value of the sentence is not impaired. Thus in a medical article, in the sentence, '*Alors qu'il utilisait une toupie, sa main gauche a été prise par la machine*', *toupie* may be a vertical or milled cutter or shaper of a moulding-machine or any kind of lathe; no further clue is given in the text, from either the linguistic context or the situation. The only important facts about the *toupie* are (1) that its operator is a joiner, (2) that he can catch his hand in it, (3) that it can then cause a 10 cm longitudinal wound on the back of the hand, next to the first metacarpal. There is scope therefore (a) for synonyms to describe the same machine-tool, (b) for citing one of a number of machine-tools, provided they have the features previously mentioned. Since the article is concerned with the treatment of the wound, the precise nature of the tool does not interest the reader. The translator should still try to find out from the source-text author, as further questions about the wound may arise, and also as a matter of professional pride.

But all translation is a compromise, a balancing. The translator distinguishes between the degree of importance in the meanings, forms, sounds in his text; he has to discriminate on a continuum from the centrally to the peripherally important. The truth value as seen by the writer, or the reader, or as a record of the facts of the case is, depending on the function of the text, his criterion.

111. Double negatives

All double negatives have a possible 'strong' or 'weak' interpretation, i.e. 'not unworthy' may mean 'extremely worthy' or 'quite worthy'.

112. Positive or negative

In his study of the grammar of a sentence, the translator frequently has to decide whether the total effect is 'just' positive or 'just' negative. There is a large difference, for any *Ammesso che . . .* between 'even if we admit that' and 'granted that'. Words like *délicat*, 'critical', 'arguable', *discutable* may be put on either side of the critical borderline. Note how some words like 'hopes', 'efforts', 'attempts', 'difficulties' must be 'resolved' positively or negatively; in fact, they are resolved negatively rather more often. A negative negates a positive in *salto in basso.* A double negative just becomes positive in *meno basso tenor di vita* ('not such a low standard of living').

113. Referential synonyms

The translator has to distinguish between the occasions calling for the use of referential synonyms (for cohesion; to avoid repetition; to supply extra information; poor or diffuse writing), before he decides how to handle them. Normally he avoids them, since they are confusing or ambiguous to the reader. He prefers repetitions, particularly if his own reader is less familiar with the subject matter than the first reader.

114. Semantic fields

Particular words that are virtually synonymous may cluster round particular semantic fields; thus an Italian region may have *programmi*, an industrial sector *piani.*

A good translation runs along a narrow ridge between synonymy and primary (instead of contextual) meaning correspondence.

115. Phatic language

A writer uses phatic language in order to establish an appropriate relationship with his reader. Such language may consist of social formulae (*formules de politesse*), German filler-words (*ja, schon*, etc.) or even alliterated words to attract attention. The translator has to distinguish the phatic form from the denotative element and render it in the appropriate terms of the source language, which are likely to have little strict semantic resemblance to those of the original, e.g. 'Yours faithfully', *hochachtungs-voll, Je vous prie d'agréer cher Monsieur l'expression de mes sentiments les plus distingués*. He also has to note consciously or unconsciously deceptive phatic phrases such as 'you know', 'believe me', 'seriously', 'honestly', 'as is well known' (Stalin), 'it's interesting to note that', 'doubtless', 'of course', 'evidently', 'obviously', etc. Which mean virtually the opposite of what they say.

116. Mental words

Translation of words denoting artifacts is likely to be less accurate than that of mental words, since minds are closer to each other than cultural phenomena. Mental words of thought and calculation are likely to translate more accurately than mental words of feeling and appraisal, since the latter draw more on metaphors. The more specific a word, the less accurate its translation, since it comprises more semantic features.

117. Evaluative language or negatives

When contradictory terms are semantically close to each other, the positive (e.g. 'competent', *congru*, 'sufficient', 'adequate', 'satisfactory', 'useful') is sometimes used in a negative sense, and a positive term in one language may have a negative equivalent in another.

118. The semantic core

Words are said to possess a stable semantic core and unstable, changing surfaces which 'fit' in various contexts. The worst problem for a translator is often when the surface fluctuates between positive and negative: thus *légaliser* may mean 'to legalize' or its virtual opposite, 'to bring under legal control'.

119. Opposition

Oppositions, like juxtaposed synonyms, may clarify distinctions: *psychologischer oder morphologischer Kopfschmerz* = psychological or physical headache, *souffrance physique ou morale* = physical or emotional suffering.

120. Clarification

In an informative text, it is always the translator's job to clarify a sentence in line with the intention behind the text. Thus: 'La gamme des solvants organiques participe à ce jeu de roulette russe', 'Every type of organic solvent is implicated in this tremendous risk.'

121. *Faux amis* and *amis fidèles*

As I have said before, the translator will usually find as many cognates with the same meanings in SL and TL as those with different meanings, and he must not hesitate to use the appropriate TL cognate. However, he must never translate any word he has not previously seen without checking it, and this is where cognates are deceptive. *Elégant* virtually covers the semantic range of 'elegant', but *inélégant* ranges from 'inelegant' through 'discourteous' to 'dishonest'. (Supermarkets warn against *clients inélégants* who do not show the content of their *cabas*.)

122. It all depends on the context

Not always. Internationalisms *ipso facto* do not depend on the context. Nor, usually, does the meaning of any compound words, and many words with affixes ('hypersensitive', 'define', *exophorie*). But many technical words with affixes have different meanings in different technologies: *exfolier, exostose*. However, the more particular the meaning of a word, the less it depends on the context. And a vast number of words have one meaning most of the time. And unless one says so, what one can make a word mean is, *pace* Wittgenstein, usually limited. But with all that, yes, it *usually* depends on the context.

123. Lexical accuracy

Accuracy in communicative translation is basically lexical. The translator can treat the grammar flexibly and adroitly within limits, recasting units to strengthen the logic of the text. But the lexis must be accurate. I have a text which gives 'ill-defined' for *aléatoire*, 'abnormality' for *déviation*, 'outlined' for *décrivit*, etc. This sort of approximation will not do.

Punctuation

124. Italics, underlining and inverted commas

A translator into English usually underlines words:

(a) when they make up the titles of printed material, plays, music, pictures, etc.
(b) when they are foreign;
(c) to distinguish, contrast or emphasize their importance.

Such words are often italicized in print, depending on the publication's house-style.

The translator (and the printer) normally uses inverted commas for:

(a) quotations;
(b) dialogue;
(c) complements of verbs of designation (e.g. *présenté comme 'rince-creme' ou 'cream rinse'*, 'known as "perfect" ';
(d) literal translation, particularly of foreign cultural words and collocations; usually in brackets indicating, often after reproducing the original, that these are unacceptable but help to explain the meaning, e.g. '*Berufsverbot*, "prohibition of employment", the FRG law which denies civil service posts to political extremists', or *publicité institutionnelle*' 'institutional advertising'. (Single contrast with double inverted commas.)

The translator may also use inverted commas (italics or inverted commas in print) for the following stylistic purposes:

(a) unfamiliar technical terms (e.g. 'powertrain' (*groupe motopropulseur d'une automobile*));
(b) names of new inventions 'horomètre' (*montre à diapason*). (The translator could risk 'horometer', based on the French *horomètre*);
(c) neologisms, viz. newly formed words or words used in a strange or unusual sense, e.g. 'Les objets mis à la disposition des usagers sont "poétisés" par la recherche d'une marque de commerce aux consonances.' *Poétisés* could be 'poeticized' (neologism for neologism) or normalized as 'given a poetic quality by . . .'. Likewise, *l'automobile qu'il va 'vendre'* = the car he (an advertiser) is about to 'sell';
(d) words used ironically, contradictorily or paradoxically, e.g. 'La responsabilité d'avoir abâtardi la publicité incombe à des "traducteurs" qui n'ont de traducteur que le nom.' Translate: 'translators in name only', or 'Quand une annonce prône le snobisme et le mimétisme social le publicitaire a-t-il le droit de proposer cet "idéal" à ses compatriotes?' Translate: 'ideal';

(e) words used to make an impression, for instance as a slogan (again contradictory), e.g. 'Le traducteur ne doit-il pas être "le spécialiste de tout"?' Translation: 'the specialist all-rounder';
(f) words deliberately misused: e.g. *die 'expressimistische' Bewegung*, the 'expressimistic' movement;
(g) words regarded as slang or jargon: 'La méconnaissance du français les oblige à s'exprimer en "joual", sous le prétexte de "faire québécois".' 'As their knowledge of French is poor, they have to speak "joual", the French Canadian dialect, with the excuse that they are behaving like Québécois';
(h) words used as though quoted, for which the author (and translator) does not want to take responsibility, e.g. 'these men were "extremists" ';
(i) where the author/translator wants to cast doubt on the truth or appropriateness of the word in the context (alternatively: 'The italics are mine'), e.g. 'He claimed that "democracy" reigned in Chile';
(j) a word used imaginatively or figuratively outside its usual context, 'L'adaptateur travaille donc sur un "produit fini" ';
(k) unusual collocations, e.g. 'hypnotisme verbal';
(l) imaginary quotations: 'On l'incitera à se rendre "dès aujourd'hui" dans un magasin' becomes 'immediately';
(m) to indicate an accepted and important concept: e.g. 'L'homme de l'esprit doit se réduire sciemment à un refus indéfini d'être quoi que ce soit', or 'She believes there can be as much "human truth" in crime novels as in any other form of literature';
(n) to isolate or distinguish a concept from its context: e.g. 'Pour ma part je n'accepte en rien le thème du "tigre" utilisé par plusieurs produits';
(o) to adapt a well-known phrase, e.g. 'Plus qu'une belle infidèle une adaptation devra être une "belle efficace" ';
(p) 'deprecatory' inverted commas to show the writer's sense of superiority, in using a word he would not normally use: e.g. 'with its primary postulate, "steep" as it is, we will not quarrel' (Fowler);
(q) using a word deliberately outside its normal context of period or region, e.g. 'Copernicus's father was a "civil servant" of the time';
(r) to indicate a new and not yet recognized term, semantic translation/or a translation label (e.g. 'social advancement' for *promotion sociale*). If the term or the label sticks, the inverted commas can later be withdrawn;
(s) to indicate reference—'the term "comma" ' or 'a word with an affix ("hypersensitive")'.

In general, when a single word or phrase is put in inverted commas, it can be translated literally, since the inverted commas relieve the translator of the responsibility for its authenticity. However, where the word in inverted commas denotes a feature peculiar to the source language or its culture, it may be transcribed, or if used as an illustration (say, a slang word of no interest to the reader) it may be omitted by the translator.

Any word used out of its normal context or in a special sense can in fact be put in inverted commas, and is often preceded by a word such as 'alleged', 'called', 'supposed', *soi-disant*, *sog.* (omitted in English if no emotive nuance is intended). The use of inverted commas can be abused by translators as it has often been by writers, but up to now translators have not perhaps made enough use of this resource.

I have attempted to analyse the practice of italics, underlining and inverted commas in English writing. In German, a theme-word (*Stichwort*) is also often italicized. The translator has to investigate the practice in all his languages.

When a word is italicized to show that it is being used in a peculiar sense (e.g. 'Die Bakterienstämme werden *ausgesiebt*'), it can either be translated literally, retaining the inverted commas ("sieved out"), or normalized, removing the inverted commas (filtered).

125. The exclamation mark

An exclamation mark is used in English as a mark of (a) surprise; (b) strong personal feeling and in particular, incredulity, sometimes as an ironical comment, on the part of the author: e.g. 'He (really) believes this!'; (c) strong recommendation, notably in advertisements and general publicity; (d) emphasis, to draw attention to what the author is saying; (e) address or apostrophe, e.g. 'Robert! You coward!'; (f) a command or request; (g) an interjection; (h) exclamation; (i) ellipses, e.g. 'If only he had arrived!'

In most Western European languages it has the same semantic force. In German it is also used in correspondence after the address formula and for public notices (*Kein Zutritt!*).

126. The question mark

In English the question mark is used to indicate (a) a question; (b) a rhetorical question; (c) the introduction of a new subject often in a sub-heading; (d) conjecture or uncertainty, sometimes in brackets after the particular word.

Rhetorical questions are more common in many foreign languages than in English, and are frequently translated/converted into statements.

127. The comma

The comma becomes critically important in the following cases:

(1) to distinguish (a) a non-restrictive ('The man, whom I met yesterday') from
(b) a restrictive relative clause ('The man I met yesterday . . .');
(2) to separate all but the penultimate and the ultimate item in a list, e.g. 'Sheep, cattle and pigs were in the farm': the comma is required after the penultimate item in otherwise ambiguous cases, e.g. 'John Brown, Cammel Laird, Vickers, and Harland & Wolff submitted tenders';
(3) in German before a 'daß' clause, and sometimes when English would have a semi-colon.

Double commas in French have two special uses:

(1) to mean 'and' and 'or': e.g. *Le traitement d'infections banales, urinaires, pulmonaires, répondant à*, 'Treatment of common urinary or (and) lung infections responding to . . . ';
(2) to signify emphasis or contrast: e.g. *Ce traitement, salutaire, est appliqué*, 'This treatment, which was beneficial . . . was applied'; *Ce traitement, nuisible, est appliqué*, 'This treatment, which however was harmful, was applied'.

128. Parenthesis

Parentheses are indicated in one of three ways: dashes, brackets and commas (double commas or comma–full-stop). Of these, dashes, which are least used, tend to interrupt the flow of a sentence conspicuously, and are often an indulgent irrelevance: e.g. 'So far it is true—and how far it is true does not count for much—it is an unexpected bit of truth', etc. (Note that dashes are used at beginning of lists in French where English would have enumerations.)

Double commas enclose an important part of the sentence, as in the second sentence above.

Brackets are used (a) to enclose, with inverted commas, a direct quotation; (b) as an alternative or equivalent version; (c) to enclose numerical or alphabetical enumerations as here; (d) in mathematics and logic to indicate self-contained groups; (e) to indicate, less conspicuously than dashes or double commas, a tactful, almost whispered parenthesis. Note the difference heightened by but not entirely due to the different word-group order between:

(F) 'Fausser compagnie, le maïs mis à part, aux plantes *dominantes*', and
(E) 'To turn one's attention brusquely away from the dominant plants (maize excepted)'.

In this sentence, *dominantes* is put in italics as a sign of stress, to indicate a key-word, a practice more common in French and German than in English punctuation.

Square brackets are not much used except in logic and by special convention.

129. Colons

When a sentence is logically (not grammatically) incomplete, and requires an explanation, an illustration or a list of items which it designates, it is normally punctuated with a colon: thus the clause succeeding it is its implicit response, its natural sequel. The first clause (the topic) frequently includes a word such as 'the following', 'there are', 'means', 'explain' or an expression of quantity. The complement is the analytical or synthetic comment on the preceding topic. The topic as it were points to the ensuing comment.

If the comment is analytical, the colon may be useful to the translator, since a rare word in the first clause will be explained in the second, e.g. 'Il aperçut des furoles: c'étaient de petites flammes qui l'entouraient'.

If the comment is synthetic, the colon should assist the translator in following the logical sequence of the SL text, and where necessary reinforcing it: e.g. 'Toute la mise en scène a une carrière: elle naît, s'épanouit et meurt; se nourissant de l'oeuvre qui lui reste transcendante'. The colon is implicitly an alternative to expressions like: 'i.e.', 'viz.', 'scil.', 'that is to say', 'for example', 'I mean'.

130. Semicolons

Semicolons are occasionally used to indicate a logical and sometimes a formal/grammatical relation between two parallel sentences; the relationship may indicate similarity or contrast, 'I work; you sleep'.

Secondly, the semi-colon is used to separate items in a series: e.g. '. . . les sommets que sont le 2e acte de la Walkyrie; le renouvellement fabuleux du rôle de Mime; les 2 scènes exquises et poignantes de Siegmund at Sieglinde; et tout le terrible Crépuscule des Dieux'.

Thirdly, the semi-colon is used to show continuity of thought or speech, particularly in reported speech, the full-stop indicating the end of the reported speech.

Fourthly, semi-colons are sometimes used to mark off the subordinate clauses of a long complex sentence.

Text analysis

131. Discourse analysis or cohesion

Language has various resources to ensure the cohesion of thought beyond the sentence, and the translator comes to rely on them as guide-lines.

(a) *Theme and rheme.* Theme states the subject of discourse, which is normally referred to in, or logically consequential upon, the previous utterance (sentence or paragraph). Rheme is the fresh element, the lexical predicate, which offers information about theme. (Within the structure of a sentence, these lexical terms are sometimes referred to as topic and comment.) 'Theme plus rheme' need not be a surface grammar sequence, and its identification will depend on a wider context. Thus the sentence: 'He discussed this subject' is a logical sequence which might be the basis for a periphrase such as, 'This subject offered him the opportunity he required for discussing it'. Lexically, 'this subject' is the theme and 'he discussed' the rheme, and therefore there is a conflict between the logical sequence ('He discussed this subject') and the more cohesive realization (possibly 'This was the subject he discussed') which the translator may have to resolve; he may have to make a compromise between the basic logical sequence, viz., animate subject/animate verb/inanimate direct object, which is clear and context-free, and a sequence determined by emphasis and cohesion factors, which may themselves be conflicting.

(b) *Anaphoric and cataphoric reference.* Anaphora, consisting of a deictic determiner (the, this, that) or pronoun, refers to something previously mentioned, whilst cataphora (deictics, pronouns or 'dummy' words such as 'here' in 'here is the news' or impersonal 'it' in 'it's interesting to note that, . . .' etc.) refers to what is to follow. Both features are sometimes overlooked in translation. In synthetic languages they are variously inflected, and often have to be replaced by 'full' nouns when translated into English.

(c) *Enumerations* (firstly, secondly, or next or then or afterwards, etc.).

(d) *Opposition*, or dialectic. Argument proceeds from thesis to antithesis, from positive to negative, from static to dynamic, from specific to genetic, and possibly back in each case, or it may start with the negative to go on to the positive. Occasionally, there is synthesis, or a neutral position is held. The oppositions may be extreme (contraries) or kept close to the middle (contradictories). This is how much narrative of all kinds is built up.

A translator has to be particularly sensitive to opposition; it often assists him in detecting the sense of rare words, neologisms and tropes; viz.: 'Il était le généraliste qui peaufine les mesures économiques'. (*Peaufine*, 'works out in detail', is in opposition to généraliste.) 'Il maniait des unités fongibles et non des êtres humains' ('disposable components', contrasted with 'human beings').

'C'est par rapport à cette notion d'entité pathologique transitoire que se pose le pronostic classique: bouffée isolée ou entrée dans la schizophrénie et que se discute l'efficacité du traitement.' Here *transitoire* and *isolée* (synonyms) are in opposition to *entrée dans*, which latter is cataphorically explained several sentences later. Hence: 'We must decide whether the disease is likely to be short-lived before we make the usual prognosis (isolated outburst or incipient schizophrenia) and discuss whether treatment will be effective.'

When sentences begin 'on the one hand', *en revanche*, etc., the translator's task is easy. But he often has to detect implied contrasts realized by one word in italics or inverted commas, or words such as 'only', 'just', 'merely', 'equally', 'also' and other functional words that indicate contrasts, or comparatives of adverbs and adjectives which refer back to a previous statement, not necessarily the last sentence. The most delicate contrasts can sometimes be discovered only by seizing the thought of the whole passage.

(e) *Redundancy*. In information theory, the function of redundancy is to counteract noise. In a text, redundancy may be bad writing, woolliness, etc. (avoiding 'monologophobia') which can be discreetly climinated by the translator. However, repetition, paraphrase, tautology and pleonasm (extended redundancy) can also be used to amplify, to clarify, to avoid false emphasis, to summarize, to assist comprehension in the face of the 'noise' of obscurity, irrelevance or complex thought. The translator has to detect the tautology before deciding whether to transfer it to the TL; in the following sentence, the opening and closing noun-phrases refer to the ending and the beginning of the same process: 'La saturation des villes oblige les principales entreprises à reconsidérer leur implantation dans les centres commerciaux traditionnels', and the translator surely has to clarify: 'As many towns are saturated, the main firms are re-examining their policy of setting up in these traditional commercial centres.' Again, any translator unacquainted with the reference would be confused by 'Palestine's Arabs swore . . . to drench the soil of that tiny country with the last drop of their blood in opposing any Big Power scheme to partition the Holy Land'.[24] Again, three consecutive sentences beginning: 'Mrs. Barbara Castle . . . The red-headed non-driver . . . The Minister who sits for Blackburn travelled . . .'"[24] are bad enough for an English reader, as Harold Evans has explained, and worse for a foreigner.

(f) *Conjunctions*. These include all linking words, interpolated clauses and phrases, disjuncts,[25] enclitics. They are often excessively used by writers to establish a colloquial style, the written equivalent of 'you know', 'sort of', 'let me think', and are more frequently in normal use in French and German than in English. Often they carry so little cognitive information (e.g. *quoi qu'il en soit*) that a translator may omit them.

(g) *Substitution.* Ruquaiya Hasan (1968) has pointed out that grammatical and lexical words are used for cohesive purposes to refer to an object or person mentioned in a sentence or the previous sentence. (This may be simply to avoid repetition.) Typical, grammatical words are 'the one', 'same', 'similar', 'equal', 'identical', 'other', which may have slightly concealed anaphoric references. R. Hasan lists lexical words (general nouns) such as 'thing', 'object', 'business', 'affair', etc. To these must be added common words such as *interlocuteur, der Motionär*, 'the speaker', *intervention*, which may have no equivalent in the TL. Frequently the translator will substitute the proper noun for the animate noun (e.g. *Herr Gauslin* for *der Motionär*) and the name of the object for the general noun. General nouns are usually marked by determiners such as *ce, un tel, solche,* etc.

(h) *Comparatives.* A comparison is always used cohesively. Thus a sentence beginning 'Der mehr elliptische ischämische Bereich liegt mit dem Zentrum, das immer am stärksten in Mitleidenschaft gezogen ist, im mittleren Vorderarmdrittel' ('The ischaemic section, which however is elliptic, is in the centre which is always most strongly affected, in the middle third of the forearm') refers the reader back to the previous sentence to find an adjective denoting geometrical shape contrasted with elliptic.

(i) *Initial negatives.* These are customarily a signal that their corresponding positives will follow, not only in contrasts such as 'not . . . but . . .', 'neither . . . nor', but in many passages beginning with a negative statement, sometimes ironically.

A translator has to look for cohesive terms if he cannot account for the sense of an item within its immediate (micro-)context. If he notes a cohesive term or its puzzling absence, he has to look beyond the sentence or paragraph he does not understand at the macrocontext, the whole passage. The following is an instance of cataphoric reference which can be detected because of the lack of logical sequence between *sculpture* and *environnement*: 'Malaval passe avec aisance de la peinture ou de la lithographie à la sculpture, à l'environnement ou à l'animation d'un lieu public.' Three columns later, this *Nouvel Observateur* article goes on: 'Malaval avait délaissé la peinture pour projeter un aménagement et pour des recherches sur l'environnement et l'animation par le son.'

Therefore, the first sentence could perhaps be translated: 'Malaval moves easily from painting or lithographs to sculpture, and then to the designs for the setting and sound-installation of a place of public entertainment.'

(j) *Punctuation.* A powerful cohesive factor (see Propositions, nos. 124–130).

(k) Most SL *rhetorical questions* become statements in English. English needs fewer connectives than other languages. French and Italian use hyphens to indicate enumerations.

132. Translation terms

It is characteristic of the still amateurish state of our art that we are burdened with such inaccurate and inadequate terms as 'loan-word' (e.g. *détente, rapprochement*) and 'loan-translation' (e.g. 'reason of state', 'National Assembly'). Is it too late to propose that they be replaced by 'transcribed word' (or 'adopted word' or 'adoption') and 'through-translation' respectively?

Wider questions

133. The impregnability of a language

The translator is in the best position to appreciate the 'total' difference between one language and another. He himself usually knows that he cannot write more than a few complex sentences in a foreign language without writing something unnatural and non-native, any more than he can speak one. He will be 'caught' every time, not by his grammar, which is probably suspiciously 'better' than an educated native's, not by his vocabulary, which may well be wider, but by his unacceptable or improbable collocations. Again, this 'total' difference appears when two passages are compared in a field such as medicine where the lexis of the two languages is close; the following French collocations chosen at random, for instance are suspect in English: *activité symptomatique; action sédative; anxiété des psychoses; à titre purement symptomatique; être inactif sur le symptome; structure d'intérêt biologique; esthétique industrielle.* A foreigner appears to go on making collocational mistakes however long he lives in his adopted country, possibly because he has never distinguished between grammar and lexicology. An educated native will also make mistakes in collocation, particularly if he is under the influence of interference, but he will correct himself intuitively. *Sprachgefuhl* means awareness of collocations. For the above reasons, translators rightly translate into their own language, and *a fortiori*, foreign teachers and students are normally unsuitable in a translation course.

134. Etymology

A knowledge of etymology can sometimes be as useful to a translator as to a language learner. (Incidentally, the discipline of translation could be described as tangential to that of language learning.) For difficult words, etymology may supply him with a 'bridge' word to take him to the TL meaning; thus for a German-speaking translator, the 'bridge word' for (It) *ghisa* is *giessen.* The whole point of learning etymology is to associate and distinguish former meanings of a word, not to confuse them with the present meaning.

135. The uses of translation

Far from being old-fashioned, a relic of classical education, etc., the ability to translate should be one of the main aims of a foreign language learner. Acquiring the four 'macroskills'[26] (ocular and auricular comprehension, oral and graphic composition) is essentially a selfish and self-centred activity. If the linguist is to have a social function, he has to 'transfer' his skills. This interlingual transference (I choose the term as a superordinate or generic term) includes all activities involving the transfer of sense from one language to another, including paraphrase, summary, précis, explanation, abstracting, definition, simultaneous, consecutive *ad hoc* and two-way interpretation as well as publication and information translation. All these activities *may* have some place in foreign language learning—I think translation is useful initially to ensure understanding when extensive explanation in a classroom is not possible, and later as a regular revision and consolidation procedure—but they are primarily activities practised for the benefit of third parties. The more important international co-operation, compromise and agreement to disagree becomes, the greater the 'transferring' linguist's (*Sprachmittlers*) responsibility. The more people go abroad, the more the linguist can help them to profit from and enjoy their visit. His job or vocation is to translate. It would be ironical if the practice of translation were not a component of his training.

136. The cult of ambiguity

The linguistics literature is too full of artificial ambiguous examples. Even without the context in a general statement a translator would normally assume that 'the police were told to stop drinking' was an example of defective syntax, since police would be more likely to be engaged in fighting alcoholism; therefore, in theory, the context conflicts with the syntax, even though the police in this country cannot stop anyone drinking (unless after hours!); again in 'Flying planes can be dangerous' (Chomsky), the gerund sense is more likely than the participle. Again in 'If the baby doesn't thrive on raw milk, boil it', the translator would see no semantic ambiguity, but would eliminate the grammatical ambiguity in his translation.

However, the translator is only concerned with such unnatural sentences when he is translating a book on linguistics. He is probably more concerned with lexical than with grammatical ambiguities, unless he is dealing with the unconscious or deliberate ambiguities of an author's thinking. In a sentence such as 'Il est inutile d'insister sur les tableaux cliniques' rendering as, 'It is unnecessary to draw attention to the clinical patterns' (because they are important), 'It is unnecessary to draw attention to the clinical patterns' (because we have plenty of other information) and 'It is useless to attach importance to . . . etc', one has three opposed translations which may or may not be clarified by the context.

137. Translation criticism

Translation criticism is applied translation theory. It has five purposes:

(a) to improve standards of translation;
(b) to provide an object lesson for translators;
(c) to throw light on ideas about translation at particular times and in particular subject-areas;
(d) to assist in the interpretation of the work of significant writers and significant translators.
(e) to assess critically semantic and grammatical differences between SL and TL.

Translation criticism has four basic procedures:

(1) to analyse the intention, predominant language function, tone, themes, register, style (syntactic and lexical), literary quality, cultural features, putative readership and setting of the SL text, and to propose an appropriate translation method;
(2) to make a detailed comparison between the SL and TL text, noting all significant semantic, stylistic, pragmatic and ideological differences (either in the whole TL text or in random passages);
(3) to assess the differences between the total impression of the SL and TL text, including in particular their interpretations of the subject-matter;
(4) to evaluate the translation.

The third procedure is often neglected: while the exposure of mistakes (in relation to the SL text and the facts of the matter, as well as the TL style and register) is important, this procedure is helpful only in relation to the translator's interpretation of the text.

I should add that translation criticism is an exercise of intelligence and imagination, and is only partially objective: Harris's (1975) attempts to quantify mistakes are futile, and both Reiss's (1977) and House's (1977a) categorizations are too rigid. (Koller (1978) and Newmark (1973) have previously criticized Reiss's misunderstanding of form-stressed texts.)

138. Etymology and translation

Ever since Bally (1932), who reacted so violently against it, etymology has been the whipping-boy of linguistics. Even Lyons (1977) who is always so careful to combine the traditionalist with the ultramodern, writes 'The etymology of a lexeme is irrelevant to its current meaning'. The remark has some truth 'operationally', but if one wants to understand a word properly one must know something of its history.

A translator may require a knowledge of etymology, which is a branch of linguistic 'science', for the following reasons:

(a) to assess the meaning of a current SL word, which may be a neologism, common word, or archaism in the language stock of a writer over a life span of up to eighty years;
(b) to discover the core and peripheral meanings of a word in a text written in a previous period;
(c) to detect and/or encourage the revival of previous senses of words, as many good writers have done;
(d) to understand the development of languages and cultures in relation to the texts they have to translate;
(e) to familiarize himself practically and generally with cognate word-relations, and the development of meaning, thus 'sensitizing' himself to the technical traps of such words as *âme, tour, utile, oreille, élément, métier, soupir, truculent, Mutter,* etc.—the surprises in the last lines of dictionary-entries.

Provided that no one goes on trying to identify the 'true' (etymo-) meaning of a word with its earliest or one of its earlier senses (which was the cause of the trouble in the schools and the pother among the structural linguists), translators and language-learners can only profit from a study of etymology.

139. Language, culture and translation

A language is partly the repository and reflection of a culture. Possibly, the most ancient features of the culture lie in the aspects of grammar associated with entities (nouns) such as animate/inanimate, male/female and animal/human/divine, with processes (verbs), such as time (present/past/future; durative/momentary; progressive/habitual/repetitive/static/dynamic/punctual/perfective/imperfective), and with deictics (pronouns), such as space (here/there, near/far, etc., in relation to the topic). The features of past cultures remaining in the lexis of a language are more detailed and numerous, and usually more recent and transitory.

Literal translation can throw some light on the relation between one language and another, and one language and its antecedents (earlier *état de langue*). It is also a tool in intercultural comparison, but the main evidence is in texts and informants, not in the language. Language is full of dead metaphors and symbols (e.g. 'sunrise'), and cultural historians have to find out when they become dead. Hence the weakness, as has been pointed out, many times, of Whorf's thesis which relies on indiscriminate literal translation. Many metaphors, however, are still latent and can be revived ('I weighed it up in my own scale')—hence the element of truth in Whorf's thesis. Other features of language are universal, and some cultural elements appear to become universal (e.g. the sun is no longer regarded as animate, divine or having a gender, but as an object in a majority and an increasing number of cultures).

A knowledge of etymology is essential in translating documents: in particular to determine whether words are being used in their literal, figurative, symbolical or a new technical sense.

Logical thought-processes are reflected in grammar rather than lexis, and they are clear of the metaphorical element in language; as knowledge grows, grammar becomes relatively culture-free and universal. Imaginative thought-processes, reflected in the lexical element of language, make use of and recreate metaphors, and are relatively culture-bound, but always with personal and universal elements.

A translator faced with creative writing has to weigh the universal, cultural and personal elements against each other.

140. Translation and language teaching

'The chief defect of the now universally condemned "Grammar–Translation Method" was that it used bad grammar and bad translation' (Catford, 1965).

No, it was not the chief defect. The chief defect was that the method left little or no time for anything else—on the whole, bad grammar and bad translation were all that was taught. The result was that few people learned to speak or write or translate; a few learned to read and appreciate literature, though it was also the wrong kind of literary appreciation. Needless to say, there were exceptions.

Remains the question of translation's place in language-teaching. In a basic five-year school course, say aged 10–15, where one assumes careful progression and graded tests, the main purpose is to teach the intralingual skills—reading, listening, speaking, writing (not in chronological order), and the culture. The place of translation is subsidiary but important, unless the teacher prefers direct method. No one should attempt to learn any new item without understanding what the item means: the ideal way is ostensively (pointing, pictures, slides, etc.), but if that cannot be done clearly and quickly (and usually it cannot) it should be through a quick translation before the word or sentence is internalized. Secondly, brief translations from native to foreign language are useful in consolidation and testing of spoken and written foreign utterances: the exercises should consist of basic grammatical transpositions and one-to-one lexical translations combined with other forms of consolidation and testing related to context and situation. In this four-year course, written translations of any source language text with much unfamiliar material that has to be looked up in dictionaries or grammars is a waste of valuable time. If the reading skill is being trained somewhat separately through readers, a little oral translation is usually necessary, but questions on the texts (often simple) and later discussion should be in the FL. After the four-year course, the position changes. The social language skills, viz. oral and spoken translation into and out of the foreign language, can then be trained. Here, the translation into English should be challenging and difficult (it is as much a test of English and of intelligence as of the FL), whilst translation from English should be realistic, e.g. notices, criticism, reports, letters, etc., written in straightforward modern language—not the artificial type of passage sometimes used in A-level to test difficult grammatical points or obscure vocabulary. Again, translation plays an essential part in the reading courses (for general texts) which should start at any age after 16.

In my opinion, the basic four-year course is not the place or time for exercises in contrastive analysis nor any concentrated attempt to eliminate interference for its own sake, although in a larger sense language-teaching is basically an attempt to eliminate this interference. On the other hand, I do not question the value of Dodson's bilingual method (1967) for those teachers dedicated to it (cf. my attitude to the direct method). Language-teaching method is linked to the teacher's personality. Faulty methods can be exposed, leaving a wide choice of sound methods.

141. Translation as an academic exercise

The cultural value of translation is sometimes questioned, since many students tend to feel that translation has little justification as an academic discipline.

Culture has at least two distinct senses, and translators, like linguists, tend to think of it as the sum of a people's customs, products and ways of thinking. However, I am now referring to culture as high culture, or as intellectual development.

My short answer would be that not only are all thriving intellectual and artistic cultures heavily indebted to translation—take our debt to Greek, Roman and Arabic literature, as well as to the Icelandic Sagas, but many of the finest writers, the poets in particular, have translated and written about translation. Amongst German writers, the line stretches from Goethe, who translated Diderot and wrote much about translation, through the Romantics and the Symbolists (notably Rilke and George) to Brecht and Böll. In England, we perhaps start with Chaucer's 'Boece', whilst the main eighteenth-century stress is on Dryden and Pope; as George Steiner has said, there is scarcely an important English or American poet since the Victorians who has not also been a translator—one thinks particularly of Joyce, Graves and Auden. Because poetry uniquely uses all the resources of language, it has often been considered untranslatable, yet the translation of poetry is almost as old and as flourishing as poetry itself.

However, up to now I have produced evidence for the cultural value of translation without answering the question. I believe that translation is an exceptionally difficult and challenging exercise; that it demands infinite curiosity and about things as well as words, requires the consultation of people as well as books; that it is collaborative, but finally is usually the responsibility of one person; that it varies from the most abstruse inquiry about the symbolic meanings of roses or acanthuses (Cooper, 1978; Greenaway and Marsh, 1978) to the most mundane and all too common misprint or single inverted commas; that it is a splendid exercise in writing one's own language; stylistically many translations can be made better, more relevant, more lucid, more 'classical' than their originals; at the same time, it is the most scientific of literary exercises, requiring reasons for every sentence, always subject to the back-translation test, which is itself only evidence, not infallible, being applied usually to primary meanings only; thus if Wolfgang Doeppe translates Richard Aldington's 'We sat together in the trench' as, 'So hockten wir im Schützengraben', he has to give reasons for *hockten* rather than *sassen*, and it is not necessarily wrong.

Nothing demonstrates the complexity of language, and of specific texts, more vividly and explicitly than translation. Further, nothing exposes good writing and bad writing so nakedly as translation. Bad writing is bad writing in any language, and what *sounds* impressive in language X or Y may indeed be more clearly shown up as rubbish in language Z. In this sense, translation could be regarded as a refutation of any relativist theory of language.

I have spoken of the 'active' element in translation. It is important as a source of diffusion of knowledge of every kind. By understanding the development of every kind of culture in other civilizations, we have also enriched the understanding of our own.

Translation is exacting, and must be exact. Provided the original is not dreary and I have to admit that a trivial or diffuse original is hardly worth translating, and there is no doubt that computer translation (Lawson, 1979) is making progress with simple texts—translation is a superb academic exercise, particularly when it is combined with translation criticism, and discussion. It offers a particular insight into the nature of language as well as contrastive linguistic and cultural studies. As an academic exercise, the subject is only at its beginning. I have had a student doing a comparison of English Dante translations and now one is doing a dissertation on 'Translation as Ideological Appropriation' based on various translations of Rousseau's *Social Contract.* I was recently in Finland and proposed research on translations of publicity material; in the hotel I stayed at, a leaflet recommended the bar as a place for meeting a lot of gay people. I emphasize that this subject offers tremendous scope for post-graduate research. One aspect is not unlike the extraordinary position in art criticism at present: just as art historians are discovering that many paintings have been falsely attributed to great masters, so I think we shall find that much misinterpretation of foreign literatures, in particular Russian, rests on consistent mistranslation. It must not be forgotten that the more difficult a text is, the more a translator has to interpret. Again, a worthwhile academic exercise.

Lastly, I must stress that whilst poetry is a special case, technical or institutional translation is often just as, if not more, challenging and rewarding than literary translation. In England, we still have the remnants of an evil tradition that scorns trade, engineering, manufacturing, hard work, practical details in favour of Latin and Greek studies, knowledge for knowledge's sake, and idle speculative theorizing: this 'translates' into the false notion that technical translation is easy and boring because it is concerned with an exact international intertranslatable language, mere 'intracultural verbalism', whilst literary translation alone is worthy of an academic's time and study. Nothing could be more misguided. When a non-literary piece is well written, it often presents the same demands as literary translation, and when it is poorly written (jargon, non-sequiturs, etc.), the demands are sometimes even greater. Moreover, both are often equally rich in various levels of metaphor, which is the central problem of translation.

Technical translation

142. When generic becomes specific

When a generic term (hyperonym, *Oberbegriff*) is collocated as an alternative one of its specific terms (hyponyms, *Unterbegriffe*), it is forced to lose its generic sense and to take on another of its specific subordinate senses. Thus 'Le diverticule de Meckel n'a dans la majorité des cas aucune traduction clinique ou pathologique, et sa découverte est fortuite au cours d'une laparotomie'. 'In most cases, the presence of Meckel's diverticulum is not shown by any clinical or pathological evidence, and it is only detected accidentally during a laparotomy.' 'Pathological', theoretically a generic term covering all disease, is contrasted with 'clinical' (patients' signs and symptoms) and is narrowed to diagnosis by laboratory tests, X-ray examinations, etc.

143. Clarity or brevity: a verb problem

Translators have to make their own decision whether to encourage, follow or resist the general tendency in the jargons for verbs to be swallowed up in adjectives, nouns and adverbs. Any criterion of style, purity, etc., is mainly subjective (on the *Vorstellung* level), but provided the self-expressive function is not dominant in the text, the translator is justified in making the transposition (transposing!) if the text becomes clearer: 'Sa découverte nécessite l'examen d'un mètre de grêle'. 'To detect it, one must examine about a metre of the small intestine'. 'L'arsénal interventionniste actuel en résume l'historique'. 'The present stock of methods for treating it in itself constitutes an account of the disorder'.

144. Grammar *v.* Lexis

Not infrequently, a language's synonymical resources are richer and subtler in its grammar than in its lexis: a smooth collocation therefore requires a displacement of grammar rather than lexis. Thus in, 'Le medicin, en connaissant les inconvénients de certains antibiotiques avec les relaxants musculaires utilisés en anesthésie, essayera d'éviter l'administration de ces antibiotiques', one has a choice between varying *en connaissant* (a) grammatically (as/because/since/he knows, knowing, with a knowledge of), (b) lexically (knowing, being aware of, conscious of). The grammar, or a grammatical/lexical combination, often offers greater possibilities.

145. British and American English

For a British English translator, the main problems are cultural rather than linguistic after he has mastered the spelling traps in technical words (*e* for *oe, ae,* a few *k*'s for c's). *Questions d'internat* goes 'straight' into American English as *internship problems* (matters, difficulties), but '*A houseman's*' or '*housemanship*' has the wrong connotations, and 'medical training in hospitals' may be a more suitable label in British English.

Notes to propositions

[1] 'Collocation' in this essay is applied in rather a narrower sense than J. R. Firth's and is more in line with M. Joos's *Semology: a linguistic theory of meaning* (Bobbs-Merrill Reprints, Language and Linguistics No. 54). Firth, in this brilliant essay ('Modes of meaning' in *Papers in linguistics 1934–51*, Oxford University Press, 1964), is concerned with 'collocability' or 'meaning by collocation', and although he does not define collocation, he applies it to all words or word-groups with which a word may typically combine; he also analyses Swinburne's poetic diction in terms of its unusual collocations. Firth's stress on collocation and the situation of the context, which parallel Frege's *Sinn und Bedeutung*, are of great interest to a translator.

[2] *The Sunday Times*, 5 April 1973.

[3] 'Connotative' here is used in opposition to 'denotative' in the sense that the 'denotation' of the word 'Dachau' is a small town near Munich, and the 'connotation' is imprisonment and mass murder by Nazis. A connotation may be patent, as above, or latent, depending on its context. Connotation is here distinguished from intension: the word 'flower' has a smaller intension than the word 'dog rose' (fewer properties), but a larger connotation (beauty, fragility, short life, etc.). The word 'dog rose' has no connotation at all.

[4] R. Cheverney, *Les Cadres*, Juillard, Paris, 1967, p. 169.

[5] Formulated by Otto Kade in 'Zu einigen Grundlagen der allgemeinen Übersetzungstheorie', *Fremdsprachen*, 1965, p. 172, and W. Haas in 'The theory of translation' in *The theory of meaning*, ed. G. H. R. Parkinson, Oxford University Press, 1962.

[6] See R. Quirk, S. Greenbaum, G. Leech and J. Svartvik, *Grammar of contemporary English*, Longman, 1972.

[7] W. Koller, *Grundprobleme der Übersetzungstheorie*, Francke, Berne and Munich, 1972, p. 114.

[8] Example adapted from Koller, op. cit., p. 150.

[9] See 'Die Aufgabe des Übersetzers' (Essay in *Das Problem des Übersetzens*, ed. H. J. Störig, p. 166).

[10] Personal communication.

[11] From *L'Art hollandais*, p. 155.

[12] H. Read, *English prose style*, Bell, p. 158.

[13] From *World War II*, vol. II, Orbis, 1972.

[14] Stendhal's text is from his *Correspondance* (24 May 1843): 'Les intérieurs d'âmes que j'ai vus dans la retraite de Moscou m'ont à jamais dégouté des observations que je puis faire sur les êtres grossiers, ces manches à sabre qui composent une armée.' For *manches à sabre* Littre glosses: *'militaires considérés comme des machines à tuer, qui ne sont bons qu'à donner un coup de sabre.'* But it is difficult to translate the intelligence of the most intelligent of all prose writers.

[15] W. Wätzoldt, *Dürer und seine Zeit*, Phaidon Verlag, p. 320.

[16] See R. Hasan, 'Code, register and social dialect', in *Class, codes and control*, vol. II, ed. B. Bernstein, Routledge and Kegan Paul, 1971.

[17] Words used connotatively are translated differently depending on the reader. Even in the translation of this superb speech published in *The Listener* on 14 September 1972, the word 'Munich' should perhaps have been glossed.

[18] Didier, 1972.

[19] Heidelberg, 1970.

[20] See F. de Saussure, *Cours de linguistique générale*, ed. Payot, Paris, 1955.

[21] See his essay in *Language*, ed. A. Martinet, Pleiade, NRF, 1968.

[22] I give below an example of some *trouvailles*:

'On sait que quatres espèces de schistosomes sont pathogènes pour l'homme et que les manifestations pathologiques observées sont en rapport avec l'espèce du parasite et sa localisation particulière dans l'organisme humain. Classiquement, bien que la concordance ne soit pas absolue, on distingue:
— la bilharziose uro-génitale, due à un schistosome haematobium
— la bilharziose rectale, beaucoup moins fréquente, à schistosoma intercalatum (etc., etc.).

The following translation is by Havila Cooper:

'Four species of schistosomas are known to cause human disease and to produce pathological symptoms which differ according to the species of parasite and its specific localization in the human organism. Traditionally, although the species and their localization do not always correspond, the following distinctions are made:
(a) urogenital bilharziasis, due to *schistosoma haematobium*
(b) rectal bilharziasis (which is much less common), due to *schistosoma intercalatum* (etc.).'

The translation appears to me to bring out the four parallel relationships between the parasites, the disease, and their localizations more sharply than the original text. The phrase *en rapport avec* is strengthened by 'differ according to'. The unattached *concordance*, which might be lost as a general parenthetical comment, but is explicated in the translation, firmly and, I think, irresistibly relates the two main sentences to each other. The emphases in the original are convincingly redistributed. In my opinion, this translation successfully intuits the meaning within and between the words of the original text.

[23] *Class and conflict in an industrial society*, Routledge and Kegan Paul, 1959, p. 7.

[24] H. Evans, *Newsman's English*, Heinemann, p. 47.

[25] These terms are explained in the invaluable *Grammar of contemporary English* by R. Quirk, S. Greenbaum, G. Leech and J. Svartvik, Longman, 1972. Many other terms in this article are admirably defined in R. R. K. Hartmann's and F. C. Stork's *Dictionary of language and linguistics*, Applied Science Publishers, 1972.

[26] For these terms, see C. Vaughan James and S. Rouve, *Survey of curricula and performance in modern languages 1971–72*, CILT.

Bibliography

Adams, P. (ed.) (1972) *Language in thinking*, Penguin Books, Harmondsworth.
Adorno, T. W. (1973) *Negative dialectics*, Routledge and Kegan Paul, London.
Agricola, E. (1969) *Wörter und Wendungen*, VEB Bibliographisches Institut, Leipzig.
Alpert, M. (1979) Letter in *Incorporated Linguist* **18** (2) (Spring 1979) 64–65.
Arnold, M. (1928) *Essays literary and critical*, Dent, London.
Austin, J. L. (1962) *How to do things with words*, Cambridge University Press, London.
Austin, J. L. (1963) 'Performative-constative' in E. C. Caton (ed.), *Philosophy and ordinary language*, University of Illinois Press, Urbana.
Avril, P. (translated by John Ross) (1969) *Politics in France*, Pelican Books, Harmondsworth.
Bachrach, J. A. (1974) 'An experiment in automatic dictionary look-up', *Incorporated Linguist* **13** (2) 47–49.
Bally, C. (1932) *Linguistique générale et linguistique française*, Leroux, Paris.
Bar-Hillel, Y. (1964) *Language and information: selected essays on their theory and application*, Addison-Wesley, Reading, Mass.
Beekman, J. and J. Callow (1974) *Translating the word of God*, Zondervan, Grand Rapids, Mich.
Belloc, H. (1928) 'On translation' in *A conversation with an angel*, Cape, London.
Benjamin, W. (1923) 'The translator's task' in H. Arendt (ed.) (1970) *Illuminations*, Cape, London.
Blondel, J. (1969) *The Government of France*, Routledge and Kegan Paul, London.
Bolinger, D. (1965) 'The atomization of meaning' in *Language* **41**.
Booth, A. D. (1967) *Machine translation*, North-Holland, Amsterdam.
Braudel, F. (translated by M. Kochan) (1967) *Civilisation matérielle et capitalisme*, Armand Colin, Paris.
Brislin, R. W. (1976) *Translation*, Gardner Press, New York.
Brooke-Rose, C. (1958) *A grammar of metaphor*, Secker & Warburg, London.
Brower, R. A. (1966) *On translation*, Oxford University Press, New York.
Buber, M.: see Störig (1963).
Bühler, K. (1934) *Die Sprachtheorie*, Fischer, Jena (2nd edn. 1965, Stuttgart).
Butler, G. (1977) Inaugural Lecture, University of Bath (unpublished).
Cary, E. (1956) *La traduction dans le monde moderne*, Georg et Cie, Geneva.
Catford, J. C. (1965) *A linguistic theory of translation*, Oxford University Press, London.
Cauer, P. (1896) *Die Kunst des Übersetzens*, Weidmann, Berlin.
Celan, P. (translated by C. Middleton) (1972), *Penguin European poets*, Penguin Books, Harmondsworth.
Chomsky, N. (1957) *Syntactic structures*, Mouton, The Hague.
Chomsky, N. (1965) *Aspects of the theory of syntax*, Massachusetts Institute of Technology Press, Cambridge, Mass.
Chomsky, N. (1972) *Studies on semantics in generative grammar*, Mouton, The Hague.
Chomsky, N. (1976) *Reflections on language*, Temple Smith/Fontana, London.
Cicero, M. Tullius (1948) *De oratore*, Heinemann, London.
Cobb, R. (1969) *A second identity*, Oxford University Press, London.
Cobban, A. (1965) *A history of modern France*, Pelican Books, Harmondsworth.
Cooke, D. (1959) *The language of music*, Oxford University Press, Oxford.
Cooper, J. C. (1978) *Illustrated encyclopaedia of traditional symbols*, Thames & Hudson, London.
Corder, S. Pit (1973) *Introducing applied linguistics*, Penguin Books, Harmondsworth.
Coseriu, E. (1978): see Wandruszka (1978).
Crick, M. (1976) *Explorations in language and meaning*, Malaby Press, London.
Croce, B. (1922) *Aesthetics*, P. Owen, London.
Cumming, R. D. (ed.) (1968) *The philosophy of Jean-Paul Sartre*, Methuen, London.
Cummings, E. E. (1963) *Selected poems 1922–1958*, Penguin Books, Harmondsworth.
Dagut, M. B. (1976) 'Can metaphor be translated?' *Babel* xxii (1) 22–23.
Dahrendorf, R. (1969) *Class and conflict in an industrial society*, Routledge and Kegan Paul, London.
Darbelnet, J. (1977) 'Niveaux de la traduction,' *Babel* xxiii (1) 6–17.
Derrida, J. (translated by A. Bass) (1978) *Writing and difference*, Routledge and Kegan Paul, London.
Diller, H. J. and J. Kornelius (1978) *Linguistische Probleme der Übersetzung*, Niemeyer, Tübingen.
Dodson, C. J. (1967) *Language teaching and the bilingual method*, Pitman, London.

Dryden, J. (1684) 'Preface to Ovid's *Epistles*' in A. Ker (ed.) (1900) *Essays*, Oxford University Press, London.
Dummett, M. (1978) *Truth and other enigmas*, Cambridge University Press, London.
Empson, W. (1951) *The structure of complex words*, Chatto & Windus, London.
European Communities Glossary (1974) (F–E), 5th edn., Council of The European Communities, Brussels.
Evans, H. (1972) *Newsman's English*, Holt, Rinehart & Winston, New York.
Evans-Pritchard, E. E. (1975) *Theories of primitive religion*, Clarendon Press, Oxford.
Fedorov, A. V. (1958) *Vvedenje v teoriju perevoda*, Moscow.
Fedorov, A. V. (1968) *Osnovy obščej teoriji perevoda*, Moscow.
Firth, J. R. (1964) 'Modes of meaning' in *Papers in linguistics 1934–51*, Oxford University Press, London.
Firth, J. R. (1968) 'Linguistic analysis and translation' in F. R. Palmer (ed.), *Selected papers 1952–9*, Indiana University Press, Bloomington.
Francescato, F. (1977) 'Polysémie et métaphore' in L. Gräns (ed.), *Theory and practice of translation*, Land, Berne, Frankfurt.
Frege, G. (1960) 'Sense and reference' in P. Geach and M. Black, *Translations from the philosophical writings of Gottlob Frege,* Blackwell, Oxford.
Freud, S. (translated by A. A. Brill) (1916) *Wit and its relation to the unconscious*, T. Fischer Unwin, London.
Freud, S. (translated by J. Strachey) (1976) *Jokes and their relation to the unconscious,* Penguin Books, Harmondsworth, and Hogarth Press, London.
Friederich, W. (1969) *Die Technik des Übersetzens*, Hueber, Munich.
Fröland, R. (1975) *Grass-Übersetzungen*, Stockholm.
Fuller, F. (1973) *A handbook for translators*, C. Smythe, Gerrards Cross.
Garvin, P. (1955) *Prague school reader on aesthetics, literary structure and style*, Georgetown University Press, Washington DC.
Geckeler, H. (1971) *Zur Wortfelddiskussion*, Fink, Munich.
Gläser, R. (1976) 'Zur Übersetzbarkeit von Eigennamen', *Linguistische Arbeitsberichte*, No. 13, Sektion TAS, KMU, Leipzig.
Goethe, J. W. v. (1813) 'Zu brüderlichem Andenken Wielands', *Sämtliche Werke*, Propyläen edition, vol. 26, p. 94, Munich, 1909.
Goethe, J. W. v. (1814) *Noten und Abhandlungen zu besserem Verständnis des west-östlichen Divans, Sämtliche Werke,* Propyläen Edition, vol. 3, p. 554, Munich, 1909.
Goethe, J. W. v. (1826) *Sämtliche Werke*, vol. 39 (letter to Thomas Carlyle), Propyläen Edition, Munich, 1909.
Gumperz (1975) in P. P. Giglioli (ed.), *Language and Social Context*, Penguin, Harmondsworth.
Gombrich, E. H. (1972) *Symbolic images*, Phaidon, London.
Gombrich, E. H. (1978) *Meditations on a hobby horse,* Phaidon, London.
Gouadec, D. (1974) *Comprendre traduire*, Bordas, Paris.
Greenaway, K., and J. Marsh (1978) *The illuminated language of flowers*, Macdonald Jane's, London.
Goffman (1975) in P. P. Giglioli (ed.), *Language and Social Context*, Penguin, Harmondsworth.
Güttinger, F. (1963) *Zielsprache*, Maressê, Zürich.
Haas, W. (1962) 'The theory of translation' in G. H. R. Parkinson (ed.), *The theory of meaning*, Oxford University Press, London.
Halliday, M. A. K. (1961) 'Categories of the theory of grammar', *Word* **17,** 241–92.
Halliday, M. A. K. (1973) *Explorations in the functions of language*, Edward Arnold, London.
Harris, B. (1975) 'Notation and index for information congruence in translation', *Meta* **20** (3) 184–93.
Harris, B. (1977) *Papers in translatology*, Ottawa University.
Harris, B. and B. Sherwood (1977) 'Translating as an innate skill', *NATO Symposium on language, interpretation and communication*, Plenum Press, New York and London.
Hartmann, P. and H. Vernay (1970) *Sprachwissenschaft und Übersetzen*, Hueber, Munich.
Hartmann, R. R. K. and F. C. Stork (1972) *Dictionary of language and linguistics*, Applied Science Publishers, Barking.
Hasan, R. (1968) *Grammatical cohesion in spoken and written English I* (Programme in Linguistics and Language Teaching, Paper 7), Longman, London.
Helbig, G. (1977) 'Partikeln und illokutionare Indikatoren in Dialog', *Deutsch als Fremdsprache* **1** (1977) 30–44.
Helbig, G. and W. Schenkel (1969) *Valenz - und Distributionswörterbuch deutscher Verben,* Wörtesbuch zur Valeng und Distribution deutscher Verben, VEB Verlag Enzyklopädie, Leipzig.
Herder, J. G.: see M. Huber (1968).
Hoare, Q., and G. Nowell Smith (1971) *Prison notebooks of Antonio Gramsci (1947)*, Lawrence & Wishart, London.
House, J. (1977a) *A model for translation quality assessment*, Gunter Narr, Tübingen.
House, J. (1977b) 'A model for assessing translation quality', *Meta* **22** (2) 103–9.
Huber, M (1968) *Studien zur Theorie des Übersetzens*, Hain, Meisenheim am Glan.
Hugnet, G. (ed.) (1934) *Petite anthologie poétique du Surréalisme*, editions J. Buchet, Paris.
Humboldt, W. v. (1816) *Einleitung zu Agamemnon*: see Störig (1963).

Hymes, D., and J. Gumperz (1972) *Directions in sociolinguistics*, Holt, Rinehart & Winston, New York.
Jäger, G. (1975) *Translation und Translationslinguistik*, VEB Max-Niemeyer-Verlag, Halle.
Jakobson, R. (1960) 'Linguistics and poetics' in T. Sebeok (ed.), *Style in language*, Massachusetts Institute of Technology Press, Cambridge, Mass.
Jakobson, R. (1966) 'On linguistic aspects of translation': see Brower (1966).
Jakobson, R. (1971) *Selected writings*, vol. 2, Word and language, Mouton, The Hague.
Jakobson, R. (1973) *Main trends in the science of language*, Allen & Unwin, London.
James, C. V., and S. Rouve (1973) *Survey of curricula and performance in modern languages, 1971–2*, Centre for Information on Language Teaching and Research, London.
Jerome, St. (400) *Letter to Pammachius*: See Störig (1963), 1–13.
Joos, M. (1967) *The five clocks*, Harcourt, Brace & World, New York.
Joos, M. (n.d.) *Semology: a linguistic theory of meaning*, Language & Linguistics No. 54, Bobbs-Merrill, Indianapolis.
Joyce, J. (1960) *Ulysses*, Bodley Head, London.
Joyce, J. (1964) *Finnegan's wake*, Faber, London.
Jumpelt, R. W. (1961) *Die Übersetzung naturwissenschaftlicher und technischer Literatur*, Langenscheidt, Berlin/Schöneberg.
Kade, O. (1965) 'Zu einigen Grundlagen der allgemeinen Übersetzungstheorie, *Fremdsprachen*, p. 172.
Kade, O. (1968) *Zufall und Gesetzmässigkeit in der Übersetzung*, VEB Verlag Enzyklopädie, Leipzig.
Kapp, V. (ed.) (1974) *Übersetzer und Dolmetscher*, Quelle & Meyer, Heidelberg.
Katz, J. J. and J. A. Fodor (1964) 'The structure of a semantic theory' in J. A. Fodor and J. J. Katz (eds.), *The structure of language*, Prentice-Hall, Englewood Cliffs, NJ.
Keller, H. (1977) 'Retrial', *The Spectator*, 24 Sept. 1977.
Kempson, R. (1977) *Semantic theory*, Cambridge University Press, London.
Kloepfer, W. (1967) *Die Theorie der literarischen Übersetzung*, Fink, Munich.
Knox, R. A. (1957) *On English translation*, Oxford University Press, Oxford.
Koller, W. (1972) *Grundprobleme der Übersetzungstheorie*, Franke, Berne.
Koller, W. (1978) 'Kritik der Theorie der Übersetzungskritik', *IRAL* xvi, 2.
Komissarov, V. H. (1973) *Slovo o perevode*, Moscow.
Larbaud, V. (1946) *Sous l'invocation de S. Jérôme*, Gallimard, Paris.
Lawson, V. (1979) 'Tigers and polar bears: translating and the computer', *Incorporated Linguist*, **18** (3) 81–86.
Lederer, M. (1976) *Synecdoque et traduction* (Etudes de Linguistique Appliquée 24), Didier, Paris.
Leech, E. (1966) 'Animal categories and verbal abuse' in E. H. Lenneberg (ed.), *New directions in the study of language*, Massachusetts Institute of Technology Press, Cambridge, Mass.
Lenneberg, E. H. (1967) *The biological foundation of language*, Wiley, New York.
Lévi-Strauss, C. (1962) *La pensée sauvage*, Plon, Paris.
Lévi-Strauss, C. (translated anon.) (1966) *The savage mind*, Weidenfeld & Nicolson, London.
Lévi-Strauss, C. (1974) (translated by Claire Jakobson and Brooke Grundfest Schoepf) *Structural anthropology*, Penguin, Harmondsworth.
Levin, S. R. (1977) *The semantics of metaphor*, Johns Hopkins University Press, Baltimore.
Levy, J. (1969) *Die literarische Übersetzung*, Athenäum, Frankfurt.
Lewis, D. (1979) 'East German—a new language,' *GDR Monitor* **1**, 50–57, Dundee.
Lublinskaya (translated by B. Pearce) (1968) *French absolutism*, Cambridge University Press, Cambridge.
Luther, M. (1530) *Sendbrief vom Dolmetschen*: see Störig (1963).
Lyons, J. (1968) *Introduction to theoretical linguistics*, Cambridge University Press, London.
Lyons, J. (1972) 'Human language' in R. A. Hinde (ed.), *Non-verbal communication*, Royal Society and Cambridge University Press, London.
Lyons J. (1976) 'Structuralism in linguistics' in D. Robey (ed.), *Structuralism: an introduction*, Clarendon Press, Oxford.
Lyons, J. (1977) *Semantics*, vols I and II, Cambridge University Press, London.
Maillot, J. (1969) *La traduction scientifique et technique*, Eyrolles, Paris.
Malblanc, A. (1961) *Stylistique comparée du français et de l'allemand*, Didier, Paris.
Mann, T. (1974) 'Der Zauberberg', *Collected works*, vol. 1, Fischer, Frankfurt.
Martinet, A. (1960) *Eléments de linguistique générale*, Colin, Paris.
Martinet, A. (1964) *Elements of general linguistics*, Faber, London.
Matoré, G. (1953) *La méthode en lexicologie*, Didier, Paris.
Montagu, A. (1966) *The anatomy of swearing*, Rapp & Whiting, London.
Morris, C. S. (1955) *Signs, language and behaviour*, Prentice-Hall, Englewood Cliffs, NJ.
Morris, C. W. (1971) *Writings on the general theory of signs* (Approaches to Semiotics), Mouton, The Hague, Paris.
Mounin, G. (1955) *Les belles infidèles*, Cahiers du Sud, Paris.
Mounin, G. (1963) *Les problèmes théoriques de la traduction*, Gallimard, Paris.
Mounin, G. (1964) *La machine à traduire: histoire des problèmes linguistiques*, Mouton, The Hague.

Mounin, G. (1967) *Die Übersetzung; Geschichte, Theorie, Anwendung*, Nynphenburger, Munich.
Nabokov, V.: see Pushkin (1964).
Neubert, A. (1968) 'Pragmatische Aspekte der Übersetzung' in *Grundfragen der Übersetzungswissenschaft*, VEB Verlag Enzyklopädie, Leipzig.
Neubert, A. (1972) 'Der Name in Sprache und Gesellschaft', *Name und Übersetzung*, no. 27, Akademie-Verlag, Berlin.
Newmark, P. P. (1969) 'Some notes on translation and translators', *Incorporated Linguist* **8** (4) 79–85.
Newmark, P. P. (1973) 'An approach to translation', *Babel*, **19** (1) 3–19.
Newmark, P. P. (1976) 'A tentative preface to translation', *The Audio-Visual Language Journal* **14** (3) 161–9.
Newton, F. (1961) *The jazz scene*, Penguin Books, Harmondsworth.
Nida, E. A. (1964) *Towards a science of translating*, Brill, Leiden.
Nida, E. A. (1974a) *Exploring semantic structures*, Fink, Munich.
Nida, E. A. (1974b) 'Translation' in T. Sebeok (ed.), *Current trends in linguistics*, vol. 12, Mouton, The Hague.
Nida, E. A. (1975a) *Componential analysis of meaning*, Mouton, The Hague.
Nida, E. A. (1975b) *Language, structure and translation* (essays selected by A. S. Dil), Stanford University Press, Stanford.
Nida, E. A. (1977) *Translating is communicating* (unpublished).
Nida, E. A. and C. Taber (1969) *Theory and practice of translating*, Brill, Leiden.
Nietzsche, F. (1882): see Störig (1963).
Nietzsche, F. (1962) *Complete works*, Hauser.
Novalis (1798): see Störig (1963).
Nunberg, G. (1978) 'Slang, usage-conditions and l'arbitraire du signe' in *Papers from the parasession on the lexicon*, Chicago Linguistic Society.
O'Casey, S. (1958) *I knock at the door*, Macmillan, London.
Ortega y Gasset, J. (1937) *Miseria y esplendor de la traducción:* see Störig (1963).
Panofsky, E. (1970) *Meaning in the visual arts*, Penguin Books, Harmondsworth.
Pears, D. (1971) *Wittgenstein* (Fontana Modern Masters), Fontana, London.
Peirce, C. S. (1934) *Collected papers*, Harvard University Press, Cambridge, Mass.
Pottier, B. (1974) *Linguistique générale*, Klinksieck, Paris.
Pound, E. (1934) *An ABC of reading*, Faber, London.
Pushkin, A. S. (translated V. Nabokov) (1964) *Eugene Onegin*, Bollinger, New York.
Quine, W. V. (1959) 'Meaning and translation' in R. A. Brower (ed.), *On translation*, Harvard University Press, Cambridge, Mass.
Quine, W. V. (1960) *Word and object*, Massachusetts Institute of Technology Press, Cambridge, Mass.
Quirk, R. (1964) *The use of English*, Longman, London.
Quirk, R., Greenbaum, S., Leech, G., and Svartvik, J. (1972) *Grammar of contemporary English*, Longman, Harlow.
Rabin, C. (1966) 'The linguistics of translation' in *Aspects of translation* (pref. A. H. Smith), Secker & Warburg, London.
Racine, J. (translated by Tony Harrison) (1977) *Phèdre* (unpublished).
Read, H. (1928) *English prose style*, Bell, London.
Reiss, K. (1971) *Möglichkeiten und Grenzen der Übersetzungskritik*, Hueber, Munich.
Reiss, K. (1977) *Texttyp und Übersetzungsmethode. Der operative Text*, Scriptor, Kronberg.
Reum, A. (1920) *Petit dictionnaire de style*, Weber, Leipzig.
Richards, I. A. (1965) *The philosophy of rhetoric*, Oxford University Press, New York.
Richards, I. A. (1968) *Interpretation in teaching*, Routledge and Kegan Paul, London.
Rieu, E. V. (1953) 'Translation' in *Cassell's Encyclopedia of Literature,* vol. 1, Cassell, London.
Russell, R. (1979) 'The statutes of Quebec' (linguistic interference), *Meta* **24,** Montreal.
Ryle, G. (1963) *The concept of mind*, Penguin Books, Harmondsworth.
Sartre, J-P. (1960) *Critique de la raison dialectique*, Gallimard, Paris.
Savory, T. H. (1968) *The art of translation*, Cape, London.
Schleiermacher, F. (1813) *Methoden des Übersetzens:* see Störig (1963).
Schopenhauer, A. (1851): see Störig (1963).
Schwarz, W. (1970) *Principles and problems of Biblical translation*, Cambridge University Press, London.
Searle, J. R. (1979) 'Le sens littéral', *Langue Française* **42,** 15–23, Larousse, Paris.
Seleskovitch, D. (1976) 'Traduire: de l'expérience aux concepts', *Etudes de linguistique appliquée*, **24,** 36–47, Didier, Paris.
Seleskovitch, D. (1977) 'Why interpreting is not tantamount to translating languages', *Incorporated Linguist*, **16** (2) 22–33.
Seleskovitch, D. (1979) 'Traduction et mécanismes du langage' in *Parallèles 2,* University of Geneva.
Shattuck, R. (1971) *The craft and context of translation*, ed. W. Arrowsmith and R. Shattuck, University of Texas Press, Austin, Texas.

Smith, A. H. (1958) *Aspects of translation,* Secker & Warburg, London.
Smith, J. T. (1978): in A. Auswaks and R. A. Pemberton (eds): *Polyglot,* Polytechnic of Central London.
Sparer, M. (1979) 'Pour une dimension culturelle de la traduction juridique', *Meta* **24** (1) 68–94.
Spears, E. (1966) *Two men who saved France*, Eyre & Spottiswoode, London.
Spitzbart, H. (1972) *Spezialprobleme der wissenschaftlichen und technischen Übersetzung*, Max Niemeyer & Hueber, Halle.
Spitzer, L. (1948) *Linguistics and literary history: essays in stylistics*, Princeton University Press.
Steiner, G. (1966) Introduction to *Penguin book of modern verse translation*, Penguin Books, Harmondsworth.
Steiner, G. (1975) *After Babel: aspects of language and translation*, Oxford University Press, Oxford.
Steiner, G. (1978) *'On difficulty' and other essays*, Oxford University Press, Oxford.
Steiner, T. R. (1975) *English translation theory 1650-1800*, van Gorcum, Assen, Amsterdam.
Stendhal (translated by M. R. B. Shaw) (1958) *La Chartreuse de Parme,* Penguin Books, Harmondsworth.
Störig, H. J. (1963) *Das Problem des Übersetzens*, Wissenschaftliche Buchgesellschaft, Darmstadt.
Strawson, P. F. (1970a) 'On referring' in Parkinson, G. R. H. (ed.), *Theory of meaning*, Oxford University Press, London.
Strawson, P. F. (1970b) *Meaning and truth*, Oxford University Press, Oxford.
Svejtser, A. D. (1973) *Perevod i lingvistika*, Moscow.
Tesnière, L. (1959) *Eléments de syntaxe structurale*, Klinksiek, Paris.
Trier, J. (1973) *Aufsätze und Vorträge zur Wortfeldtheorie*, Mouton, The Hague.
Truffaut, L. (1968) *Grundprobleme der deutsch-französischen Übersetzung*, Georgetown University Press, Washington DC.
Tytler, A. F. (1790) *Essay on the principles of translation*, Dent, London, 1912.
Ullmann, S. (1957) *Principles of Semantics*, Blackwell, Oxford.
Valéry, P. (1946) *Monsieur Teste*, Nouvelle Revue Française, Paris.
Vasquez-Ayora, G. (1977) *Introducción a la traductología*, Georgetown University Press, Washington DC.
Vinay, J. P. (1968) 'La traduction humaine' in A. Martinet (ed.), *Langage*, Gallimard, Paris.
Vinay, J. P. and J. Darbelnet (1976) *Stylistique comparée du français et de l'anglais*, Didier, Paris.
Vincent, J. (1976) 'On translation: a first approximation,' *Annali—anglistica*, Naples.
Vygotsky, L. S. (1967) *Thought and language*, Massachusetts Institute of Technology Press, Cambridge, Mass.
Wandruszka, M. (1969) *Sprachen—vergleichbar und unvergleichbar*, Piper, Munich.
Wandruszka, M. (1978) in L. Grähs, G. Korlen and B. Malmberg (eds.), *Theory and practice of translation*, Lang, Lund.
Weightman, J. (1947) *On language and writing*, Sylvan Press, London.
Weightman, J. (1967) *Reflections of a translator*, unpublished lecture delivered at the Warburg Institute, London.
Weinreich, U. (1972) *Explorations in semantic theory*, Mouton, The Hague.
Widmer, F. (1959) *Fug und Unfug des Übersetzens,* Kiepenhauer & Witsch, Cologne and Berlin.
Wilss, W. (1978) *Übersetzungswissenschaft: Probleme und Methoden*, Ernst Klett, Stuttgart.
Winter, W. (1969) 'Impossibilities of translation' in Olshevsky, T. M. (ed.), *Problems in the philosophy of language*, Holt, Rinehart & Winston, New York.
Wittgenstein, L. (translated by G. E. M. Anscombe) (1958) *Philosophical investigations*, Blackwell, Oxford.
Wright, A. F. (1976) *Studies in Chinese thought*, University of Chicago Press, London.
Wuthenow, R. R. (1969) *Das fremde Kunstwerk: Aspekte der literarischen Übersetzung*, Vandenhoeck, Gottingen.

Name index

Subject index